Communities and Crime

In the series *Urban Life, Landscape, and Policy,*
edited by David Stradling, Larry Bennett, and Davarian Baldwin.
Founding editor, Zane L. Miller.

Also in this series:

COMMUNITIES
AND CRIME

An Enduring American Challenge

Pamela Wilcox, Francis T. Cullen,
and Ben Feldmeyer

TEMPLE UNIVERSITY PRESS
Philadelphia • *Rome* • *Tokyo*

TEMPLE UNIVERSITY PRESS
Philadelphia, Pennsylvania 19122
www.temple.edu/tempress

Library of Congress Cataloging-in-Publication Data

Names: Wilcox, Pamela, 1968– author. | Cullen, Francis T., author. | Feldmeyer,
   Ben, author.
Title: Communities and crime : an enduring American challenge / Pamela
   Wilcox, Francis T. Cullen, and Ben Feldmeyer.
Description: Philadelphia : Temple University Press, [2018] | Series: Urban life,
   landscape, and policy | Includes bibliographical references and index.
Identifiers: LCCN 2017033586 (print) | LCCN 2017046306 (ebook) | ISBN
   9781592139750 (E-book) | ISBN 9781592139736 (cloth : alk. paper) | ISBN
   9781592139743 (paper : alk. paper)
Subjects: LCSH: Crime—Sociological aspects. | Neighborhoods. | Inner cities. |
   Sociology, Urban.
Classification: LCC HV6030 (ebook) | LCC HV6030 .W54 2018 (print) | DDC
   364.973—dc23
LC record available at https://lccn.loc.gov/2017033586

Printed in the United States of America

9 8 7 6 5 4 3 2 1

We dedicate this book to our families,
the essence of our lives—
to Mike Rosenberg,
to Paula Dubeck and Jordan Cullen,
and to Carrie, Luke, and Caleb Feldmeyer

And, in respectful memory of Zane Miller,
who enthusiastically endorsed and patiently supported this effort

Contents

Communities and Crime

1

Images of Community
in Criminological Thought

W here in the city do you live? The answer to this question should be simple to provide, but it holds profound social implications. Most of us think carefully about where we might purchase a home or even rent an apartment. As we well understand, our place of residence can determine in important ways who our neighbors will be, where we will shop and what restaurants we will frequent, and which schools our children will attend. Most salient, where we reside will also affect whether the threat of criminal victimization is a daily worry or an occasional nuisance that rarely intrudes into our lives or consciousness—except perhaps when we are watching the news and learn about some awful crime in one of those "other neighborhoods."

To phrase it a touch differently, we choose to live in a particular *community* because of its reputation for a certain quality of life. We conduct an informal factor analysis—assuming that nice neighbors, good schools, well-kept houses, and a safe environment coalesce into a restricted geographical area. But, of course, not everyone can reside in such a pleasant place. In the "big sort," as Bill Bishop (2008) calls it, some of us end up in communities in which we do not know if we can trust our neighbors, must enroll our kids in schools that send few students to college, endure dilapidated housing, have our property stolen, and witness dead bodies lying on the street surrounded by police officers. There are many reasons why some among us lose the community lottery—lack of financial resources, the custom of living where we have always lived, or perhaps the barriers that still make it uncomfortable for people of color to move into "White" neighborhoods.

These observations capture what we suspect is widely known: that crime is not evenly distributed across the urban landscape. In fact, this pattern has been shown consistently since scholars, as far back as the 1800s, first started to map crime events across space. Using computers and modern data technology, contemporary studies confirm this conclusion. Criminal conduct is highly concentrated in certain neighborhoods (Weisburd, Groff, and Yang, 2012). This is not to say that lawlessness—especially minor delinquent acts, drug use, domestic disputes that turn violent, tax evasion, and perhaps other white-collar crimes—is not common in other social domains. But when it comes to predatory street crime, the "hot spots" for these offenses are located only in certain communities.

Why is this so? This project is an intellectual history of the answer that American criminologists have given to this question over the past century. At different points in time, particular *images of communities* have emerged. These images have reflected empirical reality, but they also have been social constructions—ideas that flourished because they resonated with how scholars understood the urban world. These images also have proven consequential because they have influenced which theories arose and earned allegiance and because they have justified certain crime-control policies but not others.

In short, our goal is to tell a story—to present a narrative that explains how images of communities and crime have arisen but then, in turn, have been succeeded by alternative ideas about why some neighborhoods produce so much crime. We should caution that once set forth, theoretical paradigms—including those in the community area—rarely are falsified and relegated to the criminological dustbin. Such perspectives linger for decades on end and, at times, reemerge as competing explanatory frameworks. In the end, theories never seem to perish. Rather, criminology is a field that accumulates perspectives but, at any given time, tends to pay attention mainly to the latest model.

In the remainder of this chapter, we outline the seven major images that have shaped the development of theory, research, and policy in the area of communities and crime. This introduction is intended to provide a road map that will help readers negotiate their travels through the remainder of our book. As will soon be apparent, each image is granted its own chapter in the pages ahead. Before embarking on this excursion through the intellectual history of the study of communities and crime, two issues merit comments.

First, it might seem a touch odd that we have not provided a clear definition of the organizing concept of this venture—*community* (or *neighborhood*, a term we at times use as its synonym). Our reticence reflects the conceptual ambiguity that prevails within criminology, where no supreme body exists to settle such definitional issues. We seem to be in that awkward scientific developmental stage where the concept is defined on the following basis: "Well, we all know a community when we see one!" In reality, researchers have operationalized *community* in units as small as a street block to as large as a city (and the metropolitan region around it). Census tracks are often used as proxies for communities, but mainly because they offer a geographic area on which the government collects much data. The best we can do at this point is to caution readers to remain attuned to the unit of analysis that is being used when theorists cite research in favor of their ideas. We revisit this issue in Chapter 9.

Second, the community images captured in criminology's major theoretical perspectives emerged in a particular sociohistorical context. In that sense, they were a product of their time and resonated with scholars because they seemed to "make sense." Any categorization of urban historical eras is challenging because the lines demarcating one period to the next are fuzzy rather than specific. Even so, it is possible to outline three general periods that are distinct in the sense that they experienced unique urban developments.

Lasting roughly from 1920 into the 1960s, the first era might best be labeled *the growth of the city*. The central challenge that urban residents faced was how to integrate the mass immigration, mostly of ethnic Europeans, into the inner city. Theories emphasizing social disorganization, culture conflict, and the ameliorative effects of systemic ties arose as ways of understanding this immense social change. Lasting roughly from the middle 1960s through the 1990s, a second era might be labeled *the decline of the city*. During this time, inner-city neighborhoods faced the emergence of racially segregated hyper-ghettos, deindustrialization and concentrated economic disadvantage, physical deterioration and social disorder, and rising drug markets and violent crime. Scholars often prioritized one of these conditions in arguing why the nation's cities were burdened by decline, disorder, and crime. Most of the theories reviewed in this book were developed in response to conditions of urban decline. Finally, lasting from around 2000 to the present, a third era might be labeled the *resurgence of the city*. With violent and other offenses declining and the attractiveness of urban life rising, this era offers a more optimistic view of how to address both emergent and enduring pockets of crime. It is now believed that residents have the capacity to bind together collectively to deal effectively with urban problems, including crime, despite the increasing complexity and anonymity of urbanicity.

Seven Images

Community as Socially Disorganized

Within American criminology, the potential importance of community in crime causation was established in brilliant fashion in the first half of the twentieth century by Clifford R. Shaw and Henry D. McKay. These researchers would become part of the Chicago School of criminology, which included sociologists—most raised in rural areas—who were drawn to the city to study the influx of new peoples and the challenges these groups experienced in the American urban environment. As the name Chicago School hints, these scholars mainly were drawn to Chicago and were affiliated, at one point or another, with the University of Chicago.

As they entered the study of crime, Shaw and McKay were well aware of rival theories, sometimes called "neo-Lombrosian" (Sutherland, 1947, p. 103), that sought to locate the causes of crime in individual pathology. In this view, slums were crime ridden because they were populated by the losers in the evolutionary sweepstakes—the defective members of the human species whose frailties led them to the bottom reaches of the social order. With social Darwinism as a guide, might it not be better to admit that these wicked souls constituted a dangerous class that we might hope to contain in their slums or, if necessary, behind high and sturdy prison walls?

In Shaw and McKay's view, however, such thinking ignored two important realities. First, slum residents—many recent arrivals to the shores of America—were placed into a community whose institutions were crumbling and where criminal traditions flourished. From their vantage point, lives in crime were produced not by individual traits but by residing in an environment that was *socially disorganized*. Second, as incoming groups became adjusted to American city life, they moved away from the slums and into more organized neighborhoods. If such peoples were marked by pathology, high involvement in crime should follow with them. But, alas, this did not occur: their crime rates fell as they made the transition into stable areas. Community context, not people, were criminogenic.

Thus, the image of the community as socially disorganized served both as a powerful antidote to neo-Lombrosian ideas and as a powerful explanation for why crime was concentrated in slums but not elsewhere. This image also was pregnant with the solution to crime: wait for racial/ethnic groups to move to organized communities and, in the interim, work diligently to bolster the organization of disorganized areas (e.g., through the Chicago Area Project).

Community as a System

As criminology moved into the 1960s, social disorganization theory did not vanish, but it lost most of its adherents and no longer shaped research. Although it was once seen as a defense against attempts to pathologize the disadvantaged, now it was criticized itself for being class-biased. The use of the term *disorganized* was seen as value laden and demeaning; it was argued that slum life was not disorganized but merely organized differently. Leftist scholars leveled another charge. In their view, social disorganization theory erred in ignoring the powerful interests that perpetuated urban ghettos. Slums were not produced by a natural process of the in- and out-migration of groups but were manufactured by political decisions that determined the allocation of state resources and the tolerance of residential segregation.

Finally, scholars moved away from social disorganization theory because studying communities was difficult. For one thing, using communities as a unit of analysis meant that an "N" must involve tens of communities; for another thing, the information available to measure community-level processes was in short supply. Instead, following the strategy that Travis Hirschi (1969) employed in his classic *Causes of Delinquency*, these scholars increasingly relied on the new survey technology of the self-report questionnaire to test individual-level theories. Such surveys of high school students could, with relative ease, produce data sets that had an N exceeding one thousand respondents and that could yield numerous publications—and in so doing earn authors tenure, among other academic rewards.

In 1978, however, Ruth Rosner Kornhauser published *Social Sources of Delinquency*. In this dense book, Kornhauser offered a withering critique of the major theoretical paradigms. But in so doing, she also highlighted the potential theoretical power of one version of Shaw and McKay's social disorganization theory. Kornhauser had little use for their insights on how criminal traditions took hold in "delinquency areas" and were transmitted from one generation to the next (e.g., from older siblings, gangs, neighborhood criminal networks). Instead, she made a persuasive case that neighborhood variations in crime rates could be linked to the capacity of residents to realize their collective goals—such as a safe environment. Close organization permitted goals to be achieved; disorganization meant that neighbors would lack the trust and cohesion to exercise informal control over disruptive youths and other criminal influences.

Inspired by Kornhauser, a number of scholars soon attempted to revive disorganization theory under a new label: "the systemic model." For them, the community was now imagined as a system of social networks and associational ties. Using this framework, social disorganization was seen as the inability of a community to regulate itself through effective networks and ties. Work in this tradition showed how community disadvantage, heterogeneity, and population turnover affect the breadth and depth of various associational ties and social networks presumed necessary for effective informal social control. These ties and networks, in turn, were posited to influence community rates of crime.

Importantly, in the original social disorganization theory, Shaw and McKay focused mainly on the lives of delinquent youths—what they experienced in the slums, including adults' inability to control them and their exposure to flourishing criminal traditions. In the systemic model, however, the focus shifted away from the offender to the presumably good people of the community. Crime would be prevented if community conditions allowed the nonoffenders to interact with, like, and trust one another. In crime-ridden neighborhoods, the systemic model offered the image of residents staying home at night rather than venturing out to community meetings, locking doors rather than chatting with those close by, and "not getting involved" when trouble arose.

Community as the Truly Disadvantaged

In 1987, another classic work appeared that shaped how criminologists came to understand inner-city communities—William Julius Wilson's *The Truly Disadvantaged*. Wilson was not a criminologist, and this volume touched on crime mostly in passing. But it nonetheless conveyed a reality about the urban core that resonated with a number of scholars.

Wilson was writing at a time when the United States was moving into a postindustrial era, which included competition across the globe. When he looked into slum areas, he was not reluctant to document the breakdown of core social institutions and to call these areas "disorganized." If he was taking a value-laden stand, so be it. But Wilson did not take the next step of blaming inner-city residents for their plight; he did not pathologize them. Something else was at work.

Thus, he carefully illuminated how the prevailing community fabric was frayed, if not torn asunder, by the collapse of the economy—by deindustrialization. He showed how urban communities had lost tens of thousands of well-paying jobs, as factories closed for good or moved to low-wage states or foreign lands. With employment in short supply, those who could escape the community typically did. Those staying behind were left without work and the means to marry and support a family. The slum increasingly became much like a prison, with its populace isolated from the rest of society. Life became harsh, with these disadvantaged people subjected, to use Jonathan Kozol's (1991) words, to "savage inequalities."

This image of the inner-city neighborhood as a receptacle for the truly disadvantaged sparked an important line of research. Scholars began to probe how poverty, inequality, resource deprivation, and concentrated disadvantage were the underlying sources of cultural and structural conditions in communities that nourished crime. This image also led to calls for social policies that would protect the truly disadvantaged from the kind of extreme market economy that privileges economic interests over human needs.

Community as a Criminal Culture

The ascendance of the systemic model and of deprivation theories relegated interest in criminal culture to a secondary status. Advocates of the systemic model implied—or directly argued—that traditions supportive of crime either did not exist or, if they could be documented, had little impact on behavior. For them, if beliefs mattered at all, it was because conventional values had been attenuated and thus had lost their power to regulate conduct. Other scholars recognized the existence of criminal cultures (or subcultures) but saw them as an intervening variable between structural inequalities and criminal conduct. That is, if individuals believed that breaking the law was a good thing, these attitudes would encourage such behavior. But this proximate cause of crime was ultimately controlled by the more distal root causes. Without the underlying presence of resource deprivation, antisocial definitions would cease to exist.

It should be noted, again, that culture played a central role in the social disorganization theory of Shaw and McKay. Social disorganization and the breakdown of control might have allowed criminal traditions to arise in slum neighborhoods. But once in existence, Shaw and McKay believed, these traditions took on a life of their own and became a powerful source of sustained criminal activity in a community. Again, subsequent theorists downplayed the independent, crime-generation effects of culture.

In 1999, however, interest in culture was dramatically increased with the publication of Elijah Anderson's ethnographic study, *Code of the Street: Decency, Violence, and the Moral Life of the Inner City*. Anderson certainly noted that structural disadvantage was the prime source of cultural values. But having confessed that much, he spent the bulk of his book detailing how a set of beliefs—which he termed the "code of the street"—powerfully shaped how youths and others acted in public spaces. In particular, this code called for the use of violence when an individual faced status degradation and a loss of respect. Even for youngsters from so-called decent families, the code ruled how they must act in order to avoid being seen as weak and as an attractive target for victimization.

In Anderson's theory, criminal culture is not treated as epiphenomenal or as being of minor causal significance. In the inner city, residents' moral lives were often dictated by the code and its mandates. To ignore this reality was to misunderstand why crime—especially violence—flourishes in these neighborhoods.

Community as a Broken Window

In a famous essay, James Q. Wilson and George Kelling (1982) introduced their "broken windows theory." They asked what would happen if a house had a broken window that was never fixed. Soon, they hypothesized, pass-ersby would conclude that this was a house that nobody cared about. The broken window thus sent a message to onlookers that no consequences would befall those who tossed a rock and broke another window. Not long thereafter, the house would be in complete disrepair. If only that original broken window had been replaced, then this descent into decline would not have occurred.

In a way, this is a variant of social disorganization theory in that the breakdown of order—often called "incivility" in this perspective—is held to breed fear and crime. However, a key difference must be noted. For Wilson and Kelling, the chief source of incivility or disorganization is not macro-level change or structural inequality. Instead, it is a failure of will and pru-dence on the part of criminal justice officials to crack down on minor forms of deviance—"broken windows"—that sends the message that more serious forms of lawlessness are permissible. In this perspective, formal social con-trol is the basis for informal social control.

The image of the inner-city community as a broken window earned alle-giance at a time in the 1980s and early 1990s when urban violence—especially involving drug markets selling substances such as crack cocaine—spiked and seemed intractable. How would it be possible to make city streets safe again? Wilson and Kelling had an attractive answer. They did not call for massive social welfare expenditures or even massive imprisonment of criminals. Instead, they argued that if police would do their job, the tide could be turned, and the good people could retake their community from the bad people. Thus, they were part of a policy movement that asked police to have "zero tolerance" for minor incivilities such as jaywalking, defacing walls with graffiti, littering, loitering, and public intoxication. With no broken windows left in disrepair, the public space in neighborhoods would become inviting to law-abiding citizens and uninviting to the criminal crowd. The return of a critical mass of good people to the streets would thus increase informal social control. Crime, as a result, would spiral downward.

Community as Criminal Opportunity

Community theories are primarily interested in why offenders are drawn disproportionately from neighborhoods marked by certain social condi-tions. The challenge is to discover what these residents experience that creates within them the motivation or propensity to break the law. Another group of scholars, however, argued that an alternative question is equally, if not more, important: Where do *crime events* occur within communities?

This inquiry was important because it caused scholars' attention to change from *people* to *places*. Of course, no crime will transpire if there is no motivated offender. But it is equally true that no crime will transpire is there is no criminal opportunity available. Places where crime events concentrate—often called "hot spots"—thus must be geographical locations that motivated offenders can easily access and locations where opportunities for predatory acts exist.

What, then, is an opportunity? As advanced by Lawrence Cohen and Marcus Felson (1979) in their routine activity theory, opportunity consists of two components. "Target attractiveness" is the first component. When burglarizing a house, for example, jewelry or a computer will be more attractive than a refrigerator, which is harder to transport and harder to fence. "Guardianship" is the second component. An empty house with no security system can be burglarized, but a house filled with family members and perhaps a barking dog and whose entry points are locked and alarmed is too protected to victimize.

Hot spots for crime thus tend to be places that contain attractive targets and lack capable guardianship. Only the presence of motivated offenders is needed to make crime events a regular occurrence. Still, more than this is involved. For example, how do motivated offenders find opportunities and select their targets? What is it about certain environments that makes guardianship difficult? In particular, how does neighborhood context—including its physical features and the level of disorganization—contribute to the emergence and persistence of criminal opportunities (see Weisburd, Groff, and Yang, 2012; Wilcox, Land, and Hunt, 2003)?

Notably, this approach—sometimes called "environmental criminology" or "crime science" (Clarke, 2010)—holds important implications for reducing crime in communities. Because it is focused on crime events—the here and now of the criminal act—it focuses little on how to fix offenders. That task is best left to the correctional system. But it is possible to reduce crime meaningfully if the opportunity to victimize is knifed off—if targets can be made less attractive or if guardianship can be provided. Hot spots for crime offer inviting chances for intervention. Through careful problem-solving, it is possible to develop strategies to diminish the availability of criminal opportunity. This approach to making communities safer is typically called "situational crime prevention," and, as of this moment, it is growing in popularity as a means of controlling crime.

Community as Collective Efficacy

In 1997, Robert Sampson—joined by Stephen Raudenbush and Felton Earls—published an article in the prestigious journal *Science* showing that neighborhood conditions in Chicago were closely tied to rates of violent crime. At first glance, it seemed that Sampson and his colleagues were showing once again that the social disorganization–systemic tradition retained explanatory relevance. On closer inspection, however, it became apparent that Sampson and his colleagues introduced a new conception of urban life: the city as "collective efficacy." Sampson (2012) would later articulate his theory more fully in his award-winning book, *Great American City: Chicago and the Enduring Neighborhood Effect*.

In his writings, Sampson recognized that the structural conditions that scholars reaching back to Shaw and McKay had identified intimately shaped inner-city areas. He grouped these under the conceptual umbrella of "concentrated disadvantage." But at this point, he reoriented criminological thinking in two important ways. First, he argued that the modern, post-industrial American city no longer consisted of tight-knit urban villages free from crime and disorganized areas racked by crime. The key to community safety thus was not whether people were friends who dined at one another's houses, bowled together, and participated in the same civic association. As Robert Putnam (2000) has shown, these kinds of interactions are in decline in the United States. Rather, the key to solving any problem—including a spike in crime—is the capacity of the community residents to come together and use their human, social, and political capital to secure appropriate interventions. Sampson called this capacity "collective efficacy." To act as a collective, residents had to be socially cohesive. To be effective, they had to have the shared expectation that they could rely on one another to act in concert. With regard to crime, this entailed the willingness to exert informal social control over disruptive and criminal elements.

Second, Sampson was suggesting that communities should not be seen simply as containers of good and bad conditions that then led ineluctably to low or high rates of crime. Again, he was mindful that concentrated disadvantage had a large impact on residents and on their ability to develop collective efficacy. Still, Sampson proposed that communities should not be seen as passive agents but as having the capacity to act on their own behalf. Just as self-efficacy allows for human agency, collective efficacy allows for community agency. The challenge is how to build collective efficacy within neighborhoods marked by concentrated disadvantage.

Overall, Sampson was offering a realistic but optimistic view of the contemporary American city. Enduring structural inequalities still existed and were the first link in a causal chain that resulted in high rates of crime in impoverished areas. But lowering crime no longer seemed to depend on re-creating ethnic urban villages where residents were closely tied by their heritage, religion, and institutional involvements. Rather, as is the case in many upscale urban neighborhoods, residents could live in relative anonymity but, when a problem such as crime emerged, could access their underlying collective efficacy to come together to achieve a solution. In this view, crime presents difficult challenges, but it is not immune to neighbors' collective efforts to make their community safe.

An Enduring American Challenge

American cities are places where predatory crimes disproportionately occur. A not-so-hidden cost of residing in less-affluent neighborhoods is that street crime exists not at a distance but close enough to foster trepidation and potentially impose a life-changing harm. In this very real sense, crime is an enduring challenge for those living in urban America.

In this regard, we were tempted to subtitle our book *An Enduring Urban Challenge*. But we did not because what occurs within the confines of the slums is not detached from what occurs outside these areas. For one thing, the quality of urban life—how inner cities are imagined—can affect the quality of life in an entire metropolitan region. Is the "downtown" area to be feared or avoided? Is the city a source of pride and entertainment or a decaying symbol for the decline of the whole region? For another thing, what goes on inside high-crime communities is not fully determined by their residents. Social welfare and criminal justice policies are often imposed by "us" on "them." Thus, in the political process, do we ignore these neighborhoods, or do we allocate resources to improve living conditions and reduce crime?

The images we hold about inner-city communities shape how we choose to address the enduring challenge of crime in these neighborhoods. In the time ahead, therefore, it is important what images will direct these efforts. It is possible that older images—or a mixture of them—will rival one another, with no clear winner emerging. But it is also possible that fresh images will emerge. This possibility becomes more likely because the social context of urban America is not static but dynamic. In particular, so-called slum neighborhoods are experiencing divergent crime trends. Overall, rates of predatory offenses have declined so much that criminologists are unable to explain why. At the same time, some places within these communities seem resistant to this global trend and remain dangerous. In Chapter 9, we have much more to say about the future of communities and crime and about the enduring challenge this relationship poses for the nation.

2

Community as Socially Disorganized

More than any other place, Chicago has been the center of the study of communities and crime (Sampson, 2012). There is no theoretical perspective named after any other major American cities—not New York or Boston, not Saint Louis or Atlanta, and not Los Angeles or San Francisco. But there is a Chicago School of criminology. How did this come to pass? Two factors—one demographic, one intellectual—that intersected in time and space were responsible.

When scholars in the Chicago School came to write about communities and crime, they were commenting on a city that had experienced a remarkable transformation. In 1840, Chicago was a town of only 4,470. In the next half century, however, it grew to more than one million residents, "outstripping twenty-three older cities in the process to become the second largest American city after New York" (Bulmer, 1984, p. 12). Between 1890 and 1930, the population expansion continued unabated, eventually numbering more than 3.3 million (Bulmer, 1984).

Chicago's striking growth was spurred by its emergence as an industrial center, itself made possible by its proximity to waterways and the development of railroads as a prime mover of people and products. As mass migration from Europe took hold, Chicago's economic vitality made it an attractive and common destination. African Americans constituted only 2 percent of the city's population in 1910 and 7 percent in 1930. By contrast, in 1900, fully half of Chicago's residents were not native-born Americans. They came across Europe, as the city was transformed into "an ethnic melting pot of

Germans, Scandinavians, Irish, Italians, Poles, Jews, Czechs, Lithuanians, and Croats" (Bulmer, 1984, p. 13). In 1907, the Polish population alone in Chicago reached 360,000, leading the city to rank "after Warsaw and Łódz as the third largest Polish center in the world" (Bulmer, 1984, p. 50).

The rapidity, magnitude, and intractability of Chicago's growth created a social environment of enormous contrasts and inequality. The wealthy lived on the so-called Gold Coast, and the city was the home for a symphony, art institute, architectural advance, literary community, and attractive boulevards and parks (Bulmer, 1984; Commager, 1960; Zorbaugh, 1929/1976). But vast numbers of its immigrant poor resided in crowded, dilapidated tenements and worked lengthy hours for little pay in dirty, dangerous industries depicted poignantly in Upton Sinclair's *The Jungle* (1906/1960). Living conditions were so challenging that reformers embarked on social welfare ventures to help the immigrant poor, including Jane Addams's (1910/1960) Hull-House settlement and the creation of the nation's first juvenile court aimed at "child saving" (Breckinridge and Abbott, 1912; see also Platt, 1969). As described by Lincoln Steffens—perhaps with a touch of hyperbole but also with more than a kernel of truth—Chicago was "first in violence, deepest in dirt; loud, lawless, unlovely, ill-smelling, new; an overgrown gawk of a village, the teeming tough among cities. Criminally it was wide open; commercially it was brazen; and socially it was thoughtless and raw" (cited in Commager, 1960, p. x).

These demographic shifts may have been more extensive in Chicago, but they were hardly unique; other American cities, such as New York, might have been similarly described (Zacks, 2012). What was unique, however, was a second factor: the gathering in one place of academics devoted to studying and understanding the natural social experiment unfolding in Chicago. How, they asked, could such a huge and diverse population be assimilated into a single city? Was social order possible? Were social problems inevitable? Intractable? In 1892, the University of Chicago opened its doors to its first students, in part as a result of the philanthropic largesse of the industrial baron John D. Rockefeller, who contributed $45 million. Under the guidance of President William Rainey Harper, this new private university was one of the few institutions to embrace the special mission of research and graduate education. The university included nascent social science disciplines, and Albion Small was given the task of developing the field of sociology. Over the years, the members of this department would make the study of Chicago a priority (Bulmer, 1984; Kurtz, 1984).

Small headed the Department of Sociology for thirty-two years until his retirement in 1924. Although his guidance was important, three other scholars would be more influential in creating the "Chicago School"—a name applied both within sociology generally and within criminology in particular (Bulmer, 1984; Kurtz, 1984). William Isaac Thomas, known as W. I., was foremost among these. He served as a prominent member of the faculty from 1895 until 1918, when the university terminated his employment for an alleged sexual indiscretion. After being found in a Chicago hotel room with the wife of a soldier stationed overseas, Thomas was charged with a violation of the Mann Act, a federal statute intended to bar the interstate trafficking of women for prostitution but that was applied more broadly in high-profile cases of immorality. With Clarence Darrow as his defense attorney, the court dismissed the charges, but Thomas's severance from the university stood (Bulmer, 1984; Zaretsky, 1984).

Thomas's defining work, coauthored with Florian Znaniecki, was his five-volume study, *The Polish Peasant in Europe and America*. Funded by a $50,000 grant by heiress Helen Culver, Thomas spent eight months a year in Poland from 1908 until 1913 (Bulmer, 1984). As Thomas noted, "immigration was a burning question," and he wished to investigate how a group's "home mores and norms" affected "their adjustment and maladjustment to America" (cited in Bulmer, 1984, p. 46). Studying Polish immigrants made sense, given their numbers in Chicago; in fact, between 1899 and 1910, one-fourth of all immigrants to the United States came from Poland (Bulmer, 1984). According to Lester Kurtz (1984, p. 3), Thomas "was more responsible than any other individual for the development of the so-called 'Chicago School.'" In particular, he "was a pioneer in the effort to link theory and research in a comprehensive approach that encompassed both macrosociological and microsociological analyses" (1984, p. 3). For our purposes, Thomas's key contribution is the construct he used to describe the difficulties that immigrants confronted in reestablishing community life in America: *social disorganization*. This concept would come to shape how the Chicago School scholars would explain the relationship of communities to crime.

Robert Park was a second prominent figure in the evolution of the Chicago School. Park was a newspaper reporter for a decade before attending Harvard to study with William James. He then traveled to Germany, where he was initially influenced by lectures by Georg Simmel and then earned a Ph.D. at Heidelberg University (Bovenkerk, 2010; Bulmer, 1984). Park subsequently worked with the Congo Reform Association and served for seven years as the secretary to Booker T. Washington in Tuskegee, Alabama. Organizing the International Conference on the Negro in 1912, he met W. I. Thomas, who was an invited speaker. Thomas in turn recruited Park to the University of Chicago (Bovenkerk, 2010; Bulmer, 1984). Park had a fascination for the city and its downtrodden people. He advocated an appreciation for the circumstances of others, believing that "real understanding" required not only detachment but also "imaginative participation in the lives of others, empathy as well as an acute eye" (Bulmer, 1984, p. 93; see also Matza, 1969).

In 1916, Park was joined at the University of Chicago by Ernest Burgess, who would be his close collaborator, including on the "Green Bible"— a 1,040-page volume bound in a green cover that sought to organize existing knowledge and that carried the title of *Introduction to the Science of Sociology* (1921/1969). Burgess, who lived for a period at Jane Addams's Hull-House, embraced Park's fascination with urban life (Kurtz, 1984). They shared an office in the Social Science Research Building and would "inspire an entire generation of graduate students to comb the city and its institutions, looking for patterns of social organization within natural areas of Chicago, the 'sociological laboratory'" (Kurtz, 1984, p. 4). Starting in 1918, the team taught a graduate seminar on field studies. Their syllabus described the course in the following way:

> The mobility, local distribution, and segregation of the population within the urban and suburban areas of the city of Chicago; the cultural differences and relative isolation of different classes; racial, vocational, and local groups; resulting changes in institutions, uses of leisure time, in the organization and expression of public opinion; and the traditional forms of social control. (cited in Bulmer, 1984, p. 95)

Thomas, Park, and Burgess thus combined to provide the intellectual training and tradition that would frame the study of crime in Chicago, most notably by Clifford R. Shaw and Henry D. McKay. In the Chicago School, crime would be understood as integrally related to the macro-sociological changes that determined the growth and ecology of the city. Immigrants and other city residents were not depicted as atomistic individuals driven into crime by pathological biology or pathological minds. Rather, their conduct was viewed as intimately shaped by the social conditions they experienced day in and day out.

Again, the central prism used to interpret these daily conditions was the concept of *social disorganization*. Many immigrants, it was asserted, had lived in organized communities in Europe, but the massive dislocation they—and their fellow travelers—had experienced led to their settling in disorganized communities in Chicago. The Chicago School sociologists argued that communities mattered. As Park (1923/1961, p. xxiii) observed, "If it is true that man made the city, it is quite as true that the city is now making the man."

This chapter explores this theme of the community as socially disorganized. Appropriately so, the chapter begins by considering the concept of social disorganization. From there, the chapter examines how the Chicago School scholars studied urban life and the model they used to understand the growth of the city and the varying impact its different communities had on their residents. At this point, we will be prepared to present the work of Shaw and McKay, whose exploration of "juvenile delinquency in urban areas" comprised the most enduring and influential statement of the Chicago School's theory of crime.

Social Disorganization as an Organizing Concept

When the members of the Chicago School peered into the city, they could have understood the experience of residents in diverse ways. For example, given the abject poverty and exploitive working conditions, they could have emphasized the evils of capitalism and called for a socialist revolution—the underlying theme of Upton Sinclair's *The Jungle*. They could have focused on the contradiction of holding out the promise of the American Dream while simultaneously limiting access to this goal for most of the city's impoverished—as Robert Merton (1938), who grew up in a Philadelphia slum, would come to do (see also Cullen and Messner, 2007). Although these themes might occasionally have surfaced on the edges of their work, they chose instead to understand the urban experience through an alternative theoretical concept: social disorganization.

This image of the city resonated with their lived experience. Many members of the Chicago School came from small towns. For example, Clifford Shaw and Henry McKay hailed, respectively, from rural Indiana and South Dakota (Snodgrass, 1976). These communities were agrarian, small, homogeneous, and stable. If unexciting and stifling, they had the advantage of offering organized social life. Chicago was the opposite—industrial, large, heterogeneous, and transient. It was exciting and uncontrolled, the hallmark of disorganized social life. For the "Chicagoans," observed David Matza (1969, p. 72), the "attraction of the cities—freedom, mobility, and stimulation—masked their danger and potential decay. . . . The city was both attractive and destructive."

More notably, Chicago was a city of remarkable growth and transition. The Chicago School was not studying a group of the truly disadvantaged mired for generation after generation in an inner-city slum (Wilson, 1987). Rather, they were investigating the lives of immigrants who once were enmeshed in organized agrarian communities not unlike the midwestern towns in which many of the scholars had been raised. As they settled in Chicago, the immigrants and their children faced the enormous challenge of adjusting to a radically different environment—a challenge their European ways of life were often ill equipped to address. Their culture seemed confused and conflicted with its American counterpart; their social institutions seemed to deteriorate under the strain of being relocated to an urban neighborhood marked by high transiency. For the members of the Chicago

School, the immigrants' experience was thus best described as being socially disorganized. Alas, there was a silver lining in this conceptualization. These immigrants were not bad people consigned to a life of perpetual disadvantage. In time, they would reorganize and move to new communities, where they would once again flourish.

In this context, *The Polish Peasant in Europe and America* had a defining influence on the central problem addressed by the Chicago School. Chicago was a city of immigrants and their offspring—and, as noted, of some 360,000 Polish immigrants. The school's members thus focused not on the effects of slum living per se but on the immigration experience and its impact on the social fabric of Chicago. Thomas and Znaniecki's project was, in a sense, big science. It was a multiyear study in which Thomas spent the better part of six years in Poland in hopes of understanding the nature of the transition that these "peasants" made to life in teeming tenements erected in the shadows of factories, stockyards, and railway exchanges.

In the abridged edition of their five-volume project edited by Eli Zaretski and published in 1984, Thomas and Znaniecki defined "social disorganization briefly as *a decrease of the influence of existing social rules of behavior upon individual members of the group*" (p. 191, emphasis in the original). They continued by observing that social disorganization exists on a continuum; it may range "from a single break of some particular rule by one individual up a general decay of all institutions of the group" (p. 191). In this view, normative standards perform a regulatory function. Especially when social institutions weaken, the capacity of these "social rules" to enforce conformity is attenuated.

Thomas and Znaniecki noted that social change in Poland had produced social disorganization in that country and the need for reorganization. But Polish peasants in their homeland were insulated from many problems by long-held traditions that reinforced behavioral consistency. The nature of employment, either as a small farmer on a twelve-year contract or even as a manor servant, allowed the peasants to remain on their land—a level of "high stability" that led naturally to "the formation of steady habits." In particular, the family was held together by being enmeshed in a dense social network. In Poland, husbands and wives were "part of the wider family institution. . . . Each family, therefore, took care to enforce all traditional rules of behavior upon its own married member and at the same time was ready to defend this member against any break of these rules committed" (1984, p. 272). By contrast, Polish Americans faced new situations where traditions seemed irrelevant, worked at industrial jobs marked by uncertainty, and formed marriages isolated from the "social control to which a marriage group in the old country is subjected" and glued together only by the fragility of romantic love (p. 277).

Admittedly, the Chicago School's discussion of the concept of social disorganization often lacked specificity. Its components were not clearly articulated; no effort was made to draw path diagrams showing its origins, nature, and effects. In the 1964 obscenity case of *Jacobellis v. Ohio*, U.S. Supreme Court Justice Potter Stewart stated famously that "hard core pornography" is hard to define, but "I know it when I see it." In the same way, members of the Chicago School treated social disorganization as a condition that everyone would know when they saw it.

By probing various writings, however, it is possible to extract a clearer idea of the construct (see Cullen, 1984; Kornhauser, 1978). Thus, social disorganization has two main components: cultural and institutional. At the core of social disorganization theory is the principle that social order depends on effective social control. In turn, social control is contingent on social organization. Social organization exists when there is consensus about and allegiance to social rules—or cultural norms. Such adherence to norms is itself produced by social institutions, especially the family and local community, that socialize its members effectively and sanction departures from social rules (sometimes called "informal social control").

During the immigration process, the cultural rules imported into the United States were not always compatible to an urban, industrial neighborhood. In particular, the children of immigrant parents found such traditional prescriptions to be old-fashioned and irrelevant to their lives. When such consensus breaks down and the power of norms attenuates, there is what might be called *cultural disorganization*. This situation is exacerbated when competing normative standards arise—whether about marriage and divorce or about joining a gang and jack-rolling. Cultural disorganization is most likely to occur when there is *institutional disorganization*. A central function of primary groups is to socialize their members and to provide consistent informal social control. But, as noted, the immigration experience caused institutions to weaken and lose their effectiveness at socialization and control. No longer enmeshed in a dense social web, many marriages in the New World ended in desertion and divorce. Work could be found but also lost at the whim of an unfriendly boss; uncertainty not predictability marked employment. Church parishes and civic clubs were created, but their hold on immigrants was variable. Many men, coming to America by themselves, found their only community in the crowded boardinghouses located in the slums.

Although more obscure in contemporary discussions of the concept, Chicago School scholars occasionally introduced a third feature of social disorganization: the inability of the immigrants' traditional culture and disintegrating social institutions to meet the needs of youngsters in America (Cullen, 1984). W. I. Thomas (1921/1969, p. 489) had grouped human "wishes" into four main categories: "(1) the desire for new experience; (2) the desire for security; (3) the desire for recognition; and (4) the desire for response." Socially disorganized communities left these needs unsatisfied. Frederic Thrasher (1927/1963, p. 68) argued that youth gangs arose in part out of a "quest for new experience," as a way "to break the humdrum of routine existence—this is a problem for the boy." The unconventional playgroup offers "the thrill and zest of participation in common interests, more specifically corporate action, in hunting, capture, conflict, flight, and escape" (pp. 32–33). As Thrasher observed, "gangs represent the spontaneous effort of boys to create a society for themselves where none adequate to their needs exist" by providing "a substitute for what society fails to give" (pp. 32–33).

Importantly, the members of the Chicago School argued that social disorganization could have disquieting consequences on the lives of inner-city residents. But a hallmark of the Chicago School was not simply to theorize about community effects but also to document empirically the social realities of the city. Toward this end, they developed a methodology that mixed quantitative and qualitative analysis—or, as we discuss next, that involved mapping and interacting.

Studying the City: Mapping and Interacting

As part of a newly minted research university, the sociology faculty at the University of Chicago wished not only to teach knowledge but also to create it. Increasingly, its members joined the movement to make their discipline a science through the collection of empirical data aimed at theoretical generalization. The specific object of their inquiry—and ultimately their social laboratory—was the city in which the university was located. Still, this begged the question of how the city might be studied, both in terms of the questions asked and the methods used to answer them (Park, 1925/1967a). The unique approach of the Chicago School was its integration of quantitative and qualitative methods. With regard to the study of crime and delinquency, this multimethod approach involved mapping the distribution of the conduct and interacting in depth with those who otherwise would have remained impersonal dots on a map.

Those in the Chicago School were not the first to map crime and other forms of social behavior. Throughout the nineteenth century, a number of statistical pioneers mapped various aspects of crime in European nations, the most notable of them being Michel-André Guerry, Adolphe Quetelet, and Rawson W. Rawson. Most often, these early efforts to map the distribution of crime used large units of analysis—nations, provinces, or cities (Sampson, 2012; Weisburd, Groff, and Yang, 2012). With Chicago as their focus, however, members of the Chicago School were interested in how crime and, in particular, offenders varied *within the city.* When examining where delinquents lived, for example, were these youngsters drawn evenly from across the urban landscape? Or were they concentrated in some neighborhoods and infrequently found in others? As they would find and later scholars would confirm, crime and criminals are highly concentrated in so-called hot spots (see Sampson, 2012; Sherman, Gartin, and Buerger, 1989; Weisburd, Groff, and Yang, 2012).

As will be discussed in more detail later, Chicago School researchers pored over government documents (e.g., juvenile court records) to extract where offenders lived and to pinpoint them on a map. These data allowed them to calculate the relative concentration of offenders by "natural areas." Their discovery that offenders were found disproportionately in some communities—those located near the center of the city—had significant theoretical and methodological implications. Theoretically, the question arose: Why are youths from these neighborhoods at high risk of becoming delinquents? The immediate answer was that they hailed from *socially disorganized communities.* But this answer was a gateway, not an end, to further analysis. Thus, the subsequent question inevitably arose: What was it about socially disorganized communities that prompted children to lead criminal lives and end up in juvenile court? Methodologically, this puzzle could only be solved by interacting with wayward youths and observing the settings that nourished their criminality.

Indeed, the hallmark of the Chicago School is that it was not populated by armchair academics but by scholars that trumpeted the value of personal contact with their subject matter. From his early works onward, W. I. Thomas "stressed the necessity of having concrete, objective, detailed studies of social behavior and attitudes" (Bulmer, 1984, p. 45). Thomas noted that one fellow professor had asked "to get him a bit of information from the saloons." Alas, his colleague admitted that "he himself never entered a saloon or tasted beer." By contrast, Thomas disclosed that "he explored the city," in part simply as a "matter of curiosity" (cited in Bulmer, 1984, p. 45).

Robert Park was perhaps even more influential than Thomas. As noted, Park had been a newspaper reporter for ten years—a set of skills and orientation that he imported into his sociological research and training of graduate students. Through an appreciative lens, he wished to depict the difficult lives of those overwhelmed by the challenges of disorganized neighborhoods not as deviant and pathetic but as human and struggling (Matza, 1969). Thus, he "emphasized research methods capable of catching this subjective element of human existence"—to use "personal documents and observational methods drawn from journalism and anthropology" to "lay bare social processes in a way not hitherto achieved by social scientists" (Bulmer, 1984,

p. 94). Chicago School graduate students would go into the city and conduct landmark observational studies, including Nels Anderson's (1923/1961) *The Hobo*, a study of homeless men, and Harvey Warren Zorbaugh's (1929/1976) *The Gold Coast and the Slum*, a study of two neighborhoods in the "near north side"—one affluent and flourishing and one poor and disorganized.

Notably, the members of the Chicago School used multiple methods, in addition to participant observation, to unravel how disorganized inner-city communities shaped the lives of their immigrant residents. These involved, for example, interviews, collecting and analyzing documents (e.g., letters), and case studies (Bulmer, 1984; Kurtz, 1984). In studying criminal careers, however, the most important method might well have been the life history, in which delinquents or adults would tell their "own stories" about their entry into and experiences with crime. Edwin Sutherland (1937) would eventually publish his influential life history, *The Professional Thief*. But Clifford Shaw was perhaps most devoted to this method, collecting more than two hundred life histories (Bulmer, 1984). Three of these life histories were published: his classic work on "Stanley" in *The Jack-Roller* (1930/1966), *The Natural History of a Delinquent Career* (with Moore, 1931/1976), and *Brothers in Crime* (with McKay and McDonald, 1938). Again, these detailed accounts—likened by Burgess to using a "microscope" to explore "in detail the interplay of mental processes and social relationships"—were not intended to be employed apart from quantitative data (Bulmer, 1984, p. 106). This point was made by Becker (1966, pp. ix–x):

> If we are concerned about the representativeness of Stanley's case, we have only to turn to the ecological studies [i.e., mapping] carried on by Shaw and McKay to see the same story told on a grand scale in mass statistics. And, similarly, if one wanted to understand the maps and correlations contained in ecological studies of delinquency, one could then turn to *The Jack-Roller* and similar documents for that understanding.

Understanding the City:
The Concentric Zone Theory

Contemporary students of communities and crime often investigate inner cities that are becoming smaller, losing industries, and populated by people of color. But those in the Chicago School faced the opposite social reality. Chicago was rapidly adding residents, the industrial base was expanding, and the population was drawn mainly from European immigrants. Thus, their sociological challenge was to explain not the decline of the American city but its inordinate growth. How did the city develop? And what were the consequences of it doing so by a specific process? Three themes informed the answers to these questions.

First, as articulated in a classic essay by Roderick MacKenzie (1925/1967), the Chicago School sought to apply the metaphor of plant (or animal) ecology to the study of human ecology in urban areas. In this perspective, environments are not static but dynamic—ever changing as they become vulnerable to outside "invasion." With plants, the invasion might be a new species or type of tree; with humans, it might be the arrival of a new ethnic group into a neighborhood or the encroachment of factories. "Conflict" then ensues, with the weaker species having to "accommodate" to the dominance of the stronger force. With plants or humans, this might mean moving to a less desirable location, where they might be the invader and exert dominance in the ensuing struggle. Eventually, the process leads to "assimilation of a new order of symbiosis based upon the accommodative outcomes of the previous . . . stages" (Pfohl, 1985, p. 147).

As this emergent environment unfolds, the process generates new "natural areas" that take on their own characteristics. For plants, it might be a distinctive mixture of trees and vegetation in a certain section of the forest. For humans, as MacKenzie (1925/1967, p. 77) notes, the "general effect of the continuous process of invasions and accommodations is to give to the developed community well-defined areas, each having its own peculiar selective and cultural characteristics." According to Zorbaugh (1929/1976, p. 231), the evolution of the ecological areas is shaped by "transportation, business organization and industry, park and boulevard systems, and topographical features." These elements "tend to break up the city into numerous smaller areas, which we may call *natural areas*, in that they are unplanned, natural product of the city's growth" (p. 231, emphasis in the original). Such natural areas might range from the "Gold Coast" to communities with names such as "Towertown," the Latin Quarter, and "Little Hell," the Sicilian area (Zorbaugh, 1929/1976).

Second, in a formulation at the core of the Chicago School, Ernest Burgess (1925/1967) attempted to develop a coherent theory of the "growth of the city" (see Figure 2.1). His special innovation was in conceptualizing the city as a set of five "concentric circles"—called "zones"—that radiated out from the urban center. In his framework, the "expansion" of Chicago, and of any other city, is a "process" in which individual zones grow in size and move farther out geographically. In this process, there is a "tendency of each inner zone to extend its area by the invasion of the next outer zone" (p. 50). At one time in Chicago, all four of the zones beyond Zone I (the Loop) "were in its early history included in the circumference of the inner zone, the present business district" (p. 50). Burgess (1925/1967, p. 50) described the concentric circles in the following way:

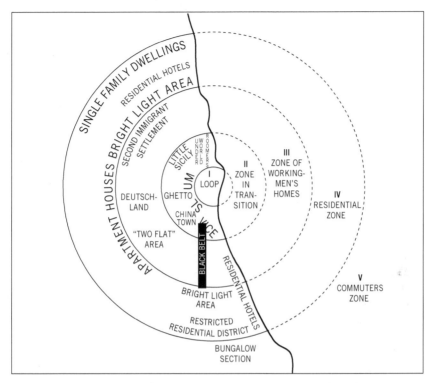

Figure 2.1 Ernest W. Burgess's Concentric Zone Theory as Applied to Chicago
Reprinted from E. W. Burgess, "The Growth of the City: An Introduction to a Research Project," in *The City*, ed. R. E. Park, E. W. Burgess, and R. D. McKenzie (Chicago: University of Chicago Press, 1967), p. 55.

This chart represents an ideal construction of the tendencies of any town or city to expand radially from its central business district—on the map "The Loop" (I). Encircling the downtown area there is normally an area in transition, which is being invaded by business and light manufacture (II). A third area (III) is inhabited by the workers in industries who have escaped from the area of deterioration (II) but who desire to live within easy access of their work. Beyond this zone is the "residential area" (IV) of high-class apartment buildings or of exclusive "restricted" districts of single family dwellings. Still farther, out beyond the city limits, is the commuters' zone—suburban areas, or satellite cities—within a thirty- to sixty-minute ride of the central business district.

Third, Burgess's concentric zone theory provided a clear visual representation and accompanying theoretical account for where *social disorganization would be located in Chicago*: the zone in transition (Zone II). This was the sector of the city that was experiencing continual invasion by the factories, transportation system, and economic organizations expanding outward from Zone I. As a community marked by inexpensive housing—rooming houses and deteriorating tenements—it was also where newly arriving ethnic groups would seek to settle, displace existing groups, and establish their own segregated areas. The concentric circle's very name—the zone in transition— highlighted its status as a social environment in flux and subject to the process of invasion, conflict, accommodation, and assimilation. The price for this transition was high, for it made the neighborhoods vulnerable to social disorganization and to all the vices this nourished, including adult crime and juvenile delinquency. It was this conceptual framework that would inform the work of the most famous criminologists within the Chicago School, Clifford R. Shaw and Henry D. McKay. It is to their theory of social disorganization that we next turn.

Explaining Crime: Shaw and McKay's Theory

In criminology texts, it is common to present Shaw and McKay's ideas as the foundational statement of "social disorganization theory." But singling out Shaw and McKay's contributions in this way conveys a misleading impression. For although an exemplar of social disorganization theorizing, their work is more accurately portrayed as a continuation of a way of thinking already well established within the Chicago School. Merton (1995, p. 5) has used the term *cognitive micro-environment* to describe a local context in which "direct interaction among teachers, students, and colleagues" allow "new ideas to emerge and develop." In this sense, Shaw and McKay were part of a micro-environment—the Chicago School—in which certain methods and concepts, especially social disorganization, were widely used to study a range of social problems, including crime (see Park, 1925/1967b; Thrasher, 1927). Shaw and McKay thus did not create this information; rather their contribution was in using it in an erudite fashion. It also is instructive that although providing compelling insights into juvenile delinquency, Shaw and McKay never articulated a clear causal model of their theory (Arnold, 2011; Snodgrass, 1972)—perhaps because they assumed that their local audience knew what they were saying. Regardless, it remained for other scholars to extract these ideas from their work and to outline and/or diagram a more formal statement of their theory (see Empey, 1982; Finestone, 1976; Kornhauser, 1978).

Shaw and McKay spent three decades together researching delinquency at the Institute for Juvenile Research in Chicago, where McKay remained following Shaw's death in 1957 (Gelsthorpe, 2010; Snodgrass, 1972). As

Snodgrass (1972, p. 128) notes, they would travel "downtown in the day to study and reform the high-crime areas just outside this giant commercial center." They were enmeshed in the Chicago School not just by propinquity but also by training. Thus, they both studied for their doctorate in sociology at the University of Chicago, although they failed to earn their Ph.D.'s because they could not meet the requirement to master a foreign language. Most important, their special individual talents allowed for one of the most influential collaborations in the history of criminology. As described by Snodgrass (1972, pp. 128–129):

> Perhaps no difference between two men could have been better suited for collaborative work. McKay was mainly the rational scientist-statistician who stayed mostly at the Institute for Juvenile Research and meticulously calculated rates, plotted the maps, ran the correlations and wrote up the findings to locate empirically and to depict cartographically the high-crime areas. Shaw was the emotional practitioner in the field, attempting to create community organization and crime prevention programs. McKay, more modest, more detached, more retiring, was the academic intellectual out to prove his point with a pen, tables, rates and interpretation. Shaw, more flamboyant, never aloof, always in motion, was the activist-organizer out to prove his point with practice and participation.

Shaw and McKay would approach the study of delinquency in urban areas in two ways: empirically and theoretically. These two components were interwoven in their work, but they are best discussed one at a time. Thus, we start by reviewing how they engaged in the epidemiology of delinquency and then present their classic social disorganization theory.

Mapping Delinquency

In 1929, Shaw published *Delinquency Areas*, which carried the lengthy subtitle *A Study of the Geographic Distribution of School Truants, Juvenile Delinquency, and Adult Offenders in Chicago*. This treatise was written "with the collaboration of" Frederick M. Zorbaugh, Henry D. McKay, and Leonard S. Cottrell. Again, this was not the first attempt to map the epidemiology of delinquency across Chicago. In 1912, Sophonisba Breckinridge and Edith Abbott recorded for Chicago "the location of the homes of all the delinquent children who became wards of the court from 1899 to 1909" (p. 150). Their maps revealed graphically that these wayward youngsters were drawn disproportionately from neighborhoods marked by poverty, population density ("congestion"), and crowded tenements. They discovered as well that "the delinquent child was also a 'child without play'" in that "the poor and congested wards of the city . . . have few parks or playgrounds" (1912, p. 154).

In his 1927 classic book *The Gang*, Frederic Thrasher also created maps to study "1,313 gangs in Chicago." On a large folded map that could be taken out of the book (not available in the 1967 abridged edition), he pinpointed the location of each group, using red symbols to indicate a gang with clubhouse (a triangle) or without a clubhouse (a dot). His cartography of Chicago also recorded railroad property, industrial property, parks, boulevards, and cemeteries. Using Burgess's concentric zone depiction of Chicago's "urban ecology" (see Figure 2.1), he then created a map on which he shaded those areas where gangs were concentrated—calling this area "gangland" (1927, p. 24). He noted that the "most important conclusion suggested by a study of the location and distribution of the 1,313 gangs investigated in Chicago is that *gangland represents a geographic and socially interstitial area of the city*" (p. 22, emphasis in the original). Anticipating the findings of Shaw and McKay, he thus discovered that delinquent gangs were concentrated in the "zone in transition" (Zone II), which was characterized by social disorganization. His theoretical explanation would thus provide a framework that Shaw and McKay could subsequently elaborate.

In *Delinquency Areas*, Shaw and his colleagues (1929, p. 22) mapped the "geographic distribution" for "eight series of individual offenders, including 5,159 male school truants, 43,298 juvenile delinquents, and 7,541 adult offenders, a total of 55,998 individuals." A "series" was a group of offenders processed in some way by the justice system and followed for a specific period of time. For example, Series IV was defined as "8,141 boys (ten to sixteen years of age) brought before the Juvenile Court of Cook County during the period 1917–23" (p. 22). The strategy of using multiple series, which Shaw and McKay would follow in other books, enabled the researchers to discern whether the findings would remain consistent across various offenders, types of measures, and periods of time. Consistency would lend confidence that the results were not methodological artifacts.

With a sample of more than fifty thousand subjects, the study was an enormous undertaking, especially in the pre-computer age. In part, Shaw and McKay's commitment to big science is one reason for the enduring influence of their work. Their method involved having a single card for each offender that "included the home address, offense, age, sex, and other items used in tabulating the composition of the several series" (Shaw, 1929, p. 23). Laying out large maps of Chicago, they plotted each of their subjects, marking down one dot for the residence of each individual offender (regardless of how many offenses this person had committed). They then relied on population data to calculate a ratio "expressed in terms of the number of offenders per hundred individuals of the same age and sex" (p. 25). They employed these data to create four types of maps: "spot maps," which again were dots on the map for each case; "rate maps," which presented the ratio of offenders by areas; "radial maps," which showed lines extending from the Loop along important streets outward to the suburbs, with rates attached to the line; and "zone maps," which showed rates of offending by concentric zones. In *Delinquency Areas*, Shaw and his colleagues did not use the zones articulated by Burgess's concentric zone theory (see Figure 2.1). Instead, they demarcated nine zones, each one mile in length, extending from the Loop outward.

In many ways, the zone maps were the most theoretically relevant because they provide an empirical test of the predictions of social disorganization theory. Consistent with the Chicago School's perspective, the rates for various outcome measures followed the pattern of being highest close to the Loop and in the zone in transition and falling in a linear gradient as the zones moved progressively away from the inner city. The correlations in findings across the series were high. In fact, Shaw and his colleagues (1929, p. 203) described as "striking" the "marked similarity in the distribution of truants, juvenile delinquents, and adult criminals in the city."

In 1942, Shaw and McKay published what is generally considered their most important contribution and one of most significant works in criminological history: *Juvenile Delinquency in Urban Areas*. Built explicitly on *Delinquency Areas*, this study was intended to bring "the delinquency data for Chicago up to date" (1942, p. 3). In the introduction to the volume, Ernest Burgess (1942, p. ix) was prescient in his observation that "this work is a magnum opus in criminology"—a project that had been "in progress for twenty years." Burgess noted that the analysis "now covers twenty cities" and "includes cases of tens of thousands of juvenile delinquency" (p. ix). He reported that the "findings were astonishingly uniform in every city. The higher rates were in the inner zones, and the lower rates were in the outer zones" (p. ix.). These data "establish conclusively a fact of far-reaching significance, namely, that the distribution of juvenile delinquency in time and space follows the pattern of the physical structure and social organization of the American city" (p. ix). Further, it was clear that juvenile delinquency was due to "social disorganization, or the lack of organized community effort to deal with those conditions" (p. xi).

In 1969, more than a decade after Shaw's death, McKay issued a revised edition of *Juvenile Delinquency and Urban Areas*, again updating the Chicago statistics and adding new information on other cities (with the assistance from scholars with knowledge of those cities). Two features, found in both the 1942 and 1969 versions, merit attention. First, the issue of the "growth of the city" is raised and discussed in light of Burgess's concentric zone theory. The five zones are explained in the text (on pp. 18–19 in both books). Later, the series data are presented by zones using the Burgess five-zone framework (see Figure 2.1). The high-to-low gradient in offending from Zone I to Zone V is shown repeatedly for different series. Again, this finding has theoretical implications because it allows the concentration of offending to be linked more clearly to social disorganization.

Second, because their data collection was extended, Shaw and McKay were able to compare offending rates mapped by zones over a lengthy period of time—for example, they could now study juvenile court commitments of delinquents for the series of 1900–1906, 1917–1923, and 1927–1933 (Shaw and McKay, 1942, p. 74). They reported consistent stability in offending even though the ethnic groups residing in the high-crime zone in transition had changed during this period. Through the process of invasion and succession, new groups had moved into these communities as the extant residents reorganized socially and moved to the outer zones. This finding led Shaw and McKay to the theoretically critical conclusion that immigrant ethnic groups (or racial groups) were not inherently pathological; there was nothing about the Poles, Irish, Italians, or any other people that consigned them to a criminal way of life. Rather, crime was a product of the nature of communities—specifically of social disorganization. As the members of ethnic groups moved from the zone in transition to Zones III, IV, and V, their involvement in criminal activities declined accordingly. As stated by Shaw and McKay (1969, p. 385), "High or low rates of delinquents are not permanent characteristics of any ethnic or racial group. Each population group experienced high rates of delinquents when it occupied the areas of first settlement, and these rates went down as the groups either move out to better areas or move toward stability in the same areas."

Explaining Delinquency

It is clear from the data included in this volume that there is a direct relationship between conditions existing in local communities of American cities and differential rates of delinquents and criminals. Communities with high rates have social and economic characteristics which differentiate them from communities with low rates. Delinquency . . . has its roots in the dynamic life of the community.

This quotation begins the conclusion of *Juvenile Delinquency and Urban Areas* (1942, p. 435). Once again, Shaw and McKay reiterate that wayward conduct is not evenly or randomly distributed but concentrated in certain communities—those that are socially disorganized. This leads to two interrelated questions: What causes communities to become criminogenic—that is, disorganized? And what occurs within a disorganized community that causes youngsters and adults to engage in crime?

The first issue—the social forces that produce disorganization—can be addressed generally and then specifically. In general, Shaw and McKay embrace the Chicago School's human ecological view of the city's growth (described above), which produces expanding zones and an inner city mired in poverty and in constant transition. The immigrants' social institutions, developed for life in agrarian communities in Europe, are ill suited to the demands of modern industrial life and thus disintegrate. In other words, social disorganization ensues.

Other scholars, however, have tried to extract a set of specific factors or variables from Shaw and McKay's writings that can, in a more formal way, be used as predictors of social disorganization. For example, Empey (1982, pp. 189–190) lists four "conditions associated with high-delinquency areas." These are "physical deterioration and population loss"; "economic segregation"; "racial and ethnic segregation"; and "high incidence of social ills." The most cited statement is found in Kornhauser's (1978) *Social Sources of Delinquency*. Analyzing various portions of *Juvenile Delinquency and Urban Areas*, she identifies four "ecological causes" of social disorganization: "economic segregation," which then leads to "low economic status," "heterogeneity," and "mobility" (1978, p. 73).

The second issue—why social disorganization is criminogenic—was addressed through two constructs: control and cultural transmission. Shaw and McKay's explanation was not innovative in that it drew heavily from earlier scholars in the Chicago School, such as Thrasher (1927), who made quite similar arguments. Further, their books were primarily oriented to the presentation of data and not to theoretical discussion. Their "theory" thus was never clearly presented in, for example, propositional form (as did Edwin Sutherland), but rather was embedded in different places in their writings, including their life histories, such as *The Jack-Roller*, and journal articles (see, e.g., McKay, 1949; Shaw, 1929). Still, the central components of their thinking can be identified.

First, consistent with the Chicago School starting from Thomas and Znaniecki's study of the Polish peasant, Shaw and McKay argued that social disorganization involved the breakdown of controls over youngsters. As the offspring of immigrant or first-generation parents, these youths lived in communities in which conventional institutions had weakened and in which cultural values were conflicting and not solidly aligned behind normative conduct. In these delinquency areas, said Shaw (1929, p. 410), "the primary group and conventional controls that were formerly exercised by the family and neighborhood have largely disintegrated. Thus delinquent behavior, in the absence of the restraints of a well-organized moral and conventional order, is not only tolerated but becomes more or less traditional."

Second, Shaw and McKay argued that the weakening of control allowed criminal traditions to arise that were then transmitted within socially disorganized areas. In *Juvenile Delinquency and Urban Areas* (1942), they devoted Chapter 7 to this issue: "Differences in Social Values and Organizations among Local Communities." The core insight is that organized communities—those in Zones III, IV, and V—are capable not only of exerting control over youths but also of shielding them from contact with criminal influences. By contrast, youths in disorganized communities—those in Zone II—are confronted with conflicting cultural systems, coming into contact with both conventional and criminal social values and organization. Thus, Shaw and McKay (1942, p. 164) noted that:

> in the area of low rates of delinquents there is more or less uniformity, consistency, and universality of conventional values and attitudes with respect to child care, conformity to law, and related matters; whereas in the high-rate areas systems of competing and conflicting moral values have developed. Even though in the latter situation conventional traditions and institutions are dominant, delinquency has developed as a powerful competing way of life. It derives its impelling force in the boy's life from the fact that it provides a means of securing economic gain, prestige, and other human satisfactions and is embodied in delinquent groups and criminal organizations, many of which have great influence, power, and prestige.

Shaw and McKay (1942, p. 166) continued, noting explicitly that the process being articulated had been described by Edwin Sutherland as "differential association" (see footnote 1 on p. 166):

> Children living in such communities are exposed to a variety of contradictory standards and forms of behavior rather than to a relatively consistent and conventional pattern. More than one type of moral institution and education are available to them. A boy may be familiar with, or exposed to, either the system of conventional activities or the system of criminal activities, or both. Similarly, he may participate in the activities of groups which engage mainly in delinquent activities, those concerned with conventional pursuits, or those which alternate between the two worlds. His attitudes and habits will be formed largely in accordance with the extent to which he

participates in and becomes identified with one or the other of these several types of groups.

Importantly, the life histories compiled by Shaw (with McKay's assistance) vividly portrayed the lack of control that allowed Zone II youngsters to roam free on city streets and, in particular, the learning experiences that led them into criminal careers. Often, such cultural transmission started in the home. Stanley, the subject of *The Jack-Roller*, thus describes in his life history how stepbrother William, five years his senior, "taught me how to be mischievous; how to cheat the rag peddler when he weighed up our rags. He would distract the peddler's attention while I would steal a bag of rags off the wagon" (Shaw, 1930/1966, p. 32). Stanley's stepmother not only failed to exercise control but also sent the two brothers "to the railroad yard to break into box-cars" to steal "foodstuffs, exactly the things my stepmother wanted"; she would later realize "that she could send me to the market to steal vegetables for her" (pp. 32–33). In his teens, Stanley would associate with other "crooks . . . young boys like me but they were more wise to the world and tougher" (p. 96). The four teenagers formed "The United Quartet Corporation," which provided a group that would reinforce Stanley's criminality and teach him the techniques needed to jack-roll a vulnerable target (e.g., an inebriated patron leaving a bar) (pp. 96–97). Learning also took place in correctional institutions, one of which Shaw termed "The House of 'Corruption'" (p. 149). As Stanley commented about the experience of leaving prison, he was "completely alone in the world except for my buddies in crime. . . . I was educated in crime" (pp. 162–163).

Finally, because Shaw and McKay attributed delinquency to both weak controls and criminal cultural transmission, their theory has been described as a "mixed model" (Kornhauser, 1978, p. 26). This characterization reflects subsequent developments within criminology that created distinct perspectives that fell under the rubrics of control theory and cultural deviance (or differential association) theory (see Hirschi, 1969; Kornhauser, 1978). Said to have incompatible assumptions, these approaches are depicted as rivals to be tested empirically in a winner-take-all contest (see, e.g., Alarid, Burton, and Cullen, 2000; Chouhy, Cullen, and Unnever, 2016; Jonson et al., 2012). When Shaw and McKay first formulated their ideas, however, this theoretical debate was nonexistent. In all likelihood, they would have resisted any effort to unpack control and culture into separate spheres because both social factors were integral to the Chicago School's conceptualization of social disorganization.

Thus, a fundamental consequence of social change and disintegration was the weakened capacity of core institutions to supervise and socialize youngsters. At the same time, once freed from restraint, the youths in these

Zone II communities were not viewed as having content-free minds and as pushed into crime by the irresistible impulse to seek immediate gratification. As Shaw and McKay probed their thinking through the case studies reported in the life histories, they could see that these youths had learned cognitions or definitions of the situation that shaped the extent and type of their criminal involvement. To ignore either control or cultural transmission would have made no sense to them; it would have truncated the very reality that Shaw and McKay so vividly witnessed in their lengthy study of Chicago's delinquency areas.

Conclusion

Although the members of the Chicago School, including Shaw and McKay, worried about the disquieting social ills experienced in the zone in transition, they also possessed an underlying optimistic belief regarding social change. Human ecological theory rejected the permanency of disorganization and its disquieting consequences. As noted, disorganization was viewed as a property of communities, not of any particular ethnic or racial group. Certain neighborhoods might endure stability of crime but not the groups that had settled in them. In time, as their social institutions adjusted to American urban life, these peoples would *reorganize* and move to the outer zones in the city. Once there, their children would be exposed to strong institutions and a dominant conventional culture. Because they no longer resided in a delinquency area—and thus were free from the consequences of social disorganization—their involvement in crime would decline precipitously.

In the meantime, the Chicago School did not advise abandoning inner-city communities as hopelessly disorganized and beyond redemption. As part of the liberal Progressive movement, they believed that the social sciences could be used to improve the lives of society's casualties (Pfohl, 1985; Rothman, 1980). Their reforms included developing settlement houses to bring culture and welfare to the immigrant poor (such as Hull-House), establishing professions such as social work to provide professional welfare services, and inventing a juvenile court aimed at saving wayward children (Platt, 1969). Most notably, in the early 1930s, Clifford Shaw and his colleagues implemented the Chicago Area Project, a delinquency-prevention program that included recreational opportunities, the creation of a committee composed of local residents to direct intervention programs, and mediation with authorities to explain a youngster's conduct and with the youths themselves to see the wisdom of staying out of trouble (a practice called "curbside counseling") (for more details, see Kobrin, 1959; Schlossman et al., 1984). Again, the goal of this multifaceted program was both to insulate juveniles from criminogenic risks and to foster an indigenous movement to reorganize the local community (more generally, see McKay, 1949).

For subsequent criminologists, however, this generally optimistic view would be difficult to sustain as the nature of the American city changed. The omnipresence of mass immigration and constant assimilation had buoyed the idea that disorganization and delinquency were a natural consequence of the process of city growth. But as the United States moved into a post-immigration period marked eventually by urban stasis if not decline, attributing crime to ongoing social change was no longer convincing. Race was the added salient consideration, as inner cities were increasingly transformed from a circulation of White ethnic groups to permanent Black hyper-ghettos offering the intergenerational transmission of poverty rather than escape to outer zones for reorganization and prosperity. As later chapters reveal, constructs as the "truly disadvantaged" (Wilson, 1987) and "concentrated disadvantage" (Sampson, Raudenbush, and Earls, 1997) would come to dominate scholarly discourse. Pfohl (1985, pp. 168–169) has captured this alternative image of community and crime:

> People are said to engage in deviance because social disorganization has robbed them of norms and constraints. Neglected is the possibility that people deviate because social stratification has robbed them of human resources and a sense of dignity. Isn't it possible that poor people may experience high rates of what the society officially defines as deviant, not because they lack organized normative constraints, but because they are frustrated, angry, or seeking escape from the oppression of a stratified social existence?

3

Community as a System

For much of the 1950s and 1960s, scholars turned away from the Chicago School's approach to studying how the nature of communities shapes the distribution of crime across neighborhoods. Shaw and McKay's work was often seen as value laden in that it used a construct—social disorganization—that seemed to suggest inner-city neighborhoods were pathological. Criminologists increasingly turned their attention to investigating why some individuals were more likely than others to break the law. Differential association, strain, and control theories emerged as popular explanatory frameworks. To the extent that community-level works were undertaken, they tended to be informed by these perspectives and not exclusively by the Chicago School.

The changing social context of America's cities, however, made it difficult to ignore the troubled—even pathological—nature of community life. Interest in the area of communities and crime thus resurfaced in the late 1970s and early 1980s. With American cities in economic decline, urban decay spreading seemingly without restraint, Whites fleeing to the suburbs, and social problems concentrating in inner-city neighborhoods, the time was ripe for scholars to explore once again how the social context of neighborhoods might prove criminogenic.

Parts of this chapter previously appeared in Wilcox and Land (2015). Reprinted with permission from Transaction.

And once again, as they peered into urban communities, what scholars saw—what they would come to depict as the core problem underlying crime in inner-city neighborhoods—was not foreordained. In fact, as will be seen in later chapters, various scholars offered different answers to the question of why some communities have more crime than others. In this chapter, we consider how one group of influential scholars addressed this issue by embracing the sociology of the Chicago School. They articulated an image of the city, and the troubled neighborhoods within, *as a system.* This perspective, which continues to shape criminological thinking, would become known as the *systemic model.* Building on the work of Shaw and McKay in a critical but appreciative fashion, this approach urged that urban communities be seen as a *system of social networks and associational ties.* These networks and ties are the basis of the capacity of neighborhood residents to successfully exercise *informal social control.* Communities in which such social ties were frayed—those that Shaw and McKay called *socially disorganized*—were considered incapable of achieving their goal of maintaining safety and peace through informal means. As a result, crime in these neighborhoods would flourish.

This understanding of crime and community meshed with the state of inner cities in the mid-1970s and beyond. Urban neighborhoods increasingly manifested the signs of being socially disorganized. Families broke apart, housing projects were covered with graffiti and allegedly run by gangs, and schools seemed to have forfeited their capacity to educate. But criminological theories are not the inevitable determinants of social context. In the end, theories also require human agency: someone has to author them. Biography and context continually intersect to make fresh ideas possible.

This chapter thus attempts to tell the story of how the systemic model of communities and crime emerged as a major explanation. Again, this explanation was based on an image that saw networks of associations serving as the core of community life—the core from which effective socialization and informal social control emerged. From this perspective, weak informal control resulted in crime, and this condition of ineffective informal control was likely in communities with weak systems of social ties among community members.

We start this story with Ruth Rosner Kornhauser, who in 1978 published her classic work, *Social Sources of Delinquency: An Appraisal of Analytic Models* (with a paperback published in 1984). As the book's subtitle suggests, Kornhauser provided a devastating appraisal of existing theories of crime, ending her analysis with a call for scholars to return to that part of Shaw and McKay's work that rooted levels of control in the degree of social organization (see Cullen et al., 2015). As we will see, scholars like Robert Sampson and Robert Bursik found Kornhauser's analysis compelling. Convinced that she had defined how theory should proceed, they initiated a research agenda heavily shaped by Kornhauser's thinking, but also blending the work of sociologists such as John Kasarda and Peter Blau. Their work in the 1980s and early 1990s revitalized Shaw and McKay's social disorganization theory in the form of a systemic model of informal social control.

Ideas are dynamic, however. As time has progressed, the systemic model has been subjected to extensive empirical investigation. This research has both confirmed and revised the model's claims so that today the most promising version of the systemic model bears the brand "new parochialism." The sections that follow trace the revitalization of social disorganization theory as a systemic model of neighborhood-network-based informal social control and, subsequently, toward a theory of new parochialism. We start with the work of Kornhauser, whose seminal book provided the systemic model's intellectual foundation.

Social Disorganization and Kornhauser's Legacy

In this section, we trace Kornhauser's reformulation of social disorganization theory, which established social disorganization theory as a macro-level control theory. Kornhauser suggested that the ecological correlates of crime observed by Shaw and McKay—including low socioeconomic status, ethnic heterogeneity, and residential mobility—weakened the capacity of communities to informally control the behavior of their members. It was variation in informal control that was held, therefore, to be the most immediate cause of community-level variation in rates of crime.

Three Models of Delinquency

Kornhauser's *Social Sources of Delinquency* was published after nearly two decades worth of work on the ideas contained on its pages. It was the published book version of her Ph.D. dissertation, presented to the Graduate School at the University of Chicago under the supervision of Morris Janowitz and Gerald Suttles. Tragically, Kornhauser suffered a stroke while the dissertation was being edited into a book manuscript. She credits her dear friend Gertrude Jaeger with providing a "labor of love" in finishing the editorial process so that *Social Sources of Delinquency* could be published by University of Chicago Press (Kornhauser, 1984, p. vii).

Although emanating most directly from her dissertation, Kornhauser began to develop the material for *Social Sources of Delinquency* in the 1960s while working at University of California–Berkeley's Center for the Study of Law and Society. During the course of her work at the center, she wrote a paper in 1963 entitled "Theoretical Issues in the Sociological Study of Juvenile Delinquency" (for a reprint of this paper, see Cullen et al., 2015).

Among other things, the paper classified different delinquency theories of the time—putting forth a theoretical classification scheme similar to what Kornhauser would eventually present many years later in *Social Sources of Delinquency*. Travis Hirschi, in fact, cited Kornhauser's unpublished paper in the opening pages of his famous 1969 book, *Causes of Delinquency*—based on his Ph.D. dissertation at Berkeley—which formulated and tested his social control theory (e.g., p. 3, footnote 3). The three major traditional theories defined by Hirschi were the same traditions recognized by Kornhauser in her appraisal of criminological/delinquency theory: strain theories, control theories, and cultural deviance theories.

Kornhauser described strain theories and control theories as united in their shared underlying assumption of societal value consensus. In other words, both traditions are based on the idea that humans essentially agree on the definitions of behaviors in terms of "right" versus "wrong" or "moral" versus "amoral." Crime and delinquency—as reflected in law as codified social norms, around which there is consensus—are thus seen as *nonnormative* behaviors from the vantage point of either a strain theorists or a control theorist. Accordingly, both theories assume that crime reflects some level of social disorganization, or breakdown in the commitment to the agreed-on social order. As such, Kornhauser (1978, 1984) actually referred to both strain theories and control theories as types of social disorganization theories. (Her use of the term *social disorganization theory* as an umbrella term, encapsulating theories based on value consensus, has largely been abandoned in more contemporary classifications of theory.)

But what causes the breakdown in the commitment to consensual values? In Kornhauser's appraisal, the answer to this question is where strain and control theories diverge. She emphasized that strain theories explained variation in commitment to social values as a function of financial needs and pressures. It is important to keep in mind that the strain theories of the time she was writing were Robert Merton's (1938) anomie-strain theory as well as Albert Cohen's (1955) and Richard Cloward and Lloyd Ohlin's (1960) variations on Merton's theory. In short, the strain theories that Kornhauser appraised suggested that an inability to address financial needs and pressures through socially acceptable means motivated a "softening" or outright repudiation of core values, with crime as the result.

In contrast, strain and unfulfilled need were considered ubiquitous from a control perspective, as explained by Kornhauser. Therefore, control theories viewed all members of society as equally "motivated" to offend, and strain and unfulfilled needs could not explain variation in commitment to consensual values. However, the costs associated with acting on motivation *were* presumed to vary. Briefly, more effective or stronger *social controls* served to better hold ubiquitous motivation in check.

Kornhauser suggested that "cultural deviance" theories departed sharply from both strain and control theories. This term served as a conceptual umbrella for perspectives otherwise known as "cultural transmission," "differential association," and "subcultural." In any event, Kornhauser emphasized that these theories shared a foundational assumption—that of value conflict—which was at complete odds with either strain or control theories. The value-conflict perspective recognizes multiple, competing value systems as opposed to a largely consensual set of norms. Crime is an outgrowth of socialization that occurs within systems that permit law-violating behaviors. Operating from the standpoint of "value conflict," then, variation in strength of commitment to values does not explain crime. In fact, from a value-conflict perspective, strong commitment to group values can actually promote crime. Within "deviant subcultures," crime and delinquency are considered normative, conforming behaviors, after all, so those most committed to the subculture's values are likely to be the most delinquent. It is thus ultimately the *conflict* that exists regarding the *content* of *different* value systems that explains crime from a cultural deviance perspective, according to Kornhauser. In this regard, "crime" exists only because some (more influential) subcultures have defined those behaviors espoused within "deviant" subcultures as "criminal."

After delineating three major theoretical traditions, Kornhauser appraised the theories in *Social Sources of Delinquency* (1978, 1984). Notably, Kornhauser acknowledged that the original version of her appraisal—in her 1963 paper, written at Berkeley's Center for the Study of Law and Society—was a critique of cultural deviance theories and a *defense* of strain theory. But in the interim between the date of that report and the publication of her dissertation, she was compelled by the evidence Hirschi presented in opposition to strain theory (Kornhauser, 1984, p. viii). Detailing Hirschi's control theory, as presented in *Causes of Delinquency*, is beyond the scope of this book. It is sufficient to say, however, that Hirschi reported data from the Richmond Youth Project that ostensibly disconfirmed the ideas associated with Mertonian strain explanations for individual delinquency. For example, such strain theories assumed that strain arose from economic needs and pressures. Hirschi's data revealed "no important relationship between social class as traditionally measured and delinquency" (1969, p. 75). Hirschi's analysis also questioned the strain theory idea that higher levels of aspirations (i.e., success goals) would leave one with a higher likelihood for crime/delinquency.

> The delinquent . . . does not aspire with some force to material things while rejecting the middle-class lifestyle. . . . In general, the values, aspirations, and goals the strain theorist uses to produce pressure

are related to delinquency in the direction opposite to that he predicts when realistic expectations are held constant. The greater one's
acceptance of conventional (or even quasi-conventional) success
goals, the *less* likely one is to be delinquent, regardless of the likelihood these goals will someday be attained. (p. 227, emphasis added)

Kornhauser was not the only one struck by Hirschi's work, which ultimately supported the idea that it was weakened control in the form of conventional attachments, commitments, involvement, and belief that explained
variation in crime. By the time Kornhauser published *Social Sources of
Delinquency*, Hirschi's control theory—commonly known as social bond
theory—was on its way to becoming one of the most widely tested and
empirically supported individual-level theories of crime. In *Social Sources of
Delinquency*, Kornhauser used such evidence to vigorously embrace a reconceptualization of Shaw and McKay's work that was most congruous with a
control theory of delinquency. Her assessment in many ways shaped the
direction of social disorganization theory as a "macro-level control theory" into
the 1980s and beyond. Her reconceptualization of social disorganization theory
and its impact on subsequent work are described in more detail throughout
the remainder of the chapter, but first Kornhauser's critiques of the two rivals
to control theories are briefly summarized. To be sure, her riveting critiques
of both strain and cultural deviance theories were equal in fervor to her
embracement of control theories.

Criticizing Strain Theory

Kornhauser discredited strain theories on several grounds. She stated her
dislike of Merton's notion of a goals-means discrepancy that was the supposed source of strain in his theory. Merton viewed American culture as
overemphasizing the economic-success goal relative to cultural norms
regarding the means by which economic success is achieved. Kornhauser
viewed his distinction between the "goals of economic success" and the
"means by which to attain those goals" as falsely dichotomizing cultural
values (see, in particular, 1984, pp. 162–167). Quite simply, she saw Merton's
"belief in the cultural supremacy of money over virtue" as flawed (p. 163).
Despite this fundamental problem, Kornhauser still acknowledged that
strain was something individuals could experience; in fact, she assumed that
most did. She much preferred relying on Émile Durkheim as opposed to
Merton, however, for understanding the source of strain: "Strain is not *produced* by culture, but by the weakness or absence of culture" (1984, p. 165).
Since strain in this form "markedly afflicts all persons" (1984, p. 49), in her
view, individuals exhibited far greater variation in control than strain.

Furthermore, she argued that, even in the face of high levels of strain, controls must be loosened before a strained individual would commit a crime. In other words, "strain will not cause delinquency unless it simultaneously weakens controls" (1984, p. 49). In contrast, Kornhauser suggested that weakened controls can affect crime, independent of strain.

Criticizing Cultural Deviance Theory

Kornhauser's appraisal of the control, strain, and cultural deviance traditions consisted of a particularly damning critique of cultural deviance theories. She characterized cultural deviance theories as having untenable foundational assumptions, including ideas such as "man has no nature, socialization is perfectly successful, and cultural variability is unlimited" (1984, p. 34). That quote, in fact, has been one of the more widely cited examples of her contentiousness regarding cultural deviance theories, sparking intense debate among criminologists even decades after it first appeared in print (e.g., Akers, 1996; Hirschi, 1996). Kornhauser's interpretation of cultural deviance theory as expressed in that quote, along with her dismissal of the theory, are discussed in the following paragraphs.

First, Kornhauser suggested that cultural deviance theories implied a view of humans as having no nature (no human nature, that is). She claimed that implicit in the theory was an assumption that humans had only social natures and were thus purely socialized products of their culture. Simply put, Kornhauser found the idea that humans had no drives, needs, or impulses that were unrelated to socialization absurd: "Now it is one thing to say that human nature is unknown and unknowable. It is quite another to say that there are *no* impulses in man resistant to socialization" (1984, p. 35). She sarcastically referred to the "automaton conformist" view of humanity within the cultural deviance paradigm, with a nature that is "wholly passive, docile, tractable, and plastic" (1984, p. 35).

Relatedly, Kornhauser also interpreted cultural deviance theory's premise that crime resulted from conformity to rather than violation of group norms as implying that criminals were "perfectly socialized" by their subculture. Citing Edwin Sutherland and Donald Cressey's (1955) differential association theory as an example of a cultural deviance theory, she suggested that their theory implied that:

> children internalize the values of the groups to which they belong or with which they have contact. Should these groups have delinquent values, commitment to delinquent values ensues, followed in due course by delinquent behavior. Delinquent behavior results *only* from difference in the *content* of socialization, not from differences in the

degree to which socialization has been successful. Socialization is never more or less effective; it is always equally effective. (1984, p. 194)

The implication of perfect socialization troubled Kornhauser for a number of reasons. For instance, she felt the undertones of "perfect socialization" embedded within Sutherland and Cressey's work represented a misrepresentation of the reality of learning. She claimed that they ignored the notion that humans respond to stimuli (in the form of values) not simply because they are found in great quantities in a culture but because they lead to *fulfillment of some need*. In short, behaviors can be rewarding or costly; she saw this aspect completely ignored in a differential association theory that linked criminal behavior solely to an excess of definitions favorable to violation of law. Again, her remarks on this issue are visceral in tone: "Socialization [from the vantage point of cultural deviance theory] does not produce a minded organism or an active self capable of selecting among stimuli those that are relevant to the self. It produces an individual stamped by the printing press of culture" (1984, p. 198).

More broadly, she criticized the theory—and its implicit assumption about perfect socialization—on the grounds that it implied that "behavior is synonymous with values." In other words, all behavior was thus assumed to be "culturally or subculturally valued behavior" (1984, p. 196). Kornhauser refused to accept this assumption; her view was that human behavior did not always represent values or culture.

Finally, Kornhauser was dismayed by what she perceived to be the assumption of "extensive dissensus" regarding values/attitudes about crime across subgroups within society (1984, p. 214). In other words, she was dubious of the very existence of "deviant subcultures." In her book, she attempted to discredit this assumption through a review of work published in the 1950s, 1960s, and 1970s indicating that attitudes about criminal behavior were similar across various population subgroups, including those defined by socioeconomic status, gender, urban versus suburban location, and level of crime in the area. She also reviewed theory and empirical evidence suggesting that delinquents were ambivalent about crime and prioritized conventional values rather than oppositional values. Furthermore, Kornhauser challenged the implication of crime emerging out of socialization within "structurally united collectivities" (i.e., the deviant subcultures) on the grounds that most crime was committed with one or two acquaintances rather than within the context of clear-cut "subgroups" (1984, p. 243). In sum, Kornhauser rejected the idea of value conflict, and she rejected the notion of subculturally driven behavior.

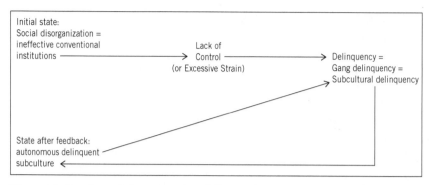

**Figure 3.1 Kornhauser's Interpretation of Shaw and McKay: A Nonrecursive
Control Model**
Reprinted from R. R. Kornhauser, *Social Sources of Delinquency: An Appraisal of Analytic Models*
(Chicago: University of Chicago Press, 1978), p. 58.

Beyond Shaw and McKay's Mixed Model

Given the backdrop of Kornhauser's classification of theories, she interpreted
Shaw and McKay's (1942) work as presenting a "mixed model." She identified
elements of strain, control, and cultural deviance theories within the explanation Shaw and McKay offered for the consistently higher rates of crime
observed within transitional areas. She interpreted Shaw and McKay's
theory as suggesting a process whereby weakened institutions (indicated
by ecological conditions related to socioeconomic status, residential instability, and heterogeneity) led to both ineffective informal social control
and excessive strain, which, in turn, led to delinquency and the formation
of delinquent subcultures. Once these delinquent subcultures were formed,
they became the primary reason for sustained delinquency, creating further
crime through the transmission of cultural values conducive to crime, in
a manner autonomous from processes of control or strain. Figure 3.1 shows
the conceptual model Kornhauser (1984, p. 58) used to depict this interpretation.

Kornhauser viewed the mixed nature of the theory as problematic in that
it integrated theoretical ideas with inherently incompatible assumptions. For
instance, she felt that value consensus was the baseline assumption of Shaw
and McKay's work. The very concept of "disorganization" (as opposed to,
say, "differential organization") implied the existence of conditions that
people would want to avoid if they could. Kornhauser (1984, p. 63) states to
this effect, "Shaw and McKay assume that values of health, life, order (lawful
conduct), economic sufficiency, education, and family stability are either the
reflection of universal human needs or are common to all members of our
society." At the same time, their incorporation of the idea that autonomous

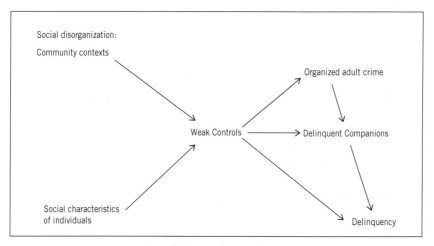

**Figure 3.2 Kornhauser's Reconceptualization of Shaw and McKay: A Recursive
Control Model**
Reprinted from R. R. Kornhauser, *Social Sources of Delinquency: An Appraisal of Analytic Models*
(Chicago: University of Chicago Press, 1978), p. 69.

deviant subcultures emerged in disorganized areas implied value conflict. A
mixed model thus appeared inherently contradictory, blending foundational
assumptions of value consensus and value conflict. She simply did not think
that a sound theory should contain such contradictions. Thus, Kornhauser
viewed the incorporation of cultural deviance into Shaw and McKay's theoretical explanation as *flawed logically.*

Kornhauser also viewed reference to cultural deviance as *causally unnec-
essary* for understanding the cross-neighborhood variation in rates of crime
that Shaw and McKay had observed. Since Shaw and McKay indicated that
weakened control and excess strain led to both delinquency and delinquent subcultures, her position was that weakened control and strain were sufficient
explanations for variation in crime within the theory. Further, as mentioned
above, she was most compelled by control theory as opposed to strain theory.
She thus proposed a reconceptualization of Shaw and McKay's theory that
was a "pure control theory," represented as a recursive path model, as opposed
to a mixed, non-recursive model. Disadvantaged community contexts (as
indicated by characteristics such as low socioeconomic status, ethnic heterogeneity, and residential instability) led to weakened community-level informal social control. Weak informal social control, in turn, caused delinquency
(lone acts as well as delinquency within group/gang contexts). Figure 3.2 is
the conceptual diagram used by Kornhauser (1984, p. 69) to depict her suggested reconceptualization.

In summary, Kornhauser's insights were fundamentally important to subsequent work in the community tradition within criminology. Through her appraisal of theoretical models, she paid great attention to Shaw and McKay's contributions at a time when interest in their theory had waned considerably. In doing so, she also offered a reconceptualization of social disorganization theory that rendered it less ambiguous in terms of causal mechanism. Her social disorganization model removed elements of strain and cultural deviance and clearly defined "weakened informal social control" as the key theoretical construct intervening between ecological conditions (i.e., low socioeconomic status, residential instability, and ethnic heterogeneity) and community rates of crime. She presented to the field an unambiguous causal model of social disorganization—one that would fuel an entire new era of research on communities and crime.

Sampson: Measuring Social Disorganization

Robert Sampson is one of the most noteworthy scholars to have used Kornhauser's suggestion of a pure control model of social disorganization theory. His utilization and expansion of her ideas shaped scholarship on community rate of crime from the 1980s to the present day. His role in the development of the systemic model of social disorganization is detailed in the following section.

Life before and after Kornhauser

In a recent autobiographical account of his scholarly evolution, Sampson suggested, "My life may be divided in the following Colemanesque way: before I read Kornhauser and after I read Kornhauser" (2011, p. 64). Sampson's statement was a play off a quote by James Coleman (1992), who had said, "My life can be divided into two parts: before I entered Fayerweather Hall (the building in which sociology is housed at Columbia), and after Fayerweather" (p. 75). For Sampson, the reading of *Social Sources of Delinquency* was life altering.

Sampson was a Ph.D. student in criminal justice at State University of New York at Albany in the late 1970s and early 1980s. There, he was heavily influenced by Michael Hindelang's empirical, data-driven approach to criminology and by Travis Hirschi's theoretical teachings. It was, in fact, in relation to a seminar led by Hirschi at Albany that Sampson offered the following reflection: "I can still feel the intellectual jolt. The occasion was a graduate seminar with Travis Hirschi on theories of deviance. It was in that seminar that a light bulb turned on. The switch was our close reading of Ruth Kornhauser's *Social Sources of Delinquency*" (2011, p. 67). In particular,

Sampson saw a clear alignment between Kornhauser's articulation of "social disorganization" as "weakened informal social control" and Hirschi's ideas on social control. Given his admiration for Hirschi as his professor, it is not surprising that Sampson was particularly drawn to the notion of conceptualizing social disorganization theory as a community-level theory of informal social control. As Sampson (2011, p. 68) suggested, "Between *Causes* and *Social Sources* I therefore became an early control theorist but with a clear interest in the macro side of things as reflected in social disorganization theory."

Structural Determinants of Disorganization

As a graduate student, postdoc, and young professor, Sampson pursued his interest in social disorganization theory, and ecological approaches more broadly, through empirical tests of the linkages between the various ecological correlates of disorganization highlighted by Shaw and McKay (1942) (e.g., low socioeconomic status, ethnic heterogeneity, and residential instability) and community rates of crime or victimization (e.g., Sampson and Castellano, 1982). The prominent work of the day (early 1980s), by scholars such as Steven Messner and Peter and Judith Blau, was focused primarily on understanding the linkage between economic/racial structures and rates of crime in terms of either (1) structural inequality–induced strain (debating the notions of relative versus absolute deprivation, in particular), or (2) subcultures of deviance/violence. In contrast, the idea that economic and racial structures were related to rates of crime because they impacted social integration and collective control was largely absent from the literature.

But in the tradition of Shaw and McKay, Sampson was explicit in offering social disorganization as a possible reason for the higher rates of crime observed in areas of economic disadvantage, heterogeneity, and residential mobility. Sampson's theoretical frame was thus important in reinvigorating scholarly interest in Shaw and McKay's theoretical ideas. Sampson's early work also emphasized the importance of community-level family disruption (e.g., rates of divorce, single-person, or female-headed households) as an additional ecological indicator of social disorganization, thus building upon Shaw and McKay's theoretical foundation (Messner and Sampson, 1991; Sampson, 1985, 1987). For example, in a 1985 article, Sampson states, "It is suggested that areas with pronounced family disorganization are less able to provide an effective network of social controls. In contrast, communities with a strong familial base are likely to be areas where families know each other and provide mutual support; consequently, there is a functional youth social control" (p. 11).

It is important to note that Sampson's earlier work did not actually measure "weakened informal control." However, given Kornhauser's insights,

Sampson presumed it to be at least one plausible intervening mechanism linking ecological characteristics and rates of crime. During the earlier stages of Sampson's career, data that could adequately test the posited intervening mechanism were simply unavailable. In fact, key studies of neighborhood-based informal social control in the era between the original publication of *Juvenile Delinquency and Urban Areas* and the mid-1980s were typically conducted on a dozen, or fewer, neighborhoods (Greenberg, Rohe, and Williams, 1982; Maccoby, Johnson, and Church, 1958; Simcha-Fagan and Schwartz, 1986). Reliably measuring community-level informal social control required survey data from large numbers of residents situated within multiple neighborhoods, so that individual survey responses could be aggregated. Furthermore, if the effects of informal social control were to be estimated in an empirically rigorous model, a large number of neighborhoods were necessary. In other words, truly testing Kornhauser's control model of social disorganization theory required access to data that employed a complex, expensive sampling design, and that sort of data was scarce until the late 1980s and early 1990s.

Can Social Disorganization Be Measured?
A Criminological Classic

The criticism that a control model of social disorganization theory could not be adequately tested as a result of data limitations was put to rest with the 1989 publication of "Community Structure and Crime: Testing Social Disorganization Theory," which Sampson authored with W. Byron Groves. Published in the *American Journal of Sociology*, this article became an instant criminological classic, as Sampson and Groves presented the first test of the "full" control model proposed by Kornhauser. In a stroke of genius, they realized that data from the British Crime Survey were ideal for testing the theory. The survey was administered, in its 1982 version, to nearly eleven thousand respondents nested within 238 ecological units (approximately neighborhoods). Sampson and Groves determined that this study design meant that a sufficient number of respondents lived within each area to take the survey answers of these individuals and then combine them to create ecological measures. That is, the survey questions could be aggregated to the neighborhood level for construction of reliable community-level variables. These variables could then be used in a neighborhood-level analysis based on 238 cases. Most important, Sampson and Groves discovered that the British Crime Survey contained questions that, when aggregated, could be used to measure dimensions of community-level informal social control.

How was community-level informal social control actually conceptualized and measured? Sampson and Groves included three variables intended to tap various dimensions of the concept, based on the *systemic perspective* that community-based informal social control is particularly rooted in systems of social ties and associational networks characterizing residents. This systemic perspective was borrowed from sociological literature on community attachment and organization in the 1970s (e.g., Kasarda and Janowitz, 1974).

Given their adoption of a systemic perspective, Sampson and Groves included a measure of *local friendship networks* as a dimension of informal social control. This measure was utilized based on the theory that dense relational ties and effective control go hand in hand. Sampson and Groves measured local friendship networks as the neighborhood-level average number of friends reported by respondents as living within a fifteen-minute walk of their homes (scored on a 1 to 5 ordinal scale). As a second dimension of informal social control, Sampson and Groves measured *participation in formal and voluntary organizations,* under the assumption that such participation tapped neighborhood institutional strength and "organizational base" (1989, p. 784). Neighborhood-level organizational participation was measured as the percentage of surveyed residents (per neighborhood) that indicated having participated in a meeting of a committee, club, or organization during the week preceding the survey. Finally, they measured the supervisory (in)capacity of neighborhood networks as the average extent to which neighborhood residents reported as problematic (on a four-point scale) *disorderly teenage youth hanging about in public.*

Sampson and Groves examined these three dimensions of "systemic" informal social control as intervening variables, linking exogenous community-level characteristics (including, more specifically, low socioeconomic status, heterogeneity, residential mobility, family disruption, and urbanization) and community rates of crime. See Figure 3.3 for a diagram of their conceptual model (Sampson and Groves, 1989, p. 783).

They constructed numerous measures of crime, drawing on a variety of survey questions. For example, they included a measure of crime that was constructed by aggregating survey responses to an item tapping residents' *perceptions of crime*—how prevalent street mugging/robbery was within their neighborhood, more specifically. They also included aggregated reports of *victimization* (of various types) experienced by residents. Finally, they included measures of "crime" based on residents' *self-reported offending behavior,* including personal violence and property theft/vandalism. By measuring crime in so many different ways—all of which avoided the potential bias associated with official/police data—Sampson and Groves were able to examine the robustness of their theoretical model. To further discern robustness, Sampson and Groves replicated their analysis of the 1982 British Crime Survey, using data from the 1984 version of the survey. This replication did more than allow Sampson and Groves to assess the

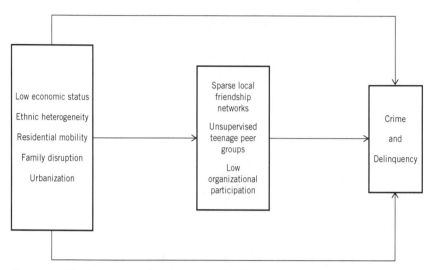

Figure 3.3 The Systemic Model of Crime and Delinquency Tested by Sampson and Groves (1989)
Reprinted from R. J. Sampson and W. B. Groves, "Community Structure and Crime: Testing Social Disorganization Theory," *American Journal of Sociology* 94 (1989): 783.

extent to which their proposed model applied in different years because the ecological units sampled in 1984 were different (larger and more heterogeneous) from those in 1982. As such, they were able to explore the extent to which the theory could be generalizable across different definitions of "neighborhood."

Although some variation in specific effects exists across the multitude of models estimated (using different dependent variables and different waves of the British Crime Survey), Sampson and Groves found overall support for social disorganization theory. Most notably, all three measures of systemic control (i.e., control presumed inherent in systems of social ties and associational networks) were found to be related to community rates of crime in the manner predicted by the theory. More specifically, there was substantial support for the idea that local friendship networks and organizational participation were negatively correlated with at least some measures of community rates of crime, whereas their measure of unsupervised peer groups was positively correlated with neighborhood crime. Additionally, substantial proportions of the effects of socioeconomic status, ethnic heterogeneity, residential mobility, and family disruption were mediated by the measures of informal control. As such, much of the effect of these variables was deemed to be indirect, operating through informal social control. Again, such findings were consistent with the predictions of the systemic model version of social disorganization theory.

This landmark study provided a model for scholars interested in social disorganization theory. In short, Sampson and Groves actually measured social (dis)organization (in systemic terms), and they showed empirically that systems of ties and social control mattered. The study generated decades of research on systemic informal social control of crime.

The Systemic Model and Tripartite Control

Sampson's contributions to the creation of the systemic model of social disorganization theory, culminating in his 1989 landmark study with Groves, cannot be overstated. However, other scholars of that era were undertaking pathbreaking work as well. Robert Bursik's scholarship, in particular, often overlapped and complemented that of Sampson.

Bursik received both his M.A. and Ph.D. in sociology at University of Chicago, the latter earned in 1980. His early post-dissertation research addressed some of the key criticisms of early social disorganization theory, most notably, the perspective of Shaw and McKay (for a review of the prevailing criticisms of the theory, see Bursik, 1988). For example, one of Shaw and McKay's most important yet controversial findings was that suggesting crime remained stable across spatial areas (e.g., communities, zones) *regardless of changes in the ethnic/racial composition of the community* that resulted from the invasion/succession process (as previously discussed in Chapter 2). It was a finding that was consistent with the Chicago School idea that local communities, including high-crime inner-city communities, exhibited a character independent of their occupants. However, skeptics questioned whether the finding could be a methodological or historical artifact (e.g., Jonassen, 1949). After all, Shaw and McKay had conducted most of their analyses "by hand" in a precomputer era. Further, most of their research was done within a historical period in which inner-city demographic shifts, in particular, were quite different from those being observed in the 1960s and 1970s.

As a (postdoctoral) affiliate of the Institute for Juvenile Research in Chicago, Bursik had access to some of the original delinquency and census data used by Shaw and McKay (stored in a file cabinet at the institute). He used these data in combination with similar data collected by the institute in 1970 in an effort to test the merits of the skepticism surrounding Shaw and McKay's findings. In an often-cited article in a 1982 edition of the *American Journal of Sociology*, Bursik and Jim Webb (a colleague at the institute) analyzed official delinquency and census data for seventy-four Chicago neighborhoods in three distinct time periods: 1940–1950, 1950–1960, and 1960–1970. Their main focus was on assessing the extent to which changes in racial/ethnic composition of a neighborhood affected changes in rates of delinquency. They found that changes in racial composition were not associated with changes in delinquency for the 1940–1950 period, but they *were* significantly related to changes in delinquency in the latter two time periods studied (see also Bursik, 1986). Change in the racial/ethnic composition of neighborhoods *did* appear to affect neighborhood crime in the post–World War II Chicago neighborhoods (for a review, see Bursik, 2015).

This analysis could have been quite damaging to the social disorganization tradition because, on its surface, it contradicted one of Shaw and McKay's major findings. Instead, Bursik extolled the virtues of Shaw and McKay's theory in his various writings about changing racial composition and changing community rates of crime (Bursik, 1984, 1986; Bursik and Webb, 1982; Heitgerd and Bursik, 1987). He interpreted the finding that racial composition was related to crime in the post–World War II era as consistent with Shaw and McKay's emphasis on the importance of community organization, including institutional stability. In particular, his work highlighted the fact that the dynamics behind the shifting racial composition of neighborhoods was quite different pre-1950 versus post-1950, largely due to Supreme Court decisions banning race-restrictive housing practices in 1948. These legal changes allowed Blacks access to communities previously unavailable to them, and rapid transition did indeed occur, as Blacks moved in large numbers into previously White neighborhoods. Bursik and his colleagues emphasized (as did McKay in the 1969 revised edition of *Juvenile Delinquency and Urban Areas*) that this rapid transition—not the changing racial makeup per se— was likely making such neighborhoods disorganized:

> Perhaps the most difficult part of the invasion/succession process is the reorganization of the social life of the invading group as it acquires dominance in the area . . . when the existing neighborhood changes almost completely within a very short period of time, the social institutions and social networks may disappear altogether, or existing institutions may persevere in the changed neighborhood but be very resistant to the inclusion of the new residents. (Bursik and Webb, 1982, pp. 39–40)

This interpretation of the correlation between changing racial composition and community crime is thus consistent with the systemic model of social disorganization theory. As such, Bursik's work on this relationship is considered important in the reemergence of the theory in the 1980s, stressing the importance of neighborhood stability, and emphasizing that neighborhood-based networks and institutional strength were important in terms of defining such stability. However, his work was also important in *extending* the conceptualization of the systemic model beyond an exclusive focus on internal neighborhood dynamics. Bursik and colleagues claimed that the demographic invasion and succession that occurred pre- versus post-1948 was due to changes in federal and state housing policies as opposed to "natural" or organic market process, as had been assumed by early Chicago School theorists. While Bursik's research supported many aspects of the systemic theoretical interpretation of Shaw and McKay's work, it also challenged and extended it in a crucial way.

Bursik addressed the criticism that social disorganization theory ignored extracommunity dynamics in understanding community-level crime patterns perhaps most notably in his 1993 book with Harold Grasmick, *Neighborhoods and Crime: The Dimensions of Effective Community Control*. In this volume, Bursik and Grasmick explicitly presented to their readers an elaborated systemic model of social disorganization theory. Building on previous statements about systemic control (Berry and Kasarda, 1977; Kasarda and Janowitz, 1974; Kornhauser, 1978; Sampson, 1988; Sampson and Groves, 1989) in combination with the work of Albert Hunter (1985), their version of the systemic model recognized three levels of social control, encompassing both informal and formal social controls. These levels of control were presumed to emerge from three distinct types of social ties: private, parochial, and public.

Private ties refer to primary, intimate interpersonal relationships, including friendship and kinship networks. *Parochial ties* refer to less intimate relations among residents of a neighborhood, such as those that would emerge in the context of institutional or organizational affiliations (i.e., church membership, ties to local schools, participation in neighborhood organizations) or in the context of neighbors' collective supervision of community youth. *Public ties* refer to relationships with persons and agencies outside the community that could supply the neighborhood with important extracommunity resources for adequate control. The most obvious examples of important public ties are relationships between community members and government agencies, including police, city council, state and federal politicians, and area business leaders.

With this tripartite conceptualization of social ties—and the social controls they were presumed to elicit—serving as the core of their model, Bursik and Grasmick's formulation of the systemic model of social disorganization is as follows: socioeconomic conditions within a community impact both the levels of residential mobility and ethnic heterogeneity in a community. More specifically, poorer socioeconomic conditions foster higher levels of mobility and heterogeneity. Higher levels of mobility and heterogeneity, in turn, weaken private, parochial, and public ties. These weakened ties are

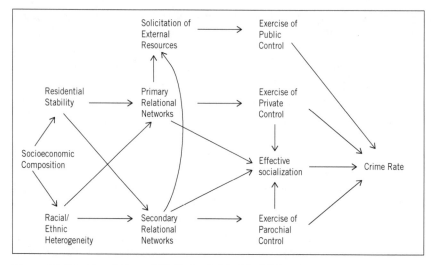

Figure 3.4 Bursik and Grasmick's Systemic Model of Crime
Reprinted from R. J. Bursik Jr. and H. G. Grasmick, *Neighborhoods and Crime: The Dimensions of Effective Community Control* (New York: Lexington, 1993), p. 39.

associated with weakened social control, resulting in relatively higher community rates of crime. Bursik and Grasmick's (1993, p. 39) depiction of these processes is shown in Figure 3.4.

The explicit recognition that social control of crime might stem from different forms of networks—both internal *and external*—was important in addressing the criticisms that social disorganization theory, and the systemic formulation thereof, ignored the extracommunity social and political forces behind the emergence of neighborhood disorganization (Bursik, 1988). However, as important as the inclusion of "public ties" and "public control" into the systemic framework is, it remains an understudied dimension of community-level systemic control of crime. The section that follows provides an overview of the empirical status of the systemic model of social disorganization theory.

Assessing the Systemic Model

How do private, parochial, and public ties fare as correlates of community rates of crime, mediating the relationship between the community structural characteristics of economic disadvantage, ethnic/racial heterogeneity, and residential mobility, at the "exogenous" end of the of the model, and community rates of crime as the outcome? As discussed above, the analysis by Sampson and Groves in 1989 is viewed as a groundbreaking test of social disorganization theory. It is generally regarded as a fundamental test of social disorganization theory's systemic model, given that that study's measurement of informal social control was based on systemic theory. The measures of community-level friendship and supervisory networks and organizational participation tapped private and parochial ties, most specifically. Although Sampson and Groves's study may be the most well known and thus the "landmark" test of the systemic model, it is certainly not the only empirical investigation. In fact, in the years following the publication of Sampson and Groves's 1989 article, research assessing the merits of the theory proliferated. Several of the more influential of these studies warrant consideration here.

Similar to the analysis provided by Sampson and Groves, most tests of the systemic model emphasize the private and parochial dimensions of systemic ties and social control. In fact, several outright replications of Sampson and Groves's study exist. One example is the 2003 study by Christopher Lowenkamp, Francis Cullen, and Travis Pratt. Lowenkamp and colleagues conducted a replication of Sampson and Groves (1989) utilizing data from the 1994 British Crime Survey. Thus, the data they analyzed involved nearly identical measures to those used by Sampson and Groves, but the data were collected a decade later. As such, Lowenkamp and colleagues sought to uncover whether the findings from Sampson and Grove's analysis were robust or a historical artifact. They reported remarkable consistency in comparing the analyses.

More specifically, in their statistical analyses, ecological features of communities—including low socioeconomic status, ethnic heterogeneity, residential mobility, family disruption, and urbanization—typically were found to be inversely related to indicators of (strong) informal social control. In turn, indicators of (strong) control were often negatively related to community crime (measured as the total victimization rate, utilizing aggregate survey responses). Furthermore, all exogenous community characteristics, with the exception of family disruption, had nonsignificant direct effects on crime, once the measures of informal control were considered. This pattern of findings suggested that the effects of low socioeconomic status, ethnic heterogeneity, residential mobility, and urbanization on community crime were substantially mediated by community-level informal social control. Again, such findings are consistent with the systemic model's predictions. Lowenkamp, Cullen, and Pratt (2003) more explicitly compared their findings with those of Sampson and Groves by conducting a statistical test of the equality of the estimates associated with each hypothesized relationship. Of the twenty-three comparisons made, only seven differences were found. In all cases where differences were found, Lowenkamp and his colleagues' estimates were consistent with the predictions of social disorganization theory;

they were simply smaller or larger in magnitude than the estimates reported by Sampson and Groves.

Another replication of the classic study by Sampson and Groves was published in 1999 by Bonita Veysey and Steven Messner. Veysey and Messner reanalyzed the 1982 British Crime Survey, utilizing the same data, theoretical model, and measures as employed by Sampson and Groves. However, Veysey and Messner used a different statistical technique (LISREL) in estimating the various paths constituting the causal model. Most of the relationships reported by Sampson and Groves were also found by Veysey and Messner. However, their analysis reported an additional important point. They found that the statistical model that best fit the data was one in which community-level ecological characteristics were specified as having direct effects on crime in addition to indirect effects on crime, operating through the indicators of informal social control. In fact, they found that a sizable portion of several community characteristics were *not* mediated by informal social control; they had residual effects on community crime that were unexplained by the intervening mechanism of control. This finding led the authors to conclude more modest support for the systemic model of social disorganization theory. To be sure, systemic control was shown to be an important mechanism, mediating some of the effects of neighborhood conditions and rates of crime. At the same time, Veysey and Messner's findings suggested that social disorganization theorists might want to explore the incorporation of other mechanisms that perhaps work alongside measures of systemic control to account for the link between structural conditions and community crime.

Numerous other studies in the 1990s and early 2000s found at least partial support for hypotheses consistent with the systemic model, especially regarding the posited relationships between intra-community ties, informal social control, and community rates of crime (see, e.g., Bellair and Browning, 2010; Warner 2003, 2007). As indicated above, fewer studies have examined the impact of public ties on crime or on ties that span parochial and public spheres (such as certain types of organizational participation). Still, attention to public ties and hybrid parochial-public ties is certainly increasing. Maria Vélez's (2001) pathbreaking study is a good example of this trend. Vélez examined community relations with local police as an intervening variable between ecological characteristics (poverty, heterogeneity, and mobility) and community rates of crime (measured as aggregated reports of victimization). She used data from sixty neighborhoods across Saint Louis, Tampa/Saint Petersburg, and Rochester. The study measured public ties in the form of aggregated (within-neighborhoods) residents' reported ties to local police and government, while also measuring private ties in the form of local friendship/kinship networks. She analyzed the effects of private and public ties in a series of models, first assessing the effects of private ties without controlling for public ties and then adding public ties to her statistical models.

Consistent with other studies, Vélez's analysis showed that, controlling for individual victimization risk factors, neighborhood-level private ties were significantly negatively related to differences in household and personal victimization. Upon adding the measure of public ties, this factor also exhibited significant, negative relationships with household and personal victimization. Further, the effects of private ties were weakened (to statistical nonsignificance) once the measure of public ties was included in the analysis. Her analysis also revealed a significant statistical interaction between neighborhood-level public ties and neighborhood-level economic disadvantage, whereby the negative effect of public ties on victimization was particularly acute in the most disadvantaged areas. These latter findings support the notion that establishing public ties is particularly important for crime and victimization prevention in the most disadvantaged communities. The communities that stand to benefit the most from public ties are those that are least likely to have such associations.

In subsequent work, Vélez, Lyons, and Boursaw (2012) studied the effects of public ties in the form of access to extracommunity economic resources such as mortgage lending. Their analysis revealed that neighborhood-level rates of home mortgage loans were negatively related to subsequent violent crime. In a somewhat similar study, Ramey and Shrider (2014) reported that extracommunity support in the form of money from Seattle's Neighborhood Matching Funds program appeared to reduce neighborhood rates of crime.

Assessing the Conditional Effectiveness of Private and Parochial Ties: Toward a New Parochialism

While a good deal of research provides support for the idea that private, parochial, and public ties can reduce levels of crime, this support is not unconditional, as implied by Velez's findings noted above. In fact, a number of other studies have suggested a rather tenuous connection between various social ties and community rates of crime such that *certain types of ties* are shown to reduce crime *under certain conditions*.

The systemic model implies that denser social networks are "better" in terms of crime control, but some evidence suggests that this ameliorative effect might not necessarily be the case. Paul Bellair's (1997) widely cited study actually indicates that "weak ties" might be as critical for community crime control as strong ties. He analyzed data from an average of two hundred respondents across sixty neighborhoods in three cities—the same data analyzed by Vélez (2001), as described above. In doing so, Bellair focused on the effects of a variety of different measures of private ties, ranging from the within-neighborhood percentage of respondents who reported getting together with neighbors "every day" (the most frequent interactions) to the within-neighborhood percentage of respondents who reported getting together with neighbors "once a year" (the least frequent interactions). In addition to these simple percentages, he also examined measures of ties that consisted of cumulative percentages—so, for example, the within-neighborhood percentage of respondents who reported getting together "once a week *or more*," "once a month *or more*," or "once a year *or more*." In brief, he found that the measure of ties that consisted of the percentage of residents reporting getting together with neighbors "once a year or more" had the most consistent and strongest negative effect across various measures of crime (measured as self-reported rates of victimization).

Bellair interpreted such findings as evidence that weak ties (indicated by infrequent interaction—such as getting together only once a year) might be quite important for crime control owing to the fact that they can be evidence of broad-ranging ties as opposed to narrow or insular ties. Such broad-ranging ties would be quite helpful for community crime control, given that broad-ranging ties are likely to involve institutional ties and extracommunity ties, thus increasing the parochial and public control available to the community above and beyond private control. Although frequent interaction (i.e., getting together with neighbors daily or weekly) might indicate quite strong private ties, it might also indicate narrowly defined, almost "cliquish" networks. Such ties could afford a community an adequate level of private control but could also leave the community lacking along the dimensions of parochial and public control. Bellair's research was instrumental in highlighting that strong private ties—which had dominated the conceptual landscape of the systemic model—might not be the panacea for community crime prevention that advocates once believed.

Other work has shown that private ties might not work to control crime, as the systemic model would predict, in all structural contexts. In particular, two studies analyzing data from one hundred Seattle neighborhoods by Barbara Warner and Pamela Wilcox Rountree emphasized this point. In each study, they examined the variable effects on crime of private ties, measured as the percentage of respondents indicating they had gotten together with neighbors for dinner, borrowed things from neighbors, or helped neighbors with problems. In their first study, Warner and Wilcox Rountree (1997) discovered that private ties were significantly negatively related to crime, as theoretically posited by the systemic model, in predominately White communities only. In predominantly Black and racially/ethnically mixed neighborhoods, in contrast, private ties were *not* related to crime.

In a follow-up study, Wilcox Rountree and Warner (1999) examined the gendered nature and context of private ties. To do so, they measured separately "female ties" and "male ties" as the percentage of female and male survey respondents within each neighborhood who had engaged in the sorts of neighboring mentioned above (having dinner with neighbors, borrowing from neighbors, and helping neighbors). While the *levels* of female versus male ties were similar, the *effects* they had on community rates of crime were quite disparate. Female ties were significantly negatively related to community rates of violence, whereas male ties had no effect. Further analysis revealed that female ties appeared most effective in controlling violent crime in communities with relatively few female-headed households—that is, in communities with a predominance of two-person households. Thus, while female-based private ties appeared particularly important for the social control of crime (in comparison to the ties of men), the effectiveness of those female ties was attenuated within community contexts characterized by a weak presence of family-rooted men. Taken together, these studies illustrate how the crime-controlling capacity of private ties can be moderated by indicators of structural disadvantage.

Another set of studies have emphasized how the crime-controlling capacity of private ties might be undermined by cultural context. In particular, such investigations have emphasized that strong private ties are less effective at curbing crime when those ties occur within communities where there is culture conflict, especially in the form of gang presence. Qualitative work by Mary Pattillo (Pattillo, 1998; Pattillo-McCoy, 1999) and Sudhir Alladi Venkatesh (1997), for instance, has shown how gang presence can make strongly tied adults less likely to informally control criminal actions themselves or to call the police for control purposes. Such reluctance to intervene occurs for several reasons. For some residents, there is simply fear of retaliation if social control were enacted. However, there is also the distinct possibility that the gang members performing criminal acts are children of family friends. Accordingly, close ties among adults creates a situation whereby the adults do not want to see their friends' kids in trouble with the law. In addition, there is often recognition on the part of the adults in the community that gang members actually provide pro-social capital to the community in addition to their unwanted criminal activity. For example, Pattillo and Venkatesh both describe gangs' sponsorship of community activities and provision of financial resources. Thus, in communities with intertwined conventional and criminal networks, a "negotiated coexistence" can emerge that can stunt informal social control (Browning, Dietz, and Feinberg, 2004). In other words, a strong licit network coexists *compatibly* alongside the illicit network; the licit networks do *not* disrupt the illicit network, as the systemic model of social disorganization theory would predict.

Venkatesh's ethnography of an urban ghetto emphasized how such negotiated coexistence is particularly likely in the most economically disadvantaged areas, where oppositional values and behaviors are often observed in the face of such depravity. Notably, Pattillo's work points out that this negotiated coexistence can occur even in middle-class communities when those middle-class communities are predominantly Black. Middle-class Black communities are much more likely than middle-class White communities to be spatially closer to poorer, crime-ridden communities. This geographical proximity makes it more likely that licit and illicit networks will be intertwined. Despite their focus on different socioeconomic contexts, both Venkatesh and Pattillo highlight the importance of cultural context in understanding crime within communities. We return to this issue in detail in Chapter 5.

The conditional nature of the ties-control relationship has also been underscored by Patrick Carr (2003), who identified "new parochialism" as a more realistic form of community-based control in modern communities than control from private ties. Carr's articulation of new parochialism emerged from his ethnographic study of the Beltway community in Chicago. Carr describes low-crime Beltway as "a typical White working-to-lower-middle-class neighborhood in a large city" (p. 1262). Carr observed that informal social control in Beltway did not emerge from strong private ties because dual-earning households were not conducive to the formation of dense private ties. Further, Beltway residents were reluctant to intervene directly in noted problems, especially those involving teens, as a result of fear (for a similar finding, see Wilkinson, 2007).

Instead, social control in Beltway stemmed from what he termed *new parochialism*: "community organizations and their links with public agencies outside the neighborhood" stimulating action on the part of residents (2003, p. 1250). In particular, Carr observed that Beltway residents engaged in more secure forms of social control that were facilitated and supported by the public sphere, such as police-led night watch programs and problem-solving groups with strong links to local politicians (see also Carr, 2012). As one example of new parochialism, Carr described the work of the neighborhood problem-solving group, in conjunction with local police and politicians, to close down a nuisance tavern via a referendum vote to revoke the tavern's license. As Carr states, "the group thus utilize[d] formal channels to solve the problem of the tavern" (p. 1270).

In sum, new parochialism involves an interconnectedness or partnership between neighborhood groups and extracommunity resources. Carr suggests that new parochialism is a common way to achieve effective control in contemporary communities—such as the Beltway neighborhood that he studied—where traditional private ties are lacking. This type of systemic control relies on residents or resident-based organizations, but it also requires the assistance from formal agencies or public officials. New parochialism thus suggests a symbiosis or interdependence among the types of ties and control identified in Bursik and Grasmick's (1993) tripartite conceptualization of the systemic model (parochial and public ties/control, in particular), rather than each exerting independent influences. Carr's notion of new parochialism is supported by subsequent research indicating that neighborhood-based organizations that bridge to the larger community are more effective at reducing crime (e.g., Slocum et al., 2013; Wo, Hipp, and Boessen, 2016).

Conclusion

This chapter traced the post–Shaw and McKay rejuvenation of community-level crime theory. By the mid-1970s, thinking about community had largely fallen off the criminological map. Kornhauser's 1978 blistering analysis of competing theories, in combination with her restatement of Shaw and McKay's theory, revived interest almost immediately. From her work, in combination with those that followed (Sampson and Bursik, most notably), the idea emerged that the key to controlling crime in a community was a system of strong ties and networks. This systemic model dominated community crime theory for the 1980s and 1990s. However, by the late 1990s and early 2000s, evidence had mounted indicating that dense private ties, in particular, were not consistently linked to strong informal social control. As such, contemporary applications of the systemic model have shifted the emphasis away from private ties as the key source of informal social control. Instead, increasing attention is placed on extracommunity linkages as key in affecting community crime, including a particular value seen on the partnering of parochial and public sources of control in the form of "new parochialism."

Although response to evidence that private ties are not always effective in controlling crime has involved greater emphasis on extracommunity linkages within the systemic model and movement toward a new parochialism, it is important to note that an alternative path to resolving the paradoxical "weak effects of strong ties" involves *collective efficacy theory* (Sampson, Raudenbush, and Earls, 1997; Morenoff, Sampson, and Raudenbush, 2001; Sampson, 2002, 2006, 2012). Collective efficacy theory accepts the systemic model's underlying premise—that variation in community-level social control explains varying crime rates. However, it rejects systems of ties as the central construct in understanding community crime, and it elevates instead the construct of collective efficacy. Collective efficacy theory is discussed in detail in Chapter 8.

4

Community as the Truly Disadvantaged

As the previous chapters describe, one of the most enduring visions of communities and crime was introduced by the Chicago School of sociology, which portrayed high-crime communities as "disorganized" and lacking strong systems of social control. However, by the 1970s and 1980s, urban neighborhoods had begun to look dramatically different than the central-city communities first described by Clifford Shaw and Henry McKay. The urban cores of U.S. cities were undergoing massive structural, economic, and demographic changes, which sparked a new vision of communities and crime—one that attributed crime to *truly disadvantaged* structural circumstances rather than social disorganization.

By the 1970s, urban areas no longer saw waves of European migrants rapidly cycling in and out of the city center. Instead, these neighborhoods had become home to large, homogeneous clusters of African Americans, who were often unable to leave the inner city and follow in the footsteps of their European predecessors. The picture of invasion and succession, immigration, and heterogeneity that formed the foundation of Shaw and McKay's theory no longer matched the reality of inner-city communities in the 1970s and 1980s. In addition, the U.S. economy began a restructuring process and transitioned away from the types of industry that first sparked the unprecedented growth seen in Chicago and other urban areas. Rather than serving as hubs of manufacturing and engines of American production, inner-city communities began to hemorrhage jobs, resources, and middle-class residents. Precisely as African Americans migrated to urban areas in the North, the United States saw a "perfect storm" of structural shifts that radically altered these communities and left many Black families marooned in jobless urban deserts with record-level crime. As William Julius Wilson (1987, 2011) described, inner-city Black neighborhoods had become home to a truly disadvantaged urban "underclass."

How did these communities become so ravaged by crime and disadvantage in a few short decades? What made this truly disadvantaged explanation of communities and crime different from Shaw and McKay's image of neighborhoods as "socially disorganized"? This chapter describes the truly disadvantaged perspective and how it offers a distinctly different vision of communities and crime than we had seen up to this point. As noted in the following sections, this perspective has some overlapping themes with the Chicago School's portrayal of urban crime. In fact, the "truly disadvantaged" perspective was inspired as Wilson watched structural changes unfold in many of the exact same Chicago neighborhoods studied by Park, Burgess, Shaw, and McKay. Yet this vision of communities and crime also differs in marked ways from the Chicago School approach, focusing its gaze more squarely on structural forces and, in many ways, providing a bleaker picture for inner-city residents than Shaw and McKay had envisioned.

From Social Disorganization to the Truly Disadvantaged

As reviewed in the previous chapters, Shaw and McKay clearly recognized that inner-city communities were disadvantaged. They famously documented the social ills in the "zone of transition," showing that it was the epicenter of crime, physical and mental illness, infant mortality, poverty, and residential instability in Chicago. It was crowded and laden with pollution from encroaching factories and meatpacking plants. In fact, nearly every marker of community social problems appeared to be concentrated in these poverty-stricken, central-city neighborhoods (Bursik, 1988; Shaw and McKay, 1942).

Despite its problems, the Chicago School perspective also suggested that the urban core was not a place of despair or hopelessness. Although inner-city neighborhoods were "disorganized," they also held hope and promise for advancement. As Matza (1969, p. 72) described, urban neighborhoods were "both attractive and destructive." They offered opportunity, freedom, and excitement, which "masked their danger and potential decay." In other words, central-city neighborhoods were "destinations" that people sought and desired despite their risks. Migrants poured into Chicago and other U.S. cities with dreams for better lives. Yes, there were pains associated with living in these communities, but the problems were seen as *temporary* circumstances and short-term pains that could produce longer-term gains.

Every ethnic group that passed through central-city Chicago experienced the same types of structural problems, disorganization, and exposure to crime and victimization. However, as Shaw and McKay observed, nearly all of these groups eventually left the zone of transition and shed the problems that plagued the inner city (Bursik, 1988; Park, 1967b; Shaw and McKay, 1942). Inner-city Chicago was like a transitional urban purgatory. No one expected to make the zone of transition their permanent home, and there was nothing in Shaw and McKay's vision suggesting that any of the groups would be permanently stuck there. Instead, crime laden inner-city neighborhoods were like a rite of passage that all migrant groups temporarily endured as they sought the American dream but eventually overcame relatively unscathed.

This image of urban neighborhoods is precisely what Chicago School researchers saw for decades. Wave after successive wave of German, Irish, Polish, Italian, and Jewish immigrants arrived in inner-city Chicago and then quickly began to assimilate, climb the ladder of social mobility, and leave the urban core. After a generation or two, each group had gone from "immigrant" to simply "American" and became rooted in mainstream U.S. society (Muller, 1993; Park et al., 1967; Portes and Rumbaut, 2006). Among the last in this line of ethnic succession were large numbers of African Americans migrating from rural and southern regions of the United States. Similar to earlier European migrants, they came in search of work, opportunity, and the upward mobility that the city had promised and delivered for so many others. However, integration was much less seamless for African Americans.

A variety of structural changes coalesced in the 1970s and 1980s that fundamentally changed the social and economic landscape of urban areas, creating a more severe and concentrated deprivation among central city neighborhoods. As scholars like Wilson (1987, 1996) and others (Blau and Blau, 1982; Massey and Denton, 1993; see Duneier, 2016) saw these changes unfold, they did not have the same hopefulness about inner-city residents' fate. The linear road to success, leading from the zone of transition to the middle-class and upper-class communities, no longer seemed guaranteed for African Americans in the urban core as they faced a more pervasive set of structural disadvantages than seen by prior residents.

Concentrated Disadvantage in the Urban Core

Although inner-city neighborhoods had been disadvantaged for decades, urban structural deprivation dramatically intensified from the 1960s to the early 1980s. These growing patterns of disadvantage and dislocation were felt among both Whites and Blacks, yet the burden of these shifts fell much more squarely on the shoulders of inner-city Black populations. Among the largest five cities, the number of Whites in poverty increased by slightly more than 20 percent during the 1970s, while the Black population in poverty grew by more than 160 percent (U.S. Census Bureau, 2015; Wilson, 1987). White unemployment nearly doubled from 1950 to 1980 but remained under 10 percent (and under 7 percent for nearly all years other than 1982). In contrast, more than one in five African Americans and approximately one in three Black teenagers were unemployed in the early 1980s (U.S. Bureau of Labor Statistics, 2016). Likewise, as Wilson (1987) notes, nearly 80 percent of Black men were active participants in the labor force in the 1930s, but by the early 1980s, only about half of Black men were participating in the U.S. labor force.

Black family structures saw an even more pronounced change. The number of Black female-headed families grew by more than 100 percent during the 1970s, while White female-headed families rose by 60 percent. Only 15 percent of Black children were born out of wedlock in the 1950s, yet this number rose to nearly 60 percent by the 1980s (U.S. Census Bureau, 2015). Indeed, it had been only a few years earlier that controversy erupted following the release of the Moynihan report (1965), which noted that a quarter of Black families were female headed in the 1960s. By the early 1980s, the inflammatory findings from the Moynihan report had been eclipsed as census figures showed that more than 40 percent of Black families and nearly 75 percent of poor Black families had female heads (U.S. Census Bureau, 2015; Wilson, 1987).

Likewise, crime trends followed suit. Homicide rates soared from about 5 per 100,000 people in the 1960s to more than 10 per 100,000 people in the 1980s and to more than 20 per 100,000 in the largest cities. Similarly, officially recorded violent crime rates more than tripled from less than 200 per 100,000 people in 1960 up to more than 700 per 100,000 by the end of the 1980s. Black communities again saw the bulk of these changes, with Black arrests for homicide and index violence that were three to four times higher than national arrest rates throughout the 1980s (Federal Bureau of Investigation, 2016). Taken together, the levels of crime and social dislocation in urban Black neighborhoods had reached unprecedented levels.

What could account for these changes in social conditions and crime in inner-city communities? For several decades, scholars largely avoided this question. After the Moynihan report was released in 1965 and became the center of intense controversy and criticism, social scientists were hesitant to study or discuss urban Black communities and families. Researchers were fearful that they might be seen as racist if their findings did not cast Black communities in a positive light and wanted to avoid the type of scrutiny that had been leveled at the Moynihan report. Furthermore, when scholars did discuss Black communities, they generally focused on advances of the Black middle class and gains of Black populations, rather than their disadvantages. Alternatively, the few liberal scholars that did discuss crime and social problems in Black neighborhoods often suggested that racism and discrimination were primarily responsible for these problems. As Wilson (1987, p. 15) noted, "It was clear to any sensitive observer that if there was to be research on the ghetto underclass that would not be subjected to ideological criticism, it would be research conducted by minority scholars on the strengths, not the weaknesses, of inner-city families and communities."

The rest of the academic community largely went silent (or was at least far less vocal) on the topics of Black families, urban communities, and crime in the decades leading up to 1980—precisely the period when urban neighborhoods saw their most dramatic social changes. Thus, when scholarly attention to these topics began to resurface in the 1980s, researchers were somewhat unprepared for what they found. The social and economic landscape in the inner city had radically shifted, and due to muted attention on the topic, researchers were left searching for a voice to explain what had happened.

However, this void in conversation was not left unfilled. As the scholarly silence on urban Black communities stretched on, the U.S. populous and political leaders gravitated toward cultural arguments to explain the plight of urban communities and Black families. Several influential pieces, including Charles Murray's famous book *Losing Ground* (1984; see also Gilder, 1981; Wilson, 1975), gained widespread attention with claims that the rise of social welfare programs had contributed to the economic decline of urban communities. Commentators such as Murray claimed that, rather than aiding poor people, welfare programs bred a culture of poverty and ultimately contributed to persistent patterns of disadvantage, unemployment, and family disruption in urban neighborhoods (Olasky, 1992). To support these claims, Murray and others pointed to the fact that urban crime, poverty, and family disruption had all expanded during the same time that the United States saw widespread expansion of social welfare programs. These explanations gained significant traction among conservative voices and political leaders and were appealing to many who saw them as "fresh" or "new" ideas. As a result, cultural perspectives and discussions of a "culture of poverty" became dominant themes in explaining the extreme levels of crime, poverty, and joblessness that had emerged in urban communities leading up to the 1980s.

In response, scholars such as Judith and Peter Blau (1982) and William Julius Wilson (1987, 1996) challenged these ideas with a new "truly disadvantaged" perspective that rekindled scholars' interests in urban communities, race, social structure, and crime. As Wilson (1987, pp. 15–16) notes, Murray's book "lit a fire" under liberal scholars and created the "spark for . . . a liberal revival" aimed at explaining the social dislocation of urban Black communities. Yet this revival of scholarly interest in race, community, poverty, and crime was also more than simply a reaction to culture of poverty claims. On the one hand, Wilson and other scholars saw that inner-city Black communities had undergone massive social and economic changes, which could not be laid solely at the feet of culture. On the other hand, he recognized that liberal views attributing Black social dislocation largely to racism had trouble explaining why Black crime and disadvantage had accelerated so quickly during an era of unprecedented civil rights gains and expanded social welfare programs for the poor. In contrast to the more liberal arguments, Wilson (1987, p. 141) said, "Skin color was part of the problem but was not all of it." Likewise, although he did not entirely dismiss cultural influences, he sharply disputed conservative claims and argued that culture was not the ultimate cause of social problems in Black communities. Instead, Blau and Blau (1982), Wilson (1987), and several others (see Duneier, 2016), redirected scholars' attention toward *structural factors* (rather than culture, discrimination, or even social disorganization) and suggested that the fundamental shifts in global and urban economies were the ultimate sources of crime and social problems that had surfaced in inner-city communities.

The Truly Disadvantaged Community

Blau and Blau

Some of the initial groundwork that helped reopen the door for structural perspectives on urban crime was first laid by Judith and Peter Blau (1977; Blau and Blau, 1982). Blau and Blau's seminal 1982 study critiqued the leading cultural explanations of crime and essentially "primed the well" for a new wave of research focusing on structural sources of crime, including Wilson's (1987) defining statements on the truly disadvantaged. Specifically, their study examined the macro-level relationships between structural context and violence across 125 of the largest metropolitan areas in the United States as a way of confronting three of the leading cultural explanations of violence: (1) the southern subculture of violence thesis, (2) theories of Black urban ghetto culture, and (3) culture of poverty arguments emphasizing toughness and aggression. As they note, prior research had often found high violent crime rates in southern locales, places with greater shares of Black residents, and places with higher rates of poverty. In response to these findings, the U.S. public and political leaders, as well as many researchers, assumed that this was due to unique cultural value systems that promoted violence in the South, in urban Black communities, and in poor neighborhoods. Blau and Blau's study offered a direct challenge to these assumptions.

Their key finding, which would become a pillar of macro-level research on social structure and crime, was that urban crime rates were largely explained by levels of *income inequality* and especially by *interracial inequality* present in a locale. Based on these findings, they suggested that if the lion's share of urban violence was explained by the structural conditions of places, then culture probably played a minor role in explaining crime differences across race, place, and region of the country. Blau and Blau's (1982, p. 126) conclusion was: "High rates of criminal violence are apparently the price of racial and economic inequalities," and that if culture did matter for urban violence, it was rooted in these larger structural forces.

At a time when cultural perspectives were dominating explanations of urban crime, Blau and Blau's study marked a turning point in research. It redirected criminologists' attention back to structural forces and illustrated the profound effects that factors such as income inequality (especially inequalities based on ascribed conditions like race) had on urban crime rates. Blau and Blau's article had set the initial foundation for a new "truly disadvantaged" perspective on urban Black crime and social dislocation, which would be more firmly cemented by William Julius Wilson's (1987) seminal book. Yet, as Wilson recounts, his personal experiences with urban Black poverty began long before the 1980s and publication of *The Truly Disadvantaged*.

William Julius Wilson

As a child, William Julius Wilson had close personal experiences with the same types of disadvantage and social dislocation he would study as an adult. Wilson grew up in western Pennsylvania, where his father worked in coal mines and steel mills. After his father died at the early age of thirty-nine from lung cancer, his mother was left to raise Wilson and his five younger siblings. The family relied on social welfare programs at times until his mother could begin supporting them through housekeeping jobs. Summarizing these experiences, Wilson (2011, p. 1) explains, "Some of the most lasting memories of my childhood have to do with enduring the physical conditions associated with deep poverty, including hunger, and the experiences of racial discrimination in a small town." These experiences would eventually help mold his career and his lasting interest in Black poverty and social dislocation. But his path to this topic was somewhat circuitous and went through a variety of other interests before returning to the topics of social structure and poverty in Black communities (Wilson, 2011).

In his graduate studies at Washington State University, Wilson studied social theory and the philosophy of science. His interest in race and urban poverty did not blossom until near the end of his graduate education when he became interested in civil rights struggles of the time and the structural changes he saw emerging for African Americans (Wilson, 2011). These experiences fed Wilson's intellectual interest in race and poverty, which had begun with his childhood experiences. This academic interest developed further when he began working as an assistant professor at University of Massachusetts, Amherst, in 1965. However, he explains that his vision of race, class, and urban social structure were not "sufficiently crystallized" until after he took a tenured position at the University of Chicago in 1972 (Wilson, 2011, p. 3).

In his own words, Wilson (2011, p. 4) believed that his chances of ending up at an elite university like the University of Chicago were "rather slim." He did not have an Ivy League pedigree, and as Sugrue (2010, pp. 73–74) notes, "Wilson was bit of a gamble for a hidebound institution like Chicago." The high quality of his work and the promise of his potential scholarship were key to his hiring. Yet Wilson also attributes his placement at the University of Chicago in part to affirmative action initiatives and to being at the right place at the right time. Regardless of the precise reasons for this placement, the "gamble" clearly paid off for the University of Chicago, and it provided Wilson with the prime opportunity and scholarly environment to develop his vision of race, inequality, and urban life.

In 1972, nearly half a century after the Chicago School perspective on urban communities and crime was developed, Wilson found himself in the same university, looking at many of the exact same neighborhoods that Shaw and McKay had studied in the early 1900s. Chicago would once again give birth to a new vision of communities and crime. Notably, Wilson saw a wholly different picture of urban life in inner-city Chicago neighborhoods, which would be reflected in his subsequent theory. He would ultimately be responsible for popularizing the image of the "community as the truly disadvantaged."

Wilson explains that he was struck by the massive social changes and mounting poverty and inequality he saw across Chicago neighborhoods. Urban neighborhoods in Chicago and other cities had seen a rise in unemployment, poverty, inequality, and especially single-parent families unlike any other seen in U.S. history. Yet the topics of Black families, poverty, and crime remained mired in controversy and silence from the scholarly community. Wilson's (1987) book, *The Truly Disadvantaged*, helped break this silence. He explained that social conditions in urban Black neighborhoods had deteriorated so severely that they could no longer be ignored. Rather than focusing exclusively on gains in the Black community, Wilson (1987, pp. 3–8) directly confronted the severe social problems in urban Black neighborhoods that had contributed to formation of a "ghetto underclass." However, Wilson's contribution was not simply that he described the structural problems in Black urban communities. It was that he offered an explanation for the plight of the ghetto underclass that starkly contrasted with conservative cultural arguments (and with some liberal perspectives focusing on racism) and that resonated widely with the U.S. public, legislators, and scholars. Wilson argued that the massive disadvantages that had emerged in urban Black communities during the 1970s and 1980s had resulted from the confluence of larger structural-economic shifts that fundamentally transformed urban communities.

Wilson's Theory of The Truly Disadvantaged

From 1960 through the 1980s, the United States began a period of *economic restructuring* in which it rapidly transitioned from an industrial and manufacturing goods-based economy to a service-based economy. In *The Truly Disadvantaged*, Wilson (1987) argued that these changes had several key effects on urban Black communities. First, it meant that manufacturing and industrial jobs that had been the lifeblood of urban economies for more than half a century began to disappear. As the U.S. economy moved into a post-industrial period, these factories and industries either closed or were pulled from inner-city areas and relocated overseas and into rural and suburban communities. As a result, African American populations faced quite different job prospects than the previous generations of migrants that had been drawn to inner-city communities. The high-paying, low-skill industrial jobs that had been plentiful were vanishing from the urban core. African American populations who came in search of these jobs were quickly faced with a situation of declining employment prospects. Within the span of two short decades, this trend had accelerated so severely that many Black populations found themselves in deindustrialized, urban deserts of abandoned factories and shuttered industries.

Second, the jobs that replaced central-city industry and manufacturing were largely service sector jobs that were mismatched with African Americans' skill sets. Black populations moved to urban communities looking for the same types of low-skill industrial work that their European predecessors had sought. Instead, they were faced with a shifting job market that increasingly required higher education, clerical experience, and work history in white-collar and service-sector jobs—all of which they had not expected when moving to inner-city neighborhoods. The promise of advancement and the industrial opportunities that had drawn newcomers to the city for decades dried up precisely as Black populations arrived. In their place, African Americans found fewer jobs that required far more training and qualifications, or they found low-skill service sector jobs (e.g., food service, janitorial/cleaning) that offered relatively meager wages. As Wilson explains, it was not that urban Black residents did not *want* to work or were *unwilling* to work (as the culture of poverty thesis suggested). It was that the work they found in urban areas had changed and no longer provided the same opportunity it had for generations of earlier migrants.

Third, Wilson argued that this decline in urban social conditions also had the unexpected effect of creating a mass exodus of middle-class Black families from inner-city communities. As job prospects deteriorated and problems like poverty and crime mounted in the inner city, stable working-class Black residents and middle- and upper-class Black families began to leave. They moved to suburbs and other communities outside the city center, where industries had relocated and that had better economic prospects, more resources, and less crime. As a result, Wilson suggested that urban communities saw a fundamental change in class structure. He notes, "In the 1940s, 1950s, and even the 1960s, lower-class, working-class, and middle-class Black urban families all resided more or less in the same ghetto areas, albeit on different streets" (1987, p. 143). Although the inner city was home to many poor families, in the past these communities also housed more affluent Black residents, which created a diverse mix of *class heterogeneity* in urban neighborhoods. In contrast, when the Black middle class poured out of central-city communities, those left behind were "almost exclusively the most disadvantaged segments of the Black community" (Wilson, 1987, p. 143).

On its surface, this sounds reminiscent of the patterns of mobility, invasion, and succession described by the Chicago School. After all, inner-city communities had been disadvantaged and poverty-stricken since the early 1900s (Park, 1967b; Shaw and McKay, 1942). Likewise, Chicago School scholars had noted decades earlier that more affluent residents had a long history of moving out of these communities once they gathered the resources to relocate. But as Wilson watched Chicago neighborhoods change, he saw that it was different this time.

Even in turn-of-the-century Chicago neighborhoods, there had always been some stable middle- and working-class residents in low-income communities who acted as a "social buffer" for other residents (Wilson, 1987, p. 144). When economic problems arose, these stable working-class and middle-class families helped urban neighborhoods "weather the storm" by insulating them from economic shocks. They often attracted businesses, employers, and social services to inner-city communities. They promoted and helped maintain schools, churches, and other supportive institutions. They were rarely wealthy, but they spent money in the community and opened and supported small businesses, which inner-city communities desperately needed during times of economic crisis. Yet by the 1980s, many of those families were gone. As a result, there was little insulation or protective buffer for the low-income residents left behind.

This created what Wilson (1987, p. 58, emphasis in the original) referred to as unprecedented *"concentration effects"* of disadvantage in urban Black communities. It was not simply that these residents suffered from poverty and had few job prospects. The problem was that after the middle-class Black families left, these problems became much more *concentrated* in the urban core. Poverty, unemployment, single-parent families, and crime had become pervasive in inner-city neighborhoods, and the residents that suffered from these conditions no longer had regular contact with more affluent families that could help mitigate economic or social problems when they arose. As such, he argued that this new urban underclass had become "socially isolated" to a degree that had not been seen in previous generations of inner-city residents (p. 60).

He explained that this pattern of *social isolation* had profound effects on urban Black communities. When contact with the middle class was severed, this cut off many poor Black families' connections to the job market. As middle-class Black residents flowed out of the inner city, social services and institutions (community centers, health-care providers, churches, retail stores) often followed. Furthermore, the exodus of stable, working-class families pulled key role models out of urban communities, leaving poor Black youths with fewer models of middle-class family life and daily work routines.

In addition, Wilson argued that these extreme patterns of disadvantage had contributed to the massive rise in single-parent families. As noted earlier, by the early 1980s nearly half of Black families with children under eighteen were in female-headed families and more than two-thirds of children born to Black women between ages fifteen and twenty-four were born outside marriage (Wilson, 1987; U.S. Census Bureau, 1983). Up until this point, these shifts had largely been attributed to cultural influences or to effects of welfare on family structure (Murray, 1984). Wilson disagreed, arguing that the rise in single-parent Black families was not due to a decline in Black family values, a dysfunctional family lifestyle, or the presence of a "matriarchal subculture" (Wilson, 1987, p. 173). Instead, he argued that Black women were choosing not to marry because there had been a sharp decline in the "male marriage pool." As male joblessness mounted, young Black women saw declining prospects for marriage and fewer available, stable partners. Notably, Wilson contrasted this with shifts in White marriage. White families had also become increasingly female headed, but nowhere near the levels seen in urban Black communities. Furthermore, the change in White family structure was largely due to a rise in divorce rather than an increase in "never married" women, as seen in Black communities. Wilson (1987, p. 73) explained the growth of "never married" Black mothers by arguing, "Despite the complex nature of the problem, the weight of existing evidence suggests that the problems of male joblessness could be the single most important factor underlying the rise in unwed mothers among poor black women."

Taken together, Wilson (1987, pp. 58–60, 143) said that extreme social isolation, expansive concentrated disadvantage, and family disruption had coalesced to create a "ghetto underclass" population of truly disadvantaged residents in inner-city neighborhoods. More importantly, his work helped change the way people thought about social dislocation in urban Black communities, illustrating that it was not simply a product of culture (from conservative arguments), nor was it due to racism and prejudice alone (from liberal arguments). Instead, he convincingly illustrated how macro-level structural shifts in the global economy had combined to create crime, family disruption, and the other growing problems found in urban communities.

The Response to The Truly Disadvantaged

Wilson's (1987) publication of *The Truly Disadvantaged* marked a key turning point in research on communities and crime. Despite its profound and long-lasting influence, Wilson's work was not immediately embraced by everyone. Some saw his ideas as quite controversial and raised serious critiques about his vision of urban communities, disadvantage, and crime. For example, Wilson's claims that the exodus of the Black middle class had contributed to social isolation and problems in the inner city drew fire from other academics (see, e.g., Billingsley, 1989). Some saw this as a critique of the Black middle class and argued that it placed responsibility for urban decline on the backs of the Black families that moved.

Researchers also strongly critiqued Wilson's "race-neutral" approach to explaining the urban decline. Wilson's earlier book *The Declining Significance of Race* (1980) had drawn heated criticism over its claims that race and racism were not the primary causes of disadvantage and decline in urban Black communities. In both *The Declining Significance of Race* and *The Truly Disadvantaged*, he argued that although race was important, economic restructuring and race-neutral structural forces offered the greatest threat for inner-city Black communities. Racism and overt discrimination toward minorities were not the primary cause of contemporary Black social dislocation in his vision of urban communities. Instead, he explained that *historic racism*, the lasting legacy of slavery, and past discrimination had positioned Blacks to be more vulnerable to the structural problems that surfaced in the mid-twentieth century. In sum, he argued that race mattered, but it was not the only (or biggest) factor driving crime, poverty, and social problems in urban Black neighborhoods. Instead, his explanation suggested that there was "more than just race" (the title and theme of his later 2009 book) driving the formation of truly disadvantaged communities.

To illustrate this idea, he pointed to the fact that both Black *and* White families in lower income brackets had fallen further behind the middle- and upper-class throughout the latter half of the twentieth century. This focus on rising within-race inequality was a key theme of his earlier book *The Declining Significance of Race* (1980). In addition, he noted that many Black middle-class families had seen large gains and improving social conditions at the same time that lower-class Black communities had faced record levels of poverty and unemployment. Wilson said that economic restructuring generated a two-tiered social system in which there was massive inequality between the "haves" and "have-nots" within both White and Black communities. Thus, he argued, it had to be something more than race and discrimination alone that led to urban Black poverty. Otherwise, why would the White poor also have fallen so much further behind the White middle class? Based on these observations, his policy suggestions for addressing urban Black poverty and crime were also race-neutral, universal policies. Rather than promoting race-specific efforts to address Black disadvantage, Wilson encouraged job growth programs and economic efforts that would help both Black and White communities and both poor and middle-class populations. As Wilson (2011, p. 14) explains, "My thinking had been that, given American views about poverty and race, a colorblind agenda would be the most realistic way to generate the broad political support that would be necessary to enact the required legislation."

Although Wilson (2009) eventually reconsidered this colorblind approach in his later work, his original race-neutral ideas sparked heated debate and criticism from other scholars (see Dill, 1989; Newby, 1989; see also Duneier, 2016). Perhaps most memorable was the criticism leveled at Wilson's work by Massey and Denton in their book, *American Apartheid* (1993). In response to Wilson's (1980) claims about the *Declining Significance of Race*, Massey and Denton argued that not only did race still matter in shaping urban decline but also that racial segregation and discrimination in the housing market was one of the primary mechanisms for creating inequality, Black disadvantage, and social problems such as crime in U.S. communities. They explained that Black and White populations were separated to such a degree that residential patterns could only be characterized as "hypersegregated" and akin to an "American apartheid" (Massey and Denton, 1993, p. 10). They asserted that the isolation of poor urban Blacks was not simply due to racially neutral economic shifts and the exodus of the Black middle class from the inner city, as Wilson had suggested. In other words, urban Black isolation "did not just happen" as an effect of economic changes. Instead, Massey and Denton (1993, p. 2) argued that it was racially motivated and was "manufactured by Whites through a series of self-conscious actions and purposeful institutional arrangements that continue today."

Despite their different stances on the role of race and racism, these scholars actually agreed on many points. Massey and Denton (1993, p. 8) acknowledge that they "agree with William Wilson's basic argument" that economic restructuring contributed to mounting disadvantages in urban Black communities. Likewise, Wilson (2011, p. 16; see also Quillian, 1999) notes that despite some heated scholarly debates with Massey and Denton, "our arguments are, in fact, complementary, not contradictory." In the end, Massey and Denton's critique was not that Wilson's structural arguments were wrong. It was simply that race and segregation mattered more in creating Black urban poverty and crime than Wilson's earlier work had implied.

Finally, another key point of controversy in Wilson's vision of communities and crime (and urban Black poverty more generally) was his use of the phrase *underclass* and focus on norms and cultural adaptations among the ghetto poor (see Covington, 1995; Gans, 1990). Wilson clearly indicated that he did not support "culture of poverty" arguments. In fact, one of his main goals in writing *The Truly Disadvantaged* was to challenge culture of poverty perspectives. Even so, Wilson (1987, p. 137) also did not rule out the idea that a "ghetto-specific culture" of *social isolation* may form in poor urban communities that contributes to crime and other social problems, a point he would later revisit with Robert Sampson in their theory of "social isolation" (Sampson and Wilson, 1995; see also Wilson, 2009).

Testing the Truly Disadvantaged Explanation of Crime

Despite some criticism, the arguments raised by Wilson (1987) and by Blau and Blau (1982) generated considerable attention among criminologists and inspired a wave of empirical research exploring the ways that deteriorating urban structural conditions (e.g., poverty, inequality, single-parent families) were tied to community patterns of crime. As researchers found connections between urban social structure and crime, they began to challenge the cultural arguments that had dominated discussions of communities and crime in prior decades. Yet the findings from this new wave of research were more mixed than scholars initially expected and did not always cleanly align with Wilson's vision.

Some studies provided clear support for the truly disadvantaged perspective on communities and crime. As noted earlier, the foundational study by Blau and Blau (1982) showed strong links between economic inequality (especially across race) and macro-level violence. Likewise, Sampson (1987) illustrated that the particularly high levels of disadvantage found in Black communities contributed to increased Black robbery and homicide rates by creating greater Black family disruption. Peterson and Krivo (1993, 1999) found that racial segregation had concentrated disadvantages in urban Black communities, which in turn contributed to higher levels of Black violence. Similarly, a host of studies found evidence linking socioeconomic disadvantage with aggregate levels of violence in neighborhoods and larger macro-level units (Standard Metropolitan Statistical Areas and counties) (Bailey, 1984; Blau and Golden, 1986; Corzine and Huff-Corzine, 1992; Krivo and Peterson, 1996; Land, McCall, and Cohen, 1990; Loftin and Parker, 1985; Messner and Golden, 1992; Sampson, 1986; Sampson and Groves, 1989; Smith, 1992; see reviews in Ousey, 2000; Peterson and Krivo, 2005). Taken together, there seemed to be convincing evidence that community patterns of crime and higher levels of urban Black violence were generated by structural, and not cultural, differences across groups and places.

However, there were some caveats with these early analyses. Many studies had relied on measures of "total" crime rates and did not disaggregate Black and White violence. Thus, they were often unable to examine whether structural conditions, such as inequality and poverty, could actually account for the different patterns of violence in Black and White communities (for a discussion, see Harer and Steffensmeier, 1992; Peterson and Krivo, 2005). Following the practices outlined by Harer and Steffensmeier (1992) and Messner and Golden (1992), subsequent studies began to address this issue by separately examining Black and White measures of structural disadvantage, inequality, and rates of violence. Yet the findings from this research were somewhat mixed and were not always consistent with a purely structural approach to explaining community patterns of crime.

Research by Harer and Steffensmeier (1992) and Shihadeh and Steffensmeier (1994) found that inequality, poverty, and other structural conditions of communities were closely linked to White rates of violence but had surprisingly little effect (or had inconsistent effects) on Black crime rates. Furthermore, this was not an isolated finding. Other studies mirrored their results, showing that structural factors were better able to explain violence in White communities than in Black communities (see Ousey, 1999; Peterson and Krivo, 1999; Phillips, 2002; Shihadeh and Ousey, 1998). Even more surprising, LaFree, Drass, and O'Day (1992) found that disadvantage not only failed to predict Black violence but also that financial success and family cohesion were actually linked to higher Black rates of violence.

These results were puzzling to say the least. The truly disadvantaged position had offered such a clear and convincing explanation for the shifts in urban crime and social structure that occurred throughout the 1970s and 1980s. Yet the empirical studies that followed offered a series of mixed findings suggesting that structural factors could not account for Black violence the same way they accounted for White rates of violence. Criminologists still contended that structural factors were a key source of violence in both Black and White communities. But if this was the case, why did factors like inequality, poverty, and unemployment fail to account for crime rates in the most "truly disadvantaged" urban Black communities that had been hit the hardest by economic restructuring?

Researchers offered several explanations. Harer and Steffensmeier (1992) and Shihadeh and Steffensmeier (1994) noted that prior research had focused on total inequality, between-race inequality, and poverty (often all at the same time) but had failed to consider *within-race* inequality. Drawing from Merton's (1938) strain theory, they argued that within-race inequality may provide a more theoretically appropriate measure of relative deprivation and, ultimately, a better predictor of strain and violence than between-race inequality or overall disadvantage. Prior studies had assumed that Blacks largely compared themselves with Whites and that Black-White inequality was generating relative deprivation, strain, and crime. However, Harer and Steffensmeier (1992) and Shihadeh and Steffensmeier (1994) argued that people are more likely to compare themselves with others who are from the same race, community, and background. Thus, they suggested that the measures of Black-White inequality and total income inequality commonly used in earlier studies may not capture relative deprivation and ultimately may not predict Black crime as well as measures of Black-on-Black inequality, which was supported in their findings.

The seminal study by Kenneth Land and his colleagues also helped clarify these puzzling findings. Land, McCall, and Cohen (1990, p. 942, emphasis in the original) recognized that this long line of mixed research likely suffered from a *"partialing fallacy,"* which could obscure the findings on social structure and crime. The problem was that researchers had included many intertwined measures of disadvantage in their models of social structure and crime (see Blau and Blau, 1982; LaFree, Drass, and O'Day, 1992; Sampson, 1987). Researchers had been trying to parse out the effects of specific community conditions on crime by saturating models with a host of structural disadvantage measures—including total inequality, between-race inequality, within-race inequality, poverty rates, employment rates—as well as related measures of family structure and educational attainment.

Harkening back to Wilson's original thoughts on the truly disadvantaged, Land, McCall, and Cohen (1990) explained that these factors were so tightly intertwined and concentrated in urban communities that they were often statistically inseparable. Separately examining effects of poverty, education, family structure, employment, and other related factors on urban crime rates essentially watered down the effects of each type of disadvantage and split the explanatory power across each measure. In turn, this could also produce seemingly odd findings in which measures of poverty or inequality failed to have significant effects on crime rates, especially in urban Black communities where these structural conditions were often more highly concentrated and intertwined. Based on these arguments, Land and his colleagues urged researchers to focus on more global measures of community concentrated disadvantage that combined multiple, related variables into a concentrated disadvantage index. Using this strategy, they saw few of the mixed findings that had plagued prior research. Instead, Land and his colleagues' analyses revealed strong links between disadvantage and urban crime rates and resounding support for the truly disadvantaged position on crime.

Similarly, Krivo and Peterson (2000) helped account for the mixed findings in prior work and illustrated why poverty and disadvantage seemed to explain crime rates of Whites but not those of Black populations. Specifically, they explained that disadvantage has a *curvilinear* effect on crime and depends on the overall levels of disadvantage present in Black and White communities. At low to moderate levels of disadvantage, an increase in poverty or other forms of deprivation adds to crime and social problems precisely as structural theories of crime would predict. However, once disadvantage reaches the extreme levels found in the most truly disadvantaged communities, its effects on crime begin to taper off. In other words, the most disadvantaged communities have reached a saturation point, in which becoming slightly "more poor" or "more unemployed" has little further impact on crime.

But why did this threshold effect of disadvantage seem to apply only to Black crime? Simply put, White communities rarely, if ever, saw the extreme types of disadvantages present among the poorest urban Black areas. As a result, disadvantage seemed to predict White crime quite well because White populations were on the lower end of the disadvantage scale, where changes in poverty, employment, and family structure were readily apparent. In contrast, urban Black populations were routinely at the higher end of the disadvantage spectrum, where effects of disadvantage on crime were already maxed out (Krivo and Peterson, 2000).

By illustrating these curvilinear effects, Krivo and Peterson helped resolve many of the puzzling findings from early analyses of Black and White crime and provided strong support for the truly disadvantaged position on crime. In contrast to many of the earlier studies, they showed that disadvantage *did* matter for both Black and White crime. However, the concentration of disadvantages in urban Black communities had made these effects on Black crime almost unobservable. In sum, Krivo and Peterson (2000, p. 558, emphasis in the original) concluded that the "crime generating processes . . . do not differ much between African Americans and Whites *when the two racial groups are similarly situated.*" However, these groups were rarely similarly situated, which was why poverty, inequality, unemployment, and other disadvantages seemed to have such different effects on Black and White crime (Peterson and Krivo, 2010).

Despite some mixed findings early on, evidence supporting the truly disadvantaged perspective on crime was mounting. Criminologists increasingly recognized that the structural shifts described by Wilson (1987) were likely a prime source of the rising crime rates seen in urban communities throughout the 1970s and 1980s. Furthermore, as scholars gravitated toward the truly disadvantage perspective, they began to reject many of the more controversial cultural perspectives on communities and crime. Scholars drew rigid dividing lines, pitting "structure versus culture." The thought was that if structural conditions were responsible for crime problems in inner-city communities, then cultural explanations for urban poverty and crime seemed less valid. As a result, cultural models of inner-city crime became taboo and were either avoided or dismissed in favor of the structural perspectives that were gaining traction. However, Sampson and Wilson's (1995) *theory of social isolation*—along with Elijah Anderson's *Code of the Street* (1999)—would soon reopen the door for cultural discussions by showing that cultural adaptations toward crime may simply be another product of living in truly disadvantaged communities.

Social Isolation among the Truly Disadvantaged

In much the same way that Wilson's theory of the truly disadvantaged shifted scholars' attention toward structural factors, Robert Sampson and William Julius Wilson's theory of social isolation helped reintroduce culture into the conversation on communities and crime by offering a structural-cultural approach that merged culture into the truly disadvantaged perspective. Some of the first seeds for this structural-cultural model were laid in Wilson's book *The Truly Disadvantaged* (1987; see also Wilson, 1980). However, the social isolation perspective did not fully materialize until Sampson and Wilson (1995) collaborated on a book chapter that would quickly become a classic in communities and crime research. Notably, Sampson and Wilson were not the only scholars to offer a structural-cultural perspective on urban communities and crime. As described in the following chapter, Anderson's (1999) portrayal of the "code of the street" paralleled several themes of Sampson and Wilson's social isolation model. Similar to Anderson's work, Sampson and Wilson (1995, p. 53) suggested that culture still had a place in explaining urban crime and argued that structural researchers had "too quickly dismissed the role of values, norms, and learning." Culture did not have to be pitted against structural explanations of crime. Instead, they showed how cultural adaptations could be part of the truly disadvantaged vision of communities and crime. However, they were careful to illustrate how their cultural perspective was a "structure first" explanation that differed from the more controversial culture of poverty arguments Wilson had so vehemently opposed.

Unlike the culture of poverty thesis, Sampson and Wilson (1995) said that social isolation was not internalized by residents as a self-perpetuating, rigid belief system. In fact, they explained that "ghetto-specific practices"—such as public displays of violence, sexuality, substance use, and machismo—are not approved by inner-city residents and are often denounced in minority communities (p. 50). Yet they also recognized that these practices could become part of the learning environment in urban neighborhoods *as a direct result of extreme social dislocation and concentrated disadvantages.*

According to Sampson and Wilson, the structural problems that coalesced in inner cities during the 1970s and 1980s may have created fertile ground for "cultural value systems and attitudes that seem to legitimate, or at least provide a basis of tolerance for crime and deviance" (1995, p. 50). Joblessness, poverty, and economic restructuring pushed the middle class out of the urban core, which left few conventional role models for inner-city youths. As a result, urban Black youths saw fewer residents modeling regular work routines, school attendance, and two-parent family structures (Sampson and Wilson, 1995; Wilson, 1987). At the same time, mounting crime rates in inner-city communities meant that crime had become commonplace and had to be managed and tolerated as part of everyday life for many urban youths. In effect, they argued that mainstream culture had become "attenuated," and thus that cultural practices that were at least somewhat permissive toward crime might develop in urban communities. Yet their key point was that these cultural practices were simply another consequence of the massive structural and economic shifts that had devastated inner-city neighborhoods. In other words, they argued that social isolation and (attenuated) culture could be part of the truly disadvantaged story of crime in urban Black neighborhoods, but ultimately this was a story in which "structure trumps culture" (Wilson, 2009, p. 21).

Although cultural arguments continued to be met with resistance, criminologists were far more accepting of Sampson and Wilson's social isolation theory and other structural-cultural arguments than they had been toward the culture of poverty. According to Sampson and Wilson, crime was not promoted in these communities; it was simply a part of the environment that had to be managed and tolerated. Ghetto-specific practices and norms also were not seen as intractable forces that took on lives of their own, nor were they seen as something unique to a single race group's belief system. Rather, Sampson and Wilson (1995, p. 41) argued that these cultural adaptations were largely due to the unequal structural conditions in which Black and White populations resided. As such, they suggested that the sources of Black and White crime were "remarkably invariant."

This theme of "invariance" served as a defining feature of their social isolation theory, suggesting that if Whites and Blacks lived in similar structural environments, then they should display similar patterns of crime. In addition, these arguments set the foundation for what would become known as the *racial invariance hypothesis*. This hypothesis claims that (1) the sources of crime are similar (or even identical) across race/ethnicity, and (2) structural factors have similar effects on crime across race. According to this idea, structural inequalities were ultimately responsible for race differences in crime, as well as Black-White differences in community organization and cultural norms toward violence. Sampson and Wilson explained that reducing the vast inequalities between Black and White communities would eventually erode these cultural differences toward crime. In other words, when Blacks and Whites were on even playing fields, we should see ghetto-specific practices fade and a narrowing of race gaps in crime. Therein laid the problem: Black and White communities were almost never on even playing fields and had little overlap in structural conditions.

As Sampson and Wilson (1995, p. 42) explained, even the "'worst' urban contexts in which whites reside are considerably better than the average context of black communities." Unfortunately, this meant that there was almost no way to observe and compare similarly situated Black and White communities, which left key questions for the racial invariance hypothesis and the truly disadvantaged perspective. Would race differences in crime actually vanish when Blacks and Whites were in similar structural circumstances? Were structural disadvantages ultimately responsible for Black-White differences in crime and for the social isolation Sampson and Wilson described? Testing these assumptions would require finding structurally similar Black and White communities, which would be no easy task.

Divergent Social Worlds and the "Racial-Spatial" Divide

As Sampson and Wilson noted, Black and White communities faced such vastly different circumstances that it was nearly impossible to make "apples-to-apples" comparisons of disadvantage and crime across race. Although many researchers wrestled with this issue, Ruth Peterson and Lauren Krivo (2010) provided the most thorough attempt to overcome this problem and compare structurally-similar Black and White communities in their seminal book, *Divergent Social Worlds.*

Krivo and Peterson were not new to the truly disadvantaged conversation on communities and crime. They had conducted numerous empirical studies identifying the effects of social structure on crime in Black and White communities, which largely supported the truly disadvantaged position. Thus, they were quite familiar with the problem Sampson and Wilson (1995) described and clearly recognized the different structural circumstances in Black and White communities. In fact, their backgrounds were testimony to the "divergent social worlds" experienced by Black and White communities throughout the United States.

As they explain, Krivo grew up in a north side Chicago neighborhood, where crime was rare and almost all residents were White (Peterson and Krivo, 2010). Krivo notes that occasionally she would encounter African Americans as they worked in local houses in her neighborhood or rode the bus to school. Outside of this limited contact, there was little opportunity for exposure to African Americans unless she traveled out of her largely White community and crossed into other areas of the city, like the Loop or the segregated south side neighborhoods. In contrast, Peterson grew up in the rural South, where Black-White segregation remained fairly rigid in public spaces (e.g., schools, churches, buses, restrooms). Although the Jim Crow era was waning during her childhood, she notes that interactions with Whites still operated under "strict rules of racial etiquette that required deference," and where "African Americans could easily get in trouble with legal authorities (and with whites in general) for minor infractions of the 'race rules'" (Peterson and Krivo, 2010, p. 2). Peterson later moved to Cleveland, which offered a wholly different experience from her childhood in the South. Interaction with Whites became a regular part of daily life. Still, at the end of the day when everyone went home, she said it was impossible not to notice that "whites and African Americans departed the bus at different stops" as they returned to their segregated, divergent social worlds (Peterson and Krivo, 2010, p. 2).

It was with this picture of a segregated Black and White society that Peterson and Krivo set about studying the way that race, place, and social structure shaped Black and White experiences with crime. When they began this line of research, Peterson and Krivo were faculty members at the Ohio State University and happened to live in the same neighborhood in Columbus. Their neighborhood, as they tell it, was "almost completely white, clearly middle-class, and nearly free of street crime" (Peterson and Krivo, 2010, p. 4). As scholars of race, place, and crime, they were struck with several burning questions—was street crime also as scarce in *non-White* neighbor-hoods that were equally middle class? Was crime equally high in White and Black neighborhoods that had matching levels of poverty, unemployment, and other disadvantages? In addition, would the "race effects" on crime vanish or be explained away once structural factors were held constant, as the truly disadvantaged position suggested?

Addressing these questions became the centerpiece of their research. However, they quickly ran into problems as they tried to compare Black and White communities. They had planned to use neighborhoods in Columbus for their research, which they did in some early analyses (see Krivo and Peterson, 1996). But they found few structurally similar Black and White neighborhoods. As they noted, there was only one predominantly Black middle-class neighborhood in Columbus. There were some poor, White communities, but those rarely matched the scale of disadvantage seen in the poorest Black neighborhoods. Echoing the claims of Sampson and Wilson, they recognized that "similarly poor and well-off white and non-white neighborhoods are virtually non-existent" (Peterson and Krivo, 2010, p. 5). Furthermore, this problem was not isolated to Columbus. They realized they would have faced the same issue in nearly any city they examined. It was clear that Whites and non-Whites remained segregated in such different social worlds that there was no easy way to compare crime and structural conditions across groups. If they wanted to make like-to-like comparisons of Black and White communities, it would require an unprecedented data collection effort that spanned dozens of cities in order to find enough struc-turally similar White and non-White neighborhoods. Peterson and Krivo welcomed the challenge, and through their National Neighborhood Crime Study (NNCS), they created one of the richest data sets on race, structure, and crime to date.

Peterson and Krivo's (2010) NNCS project and resulting book, *Divergent Social Worlds*, provided the culmination of decades of work exploring the truly disadvantaged contexts shaping race, community, and crime. As part of the NNCS project, Peterson and Krivo gathered information on structural conditions (e.g., poverty, employment, education), racial composition, segregation, and crime for 9,593 neighborhoods across ninety-one cities in the United States, offering one of the most comprehensive pictures of race, social structure, and crime across U.S. communities available to date. Their analysis of the NNCS data revealed several things.

Perhaps most notably, they found that violence and structural conditions across White and non-White neighborhoods were so markedly different that they could only be described as "divergent social worlds." Researchers such as Sampson and Wilson (1995) had long recognized that Black and White communities had vastly different levels of disadvantage and crime. Now, with these new data, Peterson and Krivo (2010) were able to illustrate just how wide the chasm truly was. With respect to crime, they found that the typical African American neighborhood had violence levels that were more than four to five times those of the average White neighborhood, though property crime rates were more comparable across race/ethnicity. Likewise, they found that only the safest 20 percent of Black neighborhoods had violence rates that were as low as those found among 90 percent of White neighborhoods.

Peterson and Krivo (2010) also found extreme divergence in the spatial arrangements and structural conditions of White and non-White neighborhoods. They explained that racial residential segregation remained so pervasive that more than a third of African Americans lived in neighborhoods that were almost all Black (at least 90 percent). In turn, these spatial arrangements led to extreme gaps in the structural conditions of White versus non-White neighborhoods. For example, only 1 percent of White neighborhoods could be considered "hyperdisadvantaged" while as many as a quarter of Black neighborhoods held this status. As they showed, Black and White communities did not simply have some structural differences. They were at opposite ends of the disadvantage spectrum with almost no overlap in levels of poverty and crime. Or as Peterson and Krivo (2010, p. 112) explained: "The distributions of disadvantage for white and non-white neighborhoods could hardly be more dissimilar . . . Thus, when comparing four types of urban neighborhoods—white, African American, Latino, and minority—the notion of 'average' disadvantage is a misnomer. Instead, there is one average for white neighborhoods, reflecting their privileges, and completely different averages for the three types of predominantly nonwhite areas, reflecting their subordinate positions in the urban hierarchy." Based on these findings, they concluded that a pervasive "racial-spatial divide" exists between White, Black, Latino, and minority neighborhoods, which is ultimately responsible for the racial differences in crime observed in their work and in prior studies (Peterson and Krivo, 2010).

In addition to providing a vivid empirical picture of the structural differences between Black and White communities, *Divergent Social Worlds* also extended the truly disadvantaged perspective by placing *race* and *segregation* at the center of the discussion more than in prior structural treatments of communities and crime. As may be recalled, Wilson's (1980, 1987, 1996) earlier arguments about social dislocation and urban crime put structure at the forefront and race in the background. He recognized that changes in the global economy had concentrated disadvantages and crime in urban Black neighborhoods. However, he saw these as *race-neutral processes* that affected both Black and White communities but that had more dire consequences for inner-city Black neighborhoods owing to their already precarious circumstances.

In contrast, race and segregation were at the heart of Peterson and Krivo's theory of the racial-spatial divide. They argued that race was not simply a piece of the puzzle. It was the central player that shapes where different groups live as well as their neighborhood conditions, life chances, and exposure to crime. Drawing from a long line of critical scholarship, Peterson and Krivo (2010, p. 21) argued that racialized structural arrangements are key to understanding why Whites and minorities have such differing experiences, noting, "The racialized social structure is clearly seen in the organization of opportunities and resources that maintain white privilege and minority oppression in a wide range of institutions. Schools, the labor market, politics, criminal justice, health care, and the like are structured in ways that reinforce a hierarchy of access and rewards across populations of color, with whites garnering the highest-quality institutional resources."

Peterson and Krivo (2010, p. 26) argued that residential segregation is the "lynchpin" responsible for this racial-spatial divide in social circumstances and crime across communities. Drawing from Massey and Denton's (1993; see also Charles, 2003; Feldmeyer, 2010; Logan, Stults, and Farley, 2004) work on racial segregation, they explained that racialized practices in real estate markets, banking and mortgage industries, and discriminatory attitudes among Whites have maintained extreme levels of segregation throughout many U.S. cities. As they illustrate, nearly two-thirds of Black or White residents in the NNCS data would have to move to different neighborhoods in order to make racial distributions even across neighborhoods in most cities (Peterson and Krivo, 2010). In addition, these segregated spatial arrangements have not been benign. Peterson and Krivo argued that segregation has effectively maintained disadvantages, disinvestment, and crime in minority neighborhoods, while stockpiling advantages in White communities. As such, Americans now routinely rely on neighborhood racial composition as a visible cue for crime and other potential risks of moving, investing, working, or going to school in a community.

In many ways, this finding provided a startling wake-up call to researchers studying race, social structure, and crime. It vividly illustrated the warning that Sampson and Wilson (1995) and Krivo and Peterson (2000) had been offering for decades: simple comparisons of Black and White neighborhoods were often inappropriate. Blacks and Whites lived in fundamentally different social worlds, and as Sampson (2009, p. 265) stated, "trying to estimate the effect of concentrated disadvantage on whites is . . . tantamount to estimating a phantom reality." Peterson and Krivo had shown that structural disadvantage was key to explaining crime for *all* race/ethnic groups. Importantly, they also showed that the "truly disadvantaged" experience of concentrated poverty and crime was something that was almost exclusively reserved for minority communities.

Last, by compiling the rich NNCS data base, Peterson and Krivo were finally able to address the question at the heart of their study of communities and crime: Do Black, White, and Latino neighborhoods have similar levels of violence when their structural conditions are essentially equal? Alas, the answer proved to be more complex than imagined. In contrast to the truly disadvantaged position, the different structural conditions in Black, White, Latino, and minority neighborhoods did not fully account for race differences in violence. Neighborhood disadvantage explained much, but not all, of race effects on community patterns of crime. Something else mattered.

Probing their data further, Peterson and Krivo examined how crime in a neighborhood might be affected by the conditions of both the larger city in which it was located and the communities close by. They discovered that these factors explained away much of the race differences in violence. Even when they were matched on measures of poverty and disadvantage, Black and White (and Latino) neighborhoods still were not quite on "even playing fields" because the *surrounding* contexts were often much more disadvantaged for non-White communities. In other words, the larger structural context was racialized in such a way that *circumstances both in a given community and in that community's surrounding neighborhoods* contributed to White advantages but led to crime and a concentration of truly disadvantaged circumstances for minority communities.

Taken together, Peterson and Krivo's theory of the racial-spatial divide and their study of *Divergent Social Worlds* using NNCS data provided one of the most comprehensive empirical analyses of the truly disadvantaged perspective to date and some of the most resounding support for this vision of communities and crime. However, as highlighted in the following section, recent research has recognized several emerging disadvantages (and a few unexpected findings) that raise additional questions for the truly disadvantaged vision of crime.

Remaining Questions and New Developments

Three decades after it was introduced, the truly disadvantaged perspective remains one of the dominant visions of communities and crime. A host of empirical studies have supported this perspective, illustrating the profound consequences of concentrated disadvantage and economic restructuring for crime in urban minority neighborhoods. Even so, important questions remain about the links between race, social structure, and community patterns of crime.

In one of the most rigorous analyses of race, place, and crime to date, Peterson and Krivo (2010) had shown that structural differences were largely responsible for differences in crime across White and non-White neighborhoods. Still, even when Black, White, Latino, and minority neighborhoods were on even playing fields, Peterson and Krivo found that some race differences in crime remained. Notably, this was not the first study to find that racial differences in crime persist net of race differences in structural circumstances. Research by Feldmeyer, Steffensmeier, and Ulmer (2013), Pratt and Cullen (2005), and Shihadeh and Shrum (2004) shows that racial composition of neighborhoods has one of the strongest and most persistent effects on community rates of violence, *even after accounting for different structural conditions of White and non-White neighborhoods.* These findings have been troubling to say the least for the truly disadvantaged perspective on crime and for theories of race, social structure, and crime (such as the racial-spatial divide and the racial invariance hypothesis). After all, if race differences in crime are simply due to structural differences across groups, then racial composition of neighborhoods should carry little weight for violence after accounting for group differences in poverty, unemployment, and other forms of disadvantage (Shihadeh and Shrum, 2004). Notably, these studies do not discount the importance of structure on crime. In fact, they all find that structural conditions explain much if not most of the connections between race and community patterns of crime. In addition, as Peterson and Krivo (2010) note, the *surrounding context* may explain much of the lingering race effects on community patterns of violence. However, even in some of the most advanced analyses, such as Peterson and Krivo's examination of the NNCS data, race effects (e.g., "percent Black") on community patterns of crime often remain, suggesting the need for further study into the connections between race, place, and crime.

Researchers also continue to raise questions about the racial invariance hypothesis, which stems directly from the truly disadvantaged vision of communities and crime. According to the racial invariance hypothesis, the sources of crime are essentially the same across race/ethnicity, and structural factors like poverty, unemployment, and education are thought to have the same effects on all race/ethnic groups. As research on race, social structure, and crime has grown, this hypothesis has gained traction and been widely embraced by criminologists. However, there is some indication that poverty, inequality, and other structural conditions may not carry exactly the same weight for crime across all race/ethnic groups. In their defining conceptual treatment of the racial invariance hypothesis, Steffensmeier et al. (2010) showed that disadvantage is indeed a key source of violence for all race/ethnic groups examined. At the same time, they also showed that there is often substantial variation in the magnitude of effects and the impact of specific measures of disadvantage across White, Black, and Latino communities.

In addition, Steffensmeier and colleagues (2010, 2011) highlight what has become a well-established finding in research on race and crime—Latinos often have surprisingly low levels of crime despite having disadvantages similar to those found in Black communities. Notably, this "Latino Paradox" raises some questions for strictly structural perspectives claiming that race/ethnic differences in crime boil down to structural differences between groups (Martinez, 2002; Sampson, 2008). If this were the case, then Latino and Black communities should have fairly similar levels of crime. However, a rapidly growing body of research has shown that Latino and immigrant communities are insulated from the effects of structural disadvantages. In many ways, this finding has provided an emerging vision of communities and crime centered around the "immigrant community," a point we return to in the following chapters. However, for the truly disadvantaged perspective, the key question is why Latino and immigrant communities are "some of the safest communities around" when they face many of the same disadvantages that are at the heart of urban Black crime (Sampson, 2008, p. 30).

Finally, a lingering question for the truly disadvantaged perspective on communities and crime is how applicable it will be going forward. Research suggests that urban communities have seen some recovery from the structural changes that first captured Wilson's attention in the 1970s and 1980s. Wilson (2009) and Peterson and Krivo (2010) note that just as scholars had embraced the truly disadvantaged vision of communities and crime, the structural landscape began to shift again. Neighborhoods racked by the most extreme concentrated disadvantages began to see some relief. Economic conditions in urban Black communities were far from stable, but they saw improvements. Disadvantage became less concentrated. Education and employment opportunities for African Americans increased. The Black middle class began to grow, and urban poverty and crime began to fall. In sum, it seemed that the worst was over and things may have been getting better.

However, despite these structural advances, in many ways, minority communities remain truly disadvantaged. Since the turn of the twenty-first century, wealth gaps between White and Black communities have widened. Segregation eased slightly, but Black communities remain severely isolated from Whites. School segregation became even more pronounced (Steffensmeier et al., 2011). In addition, despite gains among the Black middle class, "middle-class" status has remained divided and unequal. White middle-class neighborhoods routinely occupy suburban areas with greater resources. In contrast, Black middle-class residents are often unable to penetrate the barriers of White communities and remain isolated in urban areas on the periphery of poor minority neighborhoods (Pattillo-McCoy, 1999).

Scholars have also recognized other types of *emerging disadvantages* among inner-city populations that have reinforced their status as the truly disadvantaged and added to ongoing cycles of crime and deprivation in urban Black communities. Research suggests that the Great Recession of

2008 created new disadvantages and structural setbacks that erased many of the gains urban Black communities experienced in the 1990s and early 2000s. Scholars note that the mortgage crisis and resulting foreclosures during this period fostered disadvantage and crime in inner-city minority communities, many of which were targeted by the predatory lending practices that led to the great recession (see Hall, Crowder, and Spring, 2015; Peterson and Krivo 2005, 2010). Research by Perkins and Sampson (2015) examining Chicago neighborhoods shows that African Americans are far more likely to experience "compounded deprivation" (being individually poor in a poor neighborhood) than Whites or Latinos. In fact, they find that non-poor Blacks are more likely to live in poor neighborhoods than Whites who are poor themselves.

Perhaps the most substantial set of emerging disadvantages has stemmed from the era of "mass incarceration" that devastated social conditions in urban Black communities, adding to inner-city crime and social problems. Highly influential work by Michelle Alexander (2010), Bruce Western (2006), Jeff Manza and Christopher Uggen (2006), and Todd Clear (2007), among others, suggests that the prison boom and decades of mass incarceration have helped maintain truly disadvantaged structural conditions and high crime rates in many urban Black neighborhoods. Owing in large part to the war on drugs, the rate of Black (especially male) imprisonment in the late twentieth century and early twenty-first century escalated to such unprecedented levels that between one-quarter and one-third of African American men may be incarcerated in their lifetimes. As Tonry (2011, p. 28) notes, "Black men remain six to seven times more likely than white men to be inmates." Furthermore, this earned the United States the highest incarceration rate in the world and the dubious distinction of incarcerating more of its minority population than any other county, including South Africa at the height of Apartheid (Alexander, 2010).

As Alexander (2010), Clear (2007), and Western (2006) explain, these patterns of mass imprisonment reinforced all the forms of economic devastation Wilson described in urban Black neighborhoods by pulling out wage earners, breaking up families, and decreasing the earning power of families and communities. Furthermore, once released, the prison records attached to increasingly large shares of African Americans meant that they would struggle to find jobs, would be locked out of civic life and legitimate opportunities for success, and would suffer a permanent blow to their lifetime earning potential (Manza and Uggen, 2006; Pager, 2003, 2007; Western, 2006). Likewise, research by Clear (2007; see also Rose and Clear, 1998) illustrates how mass incarceration has added to the cycle of crime and violence in urban communities by destabilizing neighborhoods. Beyond its economic consequences, mass incarceration has created heterogeneity in attitudes toward crime and imprisonment as well as a population "churning" within inner-city communities as residents cycle in and out of prison. In effect, mass incarceration has socially disorganized inner-city neighborhoods and further entrenched disadvantages among urban African Americans in ways that were not predicted in the earlier structural arguments of the truly disadvantaged perspective. According to this emerging literature, mass incarceration may have simply become the new engine for creating truly disadvantaged communities.

Conclusion

Taken together, urban Black communities have seen a mix of gains and setbacks since the initial economic shifts described by William Julius Wilson. Throughout these changes, the truly disadvantaged vision of communities and crime remains as applicable as ever. Urban Black (and Latino) neighborhoods have clearly made substantial strides and seen marked improvements over the extreme deprivation observed throughout the 1970s and 1980s that first inspired Wilson's theory of the truly disadvantaged. Thus, it is not altogether surprising that both Latino and especially Black communities have experienced relatively large crime declines throughout the early twenty-first century (Parker, 2008). However, in many other ways, inner-city minority neighborhoods continue to face entrenched inequalities and emerging sets of disadvantages (like mass incarceration), which as Steffensmeier and colleagues (2011, p. 235) note is "hardly the stuff of 'good news' about race and inequality during the past 25 years." In light of this reality, as long as Black and White communities continue to exist in separate and unequal social worlds, the truly disadvantaged perspective will likely remain a core vision for understanding urban communities and crime.

5

Community as a Criminal Culture

key insight of the Chicago School was that social disorganization in the zone in transition was fertile ground for the emergence and then transmission of criminal "traditions." Indeed, the very idea of culture conflict—and then at the individual level differential association—was predicated on the view that inner-city areas are marked by an ongoing battle between a strong criminal culture and weak conventional culture. Since that time, the image of the "community as a criminal culture" has occupied a central place in the study of why neighborhoods in the urban core experience high rates of crime, especially of violent crime. Importantly, however, scholars in different generations have offered distinct theories of the sources and nature of the cultures that prevail in these communities. As will be seen, one set of theories, which emphasized delinquent and violent subcultures, emerged as urban America made the transition from the time of Shaw and McKay into the 1960s. A second set of theories, reflecting more contemporary developments such as the concentration of the "truly disadvantaged" in the central city, emerged in the latter part of the 1900s and has proceeded into the current century. This recent scholarship has been informed by a more sophisticated understanding of culture that has led to new controversies.

The image of "community as a criminal culture" first seemed to reach its apex in the 1960s—a decade marked by rising rates of crime and racial divisiveness. In this context, crime was far too readily racialized and treated as an urban, Black problem. The urban, Black experience in the 1960s was scrutinized for low rates of marriage and employment and high rates of out-of-wedlock births and welfare dependency. The stigma associated with the urban, Black experience in the 1960s was perhaps most (in)famously reinforced by the U.S. Department of Labor's Moynihan Report, presented in 1965, describing urban Black ghetto families as creating a "tangle of pathology." Though Moynihan may have been trying to emphasize the durability of the inequality facing poor, urban Blacks (Sampson, 2009), his words were often treated as conveying a self-perpetuating culture of inner-city, Black poverty.

That latter interpretation of the Moynihan Report ignited intense criticism on the grounds of insensitivity and victim blaming. As Robert Sampson (2009, p. 261) suggests in his review of the impact of Moynihan, "To this day, the term *pathology* is avoided like the plague among social scientists." And, Patricia Cohen (2010) of the *New York Times* adds, "The word 'culture' became a live grenade, and the idea that attitudes and behavior patterns kept people poor was shunned." Yet after decades of largely being relegated to the academic sidelines, the idea of urban community culture playing a role in poverty and crime is being reconsidered by a number of scholars (see, e.g., Cohen, 2010; Small, Harding, and Lamont, 2010).

This chapter discusses this historical ebb and flow of culture's perceived role in community crime. As noted, a key issue in this particular chapter is how scholars have tended to theorize about culture's role in crime-related problems in communities at various points in history. In brief, how, exactly, is community culture related to crime? As will be discussed, there seem to be two general approaches to this question. One view holds that culture in inner cities is *crime generating*. The other holds that culture in inner cities is *crime permitting*. These two views define a fundamental difference between *criminal (sub)cultural theories*, rooted in a "culture as values" perspective, and *attenuated culture theories*, viewing culture as a more of a "behavioral tool kit" to be enacted situationally.

Related to the distinction between the crime-generating versus crime-permitting role of culture in high-crime communities is an implicit difference of opinion about value conflict versus value consensus. Those who view culture as crime generating see high-crime communities as marked by conflict regarding the morality of crime, with conventional culture standing side by side with (and battling) *criminal subcultures*. In contrast, those viewing culture as crime permitting tend to view high-crime neighborhoods as having a largely unified set of values regarding the wrongfulness of crime, though the conventional culture is in a severely weakened, or attenuated, state.

This chapter attempts to detail these different views regarding the theoretical relevance of culture in community criminology. We begin by discussing crime-generating criminal subcultural theories that dominated discussions of the role of culture in the early and mid-twentieth century. By the 1970s, however, the subcultural theories were largely either heavily criticized or dismissed altogether. The emergence of the systemic model of social disorganization theory in the 1970s and 1980s brought about the favoring of crime-permitting attenuated culture theories instead. Although theories advocating criminal subcultures were still present in criminology, they tended not to emphasize *community-level* cultural processes, and instead focused on regional cultures (i.e., the southern subculture of violence), individual-level delinquent/criminal attitudes, or gang cultures (separate from their community context).

Notably, the discussion of community culture and crime took on a different flavor beginning around 1990. While still wrestling with the debate between crime-generating criminal subcultures and crime-permitting attenuated culture, greater attention is given in this later era to a unique brand of community—the "truly disadvantaged" community. As detailed in Chapter 4, deindustrialization had changed the face of inner-city communities, largely between 1970 and 1980 such that they were increasingly poor, increasingly composed of female-headed households, and increasingly Black. Scholars took note of the extreme structural disadvantage characterizing such communities, but they also observed culture in the form of "ghetto-related practices" in areas of concentrated disadvantage. The belief prevailed that deindustrialization of the inner-city—and the extreme poverty and social isolation that followed in its wake—gave rise to a "way of life" that included persistent male joblessness, teen childbearing, involvement in the drug industry, and public displays of toughness, emphasizing the use of physical violence to defend an individual's honor. Such behaviors are typically not tolerated in "mainstream" American culture, but scholars documented that these practices were accepted or even encouraged in particularly dire contexts, where mainstream habits seemed situationally irrelevant. The major sections to follow detail more fully the thinking about the role of culture in community crime across these distinct eras.

The Early and Mid-Twentieth-Century Subcultural Tradition

As developed by the Chicago School, the foundational work on communities and crime discussed the important roles of both structural disadvantage and the inter-generational transmission of cultural values. In particular, Shaw and McKay (1969, p. 170) argued that disorganized, high-crime communities not only had structural deficits in that they lacked legitimate opportunities and strong institutional and informal controls but also had "systems of competing and conflicting moral values." They contended that while growing up in these high-crime neighborhoods, youngsters were exposed to attitudes that approved of delinquency and that these criminogenic attitudes were then passed onto successive generations of youths through social learning. For reasons alluded to in earlier chapters, Shaw and McKay's social disorganization theory had largely fallen out of favor in criminology by the middle of the twentieth century. Two of the most prominent theoretical perspectives of that time were, instead, Edwin Sutherland's differential association theory and Robert Merton's anomie-strain theory. Discussions of the community origins of crime in the 1950s and 1960s thus were framed using one or both of these two traditions.

Sutherland posited that crime, just like noncriminal behavior, was learned in interaction with significant others. According to his differential association theory, techniques regarding how to commit crime are learned, but importantly, so too are motives, drives, rationalizations, and definitions of the behavior. Based on the assumption of culture conflict, or the idea that there were variable or differential "norms of conduct" in society, those who engage in crime learn to define law-violating behavior, overall, as "favorable" as opposed to "unfavorable." Most individuals are exposed to variable definitions of criminal behavior—some favorable and others unfavorable—from the range of significant others, or differential associations, in their lives. However, not all associations are of equal importance in terms of imparting their definitions of criminal behavior. Individuals are more likely to internalize the definitions of behavior learned from associations that are of long duration and high frequency, priority, and intensity. Ultimately, when an individual learns and internalizes normative definitions favorable to law violation in excess of normative definitions unfavorable to law violation, crime is a likely result.

In contrast to Sutherland's social-psychological theory, Merton's perspective was macro-structural in origin. In brief, Merton suggested that crime resulted from society's emphasis on economic success "by any means necessary." Merton claimed that the goal of monetary wealth is *the* pervasive cultural goal in the United States. Indeed, the American dream of being upwardly mobile and attaining material success was a universal prescription—something so highly extolled that everyone was mandated to value and achieve it. In this context, Merton argued, there is less cultural emphasis on norms regarding the acceptable means by which one should achieve the economic success goal (i.e., through formal education and legitimate occupations). Thus, there is a cultural imbalance in that the goal of economic success—the American dream—is emphasized over and above the means by which success is achieved. Merton stated that *anomie*—weakened or absent regulatory norms—results from this imbalance in emphasis (goals over means) in that norms lose their power to control behavior.

Beyond cultural imbalance, Merton also implicated the social structure. He claimed that social stratification in the United States results in unequal access to the legitimate means for achieving monetary success. Put more simply, there is tremendous inequality in terms of access to, for example, good schools and good jobs. For poorer segments of society, access to these legitimate, or institutionalized, means of achieving the universally prescribed cultural goal of success is blocked. Such structural obstacles, in combination with the cultural exaggeration of the goal of monetary success—at the expense of cultural norms—create a context ripe for the reliance on illegitimate means to achieve success. This context is thus likely to have a relatively high rate of crime. However, beyond this macro-level effect, Merton recognized that *individuals* experience problems of adjustment associated with living in a social context characterized by cultural imbalance and structural inequality. This sort of social context exerts strain on individuals who experience a disjuncture between culturally prescribed goals and the availability of legitimate means. Individuals can adapt to that strain in various ways; for some the response involves crime or deviance.

Criminological work in the mid-twentieth century that was interested in understanding the ecological patterning of crime, noting that crime was much higher in certain communities than others, tended to base its explanations on the ideas of Sutherland and/or Merton. Indeed, some of the more prominent scholars during this era, to be discussed below, were students of either Sutherland or Merton—or both. In the tradition of Sutherland, high-crime communities were presumed to have subcultures that championed attitudes favorable to the commission of crime. In short, crime was presumed to be normative behavior in such communities, and pro-criminal values were successfully transmitted from one generation to the next through the process of socialization. In the tradition of Merton, high-crime communities were presumed to have little access to legitimate means for achieving success (i.e., good schools, plentiful jobs), and thus they contained high concentrations of individuals experiencing strain. Some scholars integrated the two traditions by suggesting that collective strain led to a community-level response in the form of a delinquent subculture. In the sections that immediately follow, several of the more prominent theories of community crime from this era are discussed in more detail, including the work of Albert Cohen, Richard Cloward and Lloyd Ohlin, Walter Miller, and Marvin Wolfgang and Franco Ferracuti.

Cohen's Delinquent Boys: Rejecting Middle-Class Values

Albert Cohen's work on working-class delinquent boys is the first of those prominent theories. Cohen received his undergraduate training and a

Ph.D. in sociology at Harvard, where Merton was on faculty until 1938, and where Merton's mentor, Talcott Parsons, was a mainstay. In the interim between his undergraduate and doctoral studies, Cohen obtained a master's degree in sociology at Indiana University, with Sutherland as his adviser. Given this background, Cohen's blending of the traditions of Merton, Parsons, and Sutherland is clearly no accident. In brief, the theory he outlined in his famous 1955 book, *Delinquent Boys: The Culture of the Gang*, suggested that there were collective responses to problems of adjustment in the form of subcultures, or gangs. In particular, Cohen posited that collective adaptations to strain in the form of male gangs were likely to emerge in working-class communities, where a high concentration of boys experienced the frustration of not being able to measure up to mainstream, middle-class standards. The middle-class goals that Cohen discussed were broader than the economic success goal that Merton emphasized, but they were very much in the spirit of Merton's notion of strain nonetheless.

More reflective of Parsons's influence, however, Cohen detailed how working-class boys were frustrated in the school context, in particular, as a result of not being able to readily measure up to the values emphasized and rewarded in school settings, including independence, self-control, asceticism, and rationality. Consequently, gangs provided these boys with a context in which a new set of goals and norms could be established that expressly rejected middle-class values, virtually turning middle-class culture upside down. The gangs' inverted value systems furnished alternative ways through which working-class boys could achieve status. For example, gang members could achieve success by exhibiting aggression, impulsiveness, and disrespect for property. Cohen viewed the behavior that the gangs promoted as nonutilitarian and malicious.

Thus, gangs, and the crimes in which they participated, originated or emerged because of the structural obstacles to economic success facing boys in working-class communities and the collective problems of adjustment that resulted. Importantly, however, the gangs and their criminal conduct were perpetuated through cultural transmission of delinquent values. It was this cultural transmission that was the most proximal cause of crime, as the gang subculture provided definitions of behavior that favored violation of the law. Nonetheless, with Cohen's theory suggesting that such "oppositional values" were adaptations to structural inequality, the implication is that the norms and values promoted by the gangs did *not* represent autonomous subcultures (autonomous from structure) with ongoing integrity. If structural stressors were removed, Cohen's gangs would presumably wither.

Cloward and Ohlin: Types of Delinquent Subcultures

With their 1960 publication of *Delinquency and Opportunity: A Theory of Delinquent Gangs*, Cloward and Ohlin provided another theory that emphasized the emergence of unique subcultures within poorer communities. In their work, Cloward and Ohlin made an important advance over Merton's discussion of adaptations to strain. In doing so, they integrated Merton's ideas with those of Chicago-School theorists such as Sutherland, Shaw and McKay, and Solomon Kobrin (for a review, see Cullen, 1984, 1988, 2010).

Similar to Merton, who was Cloward's professor during his doctoral studies at Columbia, Cloward and Ohlin viewed delinquency as an outgrowth of social inequality, with legitimate avenues to economic success blocked for many. Thus, problems of adjustment created strain that needed to be adapted to, perhaps through criminal behavior. However, while Merton had noted that various forms of criminal or deviant adaptation were possible, he did not provide much detail as to why one form of adaptation would be chosen over another, implicitly suggesting that opportunities for illegitimate adaptive responses were equally available to all. Cloward and Ohlin specified more clearly why particular adaptations to structurally induced strain might vary, and in doing so, they challenged Merton's assumption of equality in illegitimate means. Borrowing from Cloward's earlier work (Cloward, 1959), Cloward and Ohlin claimed that, just as legitimate means were variably available, *illegitimate* means were also available to some but blocked for others. Slum communities, they noted, were differentially organized, and the level of organization shaped the availability of illegitimate opportunities and thus the nature of collective responses to strain across communities. In sum, Cloward and Ohlin claimed that adaptive responses to strain varied across communities, depending on the illegitimate opportunities available.

Similar to Cohen, Cloward and Ohlin saw the collective response to strain as gang formation. The alienation experienced by large numbers of lower-class, urban dwellers (males, in particular) living in close proximity to one another facilitated gang formation, with the gangs providing reassurance and group legitimacy to individual feelings of frustration and injustice (Cullen, 2010). However, unlike Cohen's *Delinquent Boys*, Cloward and Ohlin emphasized that values and behaviors of gangs varied. Some gangs focused on instrumental criminal enterprises, some emphasized violence, and others centered on drug use—and these different forms of gangs were referred to as "criminal," "conflict," and "retreatist" gangs, respectively. Neighborhood organization, and the resulting availability of criminal opportunities, was the major determinant for the type of gang that would emerge in any given community. The most cohesive or socially integrated slum neighborhoods tended to breed criminal gangs, as they required an organized network structure that fostered the learning of criminal trades and offered connections to opportunities for enacting such skills (e.g., access to co-offenders, access to illicit markets). As Francis Cullen suggests in his 2010 review of Cloward and Ohlin's theory, "Not everyone with a problem of adjustment can adapt by becoming a white-collar criminal or becoming a drug dealer. These options are not equally available" (p. 173).

Alternatively, conflict gangs were often observed in disorganized neighborhoods that lacked integrated social networks. The youths in such neighborhoods thus lacked a readily accessible ongoing criminal network within which they could address their problems of adjustment. To compensate, the conflict gangs that emerged in such communities focused on resolving the problem of adjustment by linking status and violence. Since means of achieving status through monetary success were not available, displays of violence were touted as status enhancing instead.

According to Cloward and Ohlin, retreatist gangs emerged in both organized and disorganized communities. In both types of areas, there were some youths unsuccessful at exercising crime or violence, thus eliminating the option of gaining status from such behaviors. For such youths, criminal or violent gangs were not viable adaptations to strain. Cloward and Ohlin offered that a retreatist subculture emphasizing drug use emerged as a collective response to the strain faced by youths who were unsuccessful at crime or violence.

Overall, all three types of gangs described by Cloward and Ohlin involved the transmission of subcultural values that promoted criminal behavior as the most proximal cause of crime. Similar to Cohen, however, Cloward and Ohlin's ties to strain theory meant that the subcultures were not viewed as purely autonomous sets of values. Instead, there was assumed consensus regarding "conventional values," and the values touted by the gangs were more situational in nature—tied to structural community conditions in terms of blocked access to legitimate and illegitimate avenues for the achievement of economic success. In particular, criminal gangs offered illegitimate means of success and thus "criminal opportunity." For Cloward and Ohlin, "opportunity" was not an aspect of the environment external to already-motivated offenders (a perspective to be discussed in Chapter 7) but was instead a process whereby motivated offenders were created. In this process, strained individuals were integrated into a network of older offenders, acquiring the skills and attitudes necessary for criminal roles, and then gaining access to situations where those criminal roles could be performed (Cullen, 1984, 1988, 2010).

Miller's Lower-Class Focal Concerns

In contrast to Cohen and Cloward and Ohlin's adaptive (and thus situational and nonautonomous) view of gang delinquency, Walter Miller is known for his "purer" cultural theory. In the 1958 article "Lower Class Culture as a Generating Milieu of Gang Delinquency," Miller suggested that there was a distinctive, long-standing "tradition" within the urban lower class. This tradition consisted of values that encouraged criminal behavior. Specifically, Miller delineated six "focal concerns" that characterized lower-class culture and promoted crime: trouble, toughness, smartness, excitement, fate, and autonomy. In its focus on getting into trouble and seeking excitement, lower-class culture conferred status on those who engaged in all sorts of crime and deviance, including fighting, stealing, drinking, drug use, or sexual promiscuity. Through a focal concern on toughness, lower-class culture especially promoted physical prowess. The emphasis on smartness in lower-class culture encouraged actions that indicate an ability to outsmart or con others. The valuing of fate discouraged earning money through legitimate hard work and instead encouraged income-generating strategies based on "luck," such as gambling. Finally, the valuing of autonomy fostered defiance of authority. From Miller's perspective, crime committed by those in the lower classes was a natural outcome of socialization within lower-class culture.

The Subculture of Violence

Marvin Wolfgang and Franco Ferracuti's 1967 publication, *The Subculture of Violence*, was similar to Miller's work in that it attempted to explain high rates of crime in urban, lower-class environments as a function of subcultural concerns. However, it differed in that it focused on the subcultural sources of *violent* crime, in particular, including *expressive homicide* most notably (i.e., "heat of passion" homicide). In the tradition of Sutherland, Wolfgang and Ferracuti theorized that, within a subculture of violence in poor urban areas, group members were taught (by other members) that violent responses to slights and conflicts were excused, condoned, and even expected. In fact, the failure to exercise violence in certain situations would be greeted with scorn, with those using nonviolent solutions at risk of being ostracized from the group. Exposure to such pro-violent definitions and reinforcements commonly led to the internalization of these pro-violent values, with high levels of violence thus being continually perpetuated within the group. Still, not all individuals exposed to these pro-violent definitions actually engaged in violence as solutions to their conflicts. Wolfgang and Ferracuti proposed that variation in personality within poor urban subcultures differentiated members more prone to violence versus those less committed to the value system.

While Wolfgang and Ferracuti's subculture of violence was originally posited in an attempt to understand higher rates of crime in poor, urban areas, it was embraced by other scholars as a way to account for higher rates of violence, especially homicide, in a variety of other geographic and social contexts. For example, the possibility of a southern subculture of violence was offered in an attempt to understand the disproportionately high rates of homicide and assault within the southern portion of the United States (see, e.g., Gastil, 1971; Hackney, 1969). From this perspective, southerners were thought to be socialized in a manner that violence in the face of conflict is tolerated or even expected (i.e., in the manner of a frontier mentality rooted in a history or duels and feuds). Other scholars used the idea of a subculture of violence to explain differential rates of crime across racial groups within the United States. In particular, a race-based subculture of violence was used to explain higher rates of violence among African Americans (e.g., Curtis, 1975).

The Declining Significance of Criminal Subcultures and the Rise of Attenuated Culture

The perspectives described above are good examples of popular theorizing about the nonrandom distribution of crime across communities during the 1950s and the first half of the 1960s. These perspectives drew on prominent scholarly theories of the time, and they were received and interpreted within the context of the prevailing social and political attitudes. Initially, these various explanations were palatable to many precisely because of the implication that criminals were "countercultural"—though, as noted above, several of these perspectives actually assumed value consensus, with oppositional subcultures arising only in the face of structural constraints (i.e., Cohen and Cloward and Ohlin). Even if social inequality played an indirect role, these theories proposed that crime ultimately existed because of unconventional (subcultural) values. Given such perspectives, who or what was to blame for crime? It was easy to use these theories to suggest that the problem of crime must be the fault of the families or social groups responsible for transmitting these values. In other words, subcultural theories were often associated with a mind-set that the groups afflicted with high rates of crime had only themselves to blame. Hence, these theories appeared quite useful in a 1950s and early 1960s America, when unquestioning loyalty to "the system," maintenance of the status quo, and fear of diversity were emphatic parts of the social climate.

The value-laden implications of subcultural theories, however, grew less popular into the 1960s, when conservative approaches to crime were challenged by those emphasizing structural inequality, class conflict, and racial threat. These latter perspectives saw the working and lower classes and racial/ethnic minorities not as holding values in opposition to those of the middle class, but as victims of a heavily stratified economic system and outright oppression at the hands of the middle and upper classes. As such, subcultural approaches began to be viewed as "blaming the victim," and their prominence in criminological theory diminished substantially.

Further lending to their decline in popularity, the subcultural theories of the mid-twentieth century had a tendency to move away from *community* dynamics and morph into *class*- and *race*-based cultural theories. The metamorphosis appeared based on the assumption that people shared subcultural values simply because of their particular race, social class, or region of residence, *regardless of whether they even knew one another* (Kornhauser, 1978). This trend diverted the field away from a focus on *cross-community* variation in crime and more in the direction of understanding cross-class, cross-race, and cross-regional differences. Recognizing how cultural explanations to such differences could reinforce social divisiveness and stereotypes, these theories were increasingly set aside as dangerously conservative.

In the more "liberal" national context beginning in the mid to late 1960s, the perspectives discussed above that had blended elements of strain and subcultural variation (i.e., Cloward and Ohlin [1960]; Cohen [1955]) began to be interpreted in a manner that stripped the theories of their community-based subcultural components. As an example, Francis Cullen—a student of Cloward's—described how this sociopolitical climate was in part responsible for the common mis-classification of Cloward and Ohlin's work as a strain theory:

> Scholars focused most completely on those aspects of *Delinquency and Opportunity* that paralleled Merton's concerns and meshed in turn with the social context . . . The prevailing ideological concern in the 1960s was with denial of legitimate, not illegitimate, opportunity. In this context, the concept of "illegitimate means" might have struck some scholars as an interesting twist, but wasn't it peripheral to solving the problems of delinquency . . . the key policy issue [of the time] was to attack this root cause by providing disadvantaged youth with equal opportunities: better schooling, better job training, access to jobs. By contrast, counting for subcultural differentiation seemed of secondary significance. (1988, p. 231)

Beyond the emerging theoretical and political distastefulness of subcultural perspectives, the 1960s also brought important empirical challenges to such perspectives. A growing number of studies simply failed to show support for the various theories outlined above. For example, Cohen's depiction of gangs as male, non-utilitarian, and malicious was viewed as overly narrow. It excluded from consideration girls'/women's criminality and delinquent gang activities done for profit (i.e., drug dealing).[1] Cloward and Ohlin's description of gangs was somewhat broader, with three ideal types outlined, but their theory was still haunted by lack of empirical verification of these forms of gangs. Of particular significance, a famous 1965 study by James Short and Fred Strodtbeck failed to verify the clear existence of these distinct subcultures. Their study of Chicago gangs revealed only one instance of a "retreatist gang" and no examples of the "criminal subculture" described by Cloward and Ohlin.

Empirical research also failed to verify that values varied substantially across class lines, racial/ethnic groups, regions of the country, or various other social groupings. Part of the difficulty subcultural theorists had in verifying the very existence of subcultural values was that values, per se, were difficult to assess. As a result, subcultural theorists interpreted criminal behavior as evidence of criminal values. This created tautological reasoning: oppositional (criminal) values, indicated by criminal behavior, were presumed to cause criminal behavior. Or, in the case of studies of the "southern subculture of violence," mere residence in the South was presumed to approximate exposure to pro-violence values. However, studies that actually measured values found little evidence of criminal values within any social stratum. For example, Short and Strodtbeck's study found that there was a uniformly high evaluation of "middle-class" values by middle-class boys, lower-class boys, and even gang members (see also Ball-Rokeach, 1973). Similarly, Hirschi's seminal test of an individual-level social control theory in *Causes of Delinquency* found few differences in values across delinquent and non-delinquent youths. Thus, the value conflict assumption on which the subcultural theories were based appeared highly questionable by the late 1960s and into the 1970s.

Systemic Theory and Attenuated Conventional Culture

Partially at the expense of subcultural theories, Hirschi's perspective on social control gained considerable momentum in the 1970s and 1980s. As discussed previously (see Chapter 3), this perspective is based on the assumption that there is *value consensus* in the sense that all segments of society condemn crime. Therefore, control theory is at complete odds with the notion of "deviant subcultures" that espouse the virtues of crime. Different cultural values—in terms of whether the content is criminal or conventional—

---

1. See Cohen and Short (1958) for an extension and discussion of "principal varieties of delinquent subcultures" (p. 23).

do not distinguish criminals from noncriminals according to control theorists. However, differences in the strength of the ties or bonds to the cultural value system can distinguish offenders from nonoffenders. Some individuals are more closely tied to the system than others owing to their personal attachments and commitments and institutional involvements. These ties serve to control behavior, keeping it in line with conventional values. Those with weakened bonds, however, are less invested in conventional values. It is not that they do not share the values; they simply have less of an investment or stake in abiding by them.

The incompatibility between control theories and "cultural deviance" theories led Kornhauser to advocate an approach to understanding community rates of crime that relied purely on variation in neighborhood-level resident-based control and that was devoid of any notion of subcultural transmission of criminal values. Following Kornhauser's lead, as discussed in Chapter 3, Shaw and McKay's work was reconceptualized in the 1970s and 1980s as a community-level systemic control model. This model posited that community indicators of "disorganization" were related to crime because they diminished the community's capacity for forming strong neighborhood-level systems of personal and institutional ties that could effectively control unwanted behavior. The systemic theory and its core assumptions (i.e., the control theory belief that there was value consensus in society) were theoretically incompatible with the idea of value conflict and, thus, criminal subcultures.

This is not to say, however, that Kornhauser dismissed culture as unimportant in understanding community rates of crime. In fact, Kornhauser used the notion of "cultural disorganization," alongside "structural disorganization," as a key component of overall community disorganization. In doing so, she presented a new way of thinking about how culture might influence community crime. First, Kornhauser viewed structural disorganization as indicated most prominently by institutional and network instability, and this aspect of disorganization went on to dominate most work in the social disorganization tradition until around the turn into the twenty-first century. Using the language of the systemic model, structural disorganization was said to be manifested in the presence of weak private and parochial ties/control. Second, however, Kornhauser contended that cultural disorganization—also referred to as cultural attenuation—was indicated by weakened and obsolete subcultures, an unstable communal culture, and the irrelevance of societal culture.

As an advocate of control theory and a harsh critic of cultural deviance theory, Kornhauser believed in subcultures; she just did not believe in deviant subcultures. In other words, she recognized that urban areas experiencing immigration were quite diverse, with many subcultures represented. From

Kornhauser's view, subcultures might express unique preferences in terms of things such as language, food, religious customs, and music. They did *not* differentially express criminal values because, in her view, the condemnation of crime was nearly universal, crossing all subcultures.

Strong subcultures of this sort could serve as an advantage for a community, as they tend to exert control over youths. However, Kornhauser offered that subcultures were unlikely to be strong in diverse, inner-city areas; instead, they were likely weak, or even obsolete. The attenuated capacity of subcultures to control youth in inner-city communities stems from such neighborhoods historically serving as areas of first-settlement for new immigrant or migrant groups. As such, the subcultures existing in these neighborhoods had been transplanted *from somewhere else*, with the likelihood being slim that they would be relevant or useful in an American inner city. For example, cultural values from a rural tightly knit community in another country might not have much relevance to kids who must negotiate life in urban America. Kornhauser explained that as subcultures were weakened, even to the point of becoming obsolete, an important source of control was lost. In such a context, subcultural values are no longer strongly enforced by families, and external control by families becomes, therefore, less effective.

However, beyond weak and/or obsolete subcultures, inner-city, crime-ridden communities also suffer from weakness in what Kornhauser referred to as "communal culture." The articulation of underlying values that unite community members, possibly across diverse subcultures, is necessary for effective community-based informal social control. If residents cannot articulate such a "community opinion," then community-based control will likely suffer. In inner-city areas with disproportionately higher rates of subcultures, there is likely a diminished capacity for achieving such communal culture.

Finally, broad societal culture—that is, mainstream American culture—must be strong within communities for effective social control. While Kornhauser assumed that all communities were composed of individual residents who largely bought into this general societal culture, the fact is that the culture is somewhat irrelevant in highly disadvantaged communities. For example, while employment (and legitimate income), stable and monogamous marriage, and in-wedlock childbearing might be valued, those values are not particularly "useful" in communities in which jobs and sources of legitimate income are scarce and the pool of "marriageable men" is shallow. Although residents in deprived communities may believe in conventional values, the conventional values are not particularly useful to many of them, and thus they are not enforced as strongly as in other, more advantaged contexts. This sort of cultural influence was articulated well in Ulf Hannerz's 1969 urban ethnography, *Soulside*, which was one of the few studies prior to

Kornhauser's work to utilize the notion of attenuated culture: "Nobody says that infidelity, broken unions, and premarital or postmarital sex are 'good,' that is, morally valuable in their own right. But on a lower level, there may be a kind of ghetto-specific cultural influence, in that the community seems to have evolved a certain measure of tolerance for a certain non-conformity as opposed to the mainstream ideal" (p. 104). In this analysis of life in a Washington, DC, ghetto, Hannerz (1969, p. 189) goes on to say, "The mainstream [societal] norm is upheld in principle, but the circumstances provide some release for behavior which is not itself valued." In communities such as the one studied by Hannerz, societal values regarding employment, legitimate income, and in-wedlock childbearing become attenuated or dis-used, but not devalued. However, in their attenuated state, they cannot as effectively be used to control the behavior of residents.

In a more recent review of Kornhauser's discussion of cultural disorganization (or, cultural attenuation), Barbara Warner and Pamela Wilcox Rountree (2000) argue that the cultural attenuation perspective is fully compatible with and complementary to a control model of community crime (i.e., the systemic model). This conceptual integration is achieved "by assuming a *conventional* normative consensus and an absence of real cultural motivation toward crime, yet, at the same time, recognizing that the presence of behaviors contradicting conventional values varies across neighborhoods . . . the presence of these behaviors then diminishes the willingness of neighbors to intervene in more serious community behaviors" (p. 47). From this perspective, cultural (and subcultural) weakness can be viewed as key in understanding cross-community variation in crime while also avoiding the notion of "oppositional values."

In sum, Kornhauser set forth a community crime model whereby ecological characteristics such as low socioeconomic status, ethnic heterogeneity, and residential mobility create both cultural and structural disorganization. Cultural disorganization is characterized by weakened and diminished enforcement of subcultural, communal, and societal values. Again, the subcultural, communal, and societal values that are weakened are presumed to be "conventional" (i.e., involving the condemnation of crime). With attenuation of conventional values comes a diminished capacity for resident-based informal social control. From this perspective, "crime is caused by the *absence* of 'good,' prosocial culture, not by the presence of 'bad' culture" (Sampson and Bean, 2006, p. 22, emphasis in the original). In contrast to cultural disorganization, structural disorganization is characterized by weak or fractured interpersonal relations and institutional ties. Structural disorganization is also posited to reduce the effectiveness of community-based control. This combined structure-culture community disorganization model is depicted in Figure 5.1.

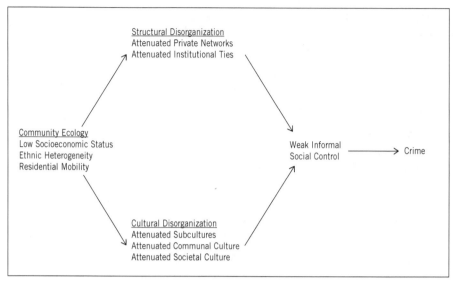

Figure 5.1 A Community Disorganization Model of Crime with Structural and Cultural Dimensions of Disorganization
Adapted from R.R. Kornhauser, *Social Sources of Delinquency: An Appraisal of Analytic Models* (Paperback ed.). (Chicago: University of Chicago Press, 1984), p. 73.

Ethnographies of Urban Ghettos: Support for an Attenuation Perspective

Alongside Kornhauser's treatment of cultural disorganization were several important ethnographic studies published between the late 1960s and 1970s, such as that by the aforementioned Hannerz. These ethnographies implicitly supported the notion that cultural attenuation, as opposed to cultural deviance, characterized impoverished "slum" neighborhoods. Gerald Suttles's famous 1968 ethnography, *The Social Order of the Slum*, is another example. Suttles begins with a characterization of the poor, racially and ethnically diverse Addams area in Chicago as follows:

> Conventional norms are not rejected but differentially emphasized or suspended for established reasons. The vast majority of residents are quite conventional people. At the same time those who continue in good standing on public measures are often exceptionally tolerant and even encouraging to those who are "deviant." . . . Taken out of context many of the social arrangements of the Addams area may seem an illusory denial of the beliefs and values of the wider society. Seen in more holistic terms, the residents are bent on ordering local

relations where the beliefs and values of the wider society do not provide adequate guidelines for conduct. (pp. 3–4)

Although Suttles suggests that provincial, territorial cultural groups emerge in such slum areas, and some appear supportive of deviance, his statements also offer that unconventional behavior is *not* primarily valued but *is* presumed to be situationally practical. Lee Rainwater reached similar conclusions in his research during the 1960s on the Pruitt-Igoe housing project in Saint Louis. In discussing the ghetto practices associated with the area—including dropping out of school, chronic unemployment, out-of-wedlock births, matrifocal families, drug addiction, and destruction of property—Rainwater (1967, p. 123) comments, *"The lower class does not have a separate system of basic values. Lower class people do not really 'reject middle class values.' It is simply that there whole experience with life teaches them that it is impossible to achieve a viable sense of self-esteem with those values"* (emphasis in the original). In short, lower-class behaviors are not reflective of lower-class aspirations or values.

Elijah Anderson's work, *A Place on the Corner*, is another ethnography that supports the view of cultural attenuation as opposed to cultural deviance in lower-class communities. Anderson's book, first published in 1978 (with a second edition in 2003), stemmed from his participant observation of a south side Chicago street corner and bar ("Jelly's") during his time as a doctoral student in sociology in the 1970s. Anderson began his research at Jelly's under the inspiration of Gerald Suttles at University of Chicago, and his work was clearly influenced by Suttles and the perspective he had offered in *The Social Order of the Slum*. Suttles ended up departing Chicago's faculty during the course of Anderson's studies, leaving, in Anderson's words, "a strongly felt vacancy" (Anderson, 2003, p. x). Anderson eventually transferred to Northwestern University to finish his Ph.D., where he continued his ethnographic research while working with Howard Becker.

In *A Place on the Corner*, Anderson details the social stratification system created through social interaction among the participants in the bar/street corner life (e.g., "the regulars," "the wineheads," and "the hoodlums"). Anderson describes a ghetto culture that is predominantly conventional in terms of value orientation, yet tolerant of unconventional behaviors when conventional behaviors seem less than useful: "Within the extended primary group at Jelly's, a 'visible means of support' and 'decency' appear to be the primary values, while 'toughness,' 'getting big money,' 'getting some wine,' and 'havin' some fun' are residual values, or values group members adopt after the 'props' supporting decency have for some reason been judged unviable, unavailable, or unattainable" (p. 209).

In sum, in the decade spanning the late 1960s to the late 1970s, important reconceptualization of the role of culture in community crime occurred. Prior to this time period, subcultural theories that emphasized oppositional, deviant values among some segments of society were the norm. By the end of that period, however, there was more discussion of value consensus. Notably, the possibility was raised that those in lower-class communities are more tolerant of behaviors counter to mainstream values because conventional values and behaviors have little practical utility in inner-city contexts. Despite this work, it was structural disorganization that took center stage in the systemic theory that dominated community-level crime theory in the 1970s and 1980s (see Chapter 3). Kornhauser's ideas about cultural disorganization and the ethnographic work that supported the concept were given relatively little attention, and scholars instead focused on weakened systems of private and parochial ties in an attempt to understand community crime. However, important seeds were sown in illustrating how cultural considerations could work within a community-control theoretical framework.

"Ghetto Behavior" in the Era of Deindustrialization

The notion of cultural attenuation discussed above allowed scholars to acknowledge the importance of community-level cultural influences without adhering to an assumption of value conflict and "cultural deviance." This perspective would be rejuvenated in an attempt to understand contemporary inner-city Black violence. The idea of cultural attenuation within a broader community disorganization framework reemerged most notably with the collaboration of Robert Sampson and William Julius Wilson in the mid-1990s, combining their respective work on the systemic model, on the one hand, and "ghetto-related behaviors," on the other hand.

The Truly Disadvantaged and Ghetto-Related Behaviors

As discussed in previous chapters, Wilson's 1987 book, *The Truly Disadvantaged*, and his 1996 book, *When Work Disappears*, detailed demographic, social, and economic changes in many U.S. inner cities, especially those in the Northeast, the Middle Atlantic, and the Midwest. These changes, along with ineffective and discriminatory policy, created a unique milieu. Segregated housing offering restricted residential choices for Blacks. Further, extensive industrial job loss, and middle-class and White out-migration from the central cites had, by 1980, created predominantly minority and deeply impoverished inner cities. These extremely poor, typically African American areas also had high percentages of households that were female headed, thus exacerbating the poverty. In brief, there was an unprecedented *concentration* of economic disadvantage in deindustrialized central cities—more residents of the inner city than ever were poor.

With such concentration effects, inner-city residents had little exposure to others with jobs, higher incomes, and family stability (i.e., two-parent households). In other words, the concentration of disadvantage within the inner cities meant that those disadvantaged residents were increasingly *socially isolated.* The concentrated disadvantage and social isolation of inner cities, in turn, served to alter the cultural landscape of the inner city. While Wilson's intention was not to offer a theory of community culture and crime, he did comment on ghetto culture in the form of tolerances of unconventional behavior, in particular. Wilson suggested that unconventional behaviors—such as idleness among young males, an emphasis on overt sexuality, teenage childbearing, and drug dealing—had become accepted in urban ghettos. However, Wilson's argument was that cultural *acceptance* or *tolerance* was *not* due to such behaviors being culturally *valued.* Instead, Wilson argues that unconventional behaviors were tolerated in disadvantaged areas as a result of few conceivable options in terms of conventional, valued behaviors. The cultural norms regarding the acceptability of unconventional behaviors were thus loosened as an adaptive response to the extreme structural disadvantage. In turn, social isolation exacerbated this disadvantage-induced "loosening" of culture. With residents in these areas increasingly cut off from nonpoor neighbors, neighbors with steady jobs, and examples of family stability, Wilson argues that there are no "social buffers," thus allowing a ghetto culture to thrive:

> In neighborhoods in which nearly every family has at least one person who is steadily employed, the norms and behavior patterns that emanate from a life of regularized employment become part of the community gestalt. On the other hand, in neighborhoods in which most families do not have a steadily employed breadwinner, the norms and behavior patterns associated with the steady work compete with those associated with casual or infrequent work. Accordingly, the less frequent the regular contact with those who have steady and full-time employment (that is, the greater the degree of social isolation), the more likely that initial job performance will be characterized by tardiness, absenteeism, and thereby, low retention. (1987, p. 61)

The near absence of models for conventional behavior more readily allows the adaptive unconventional behavior to be seen as "the only way." The unconventional behaviors—what Wilson terms "ghetto-related behaviors"—are then transmitted, not by internalization of unconventional values but by precept. The behaviors do not thrive in the urban ghettos because they are representative of values, but because they are behavioral standards that are seen with great frequency.

Race, Concentrated Disadvantage, and Cognitive Landscapes

Although Wilson had discussed culture in the form of ghetto-related behaviors in *The Truly Disadvantaged* and *When Work Disappears*, his treatment of culture was not fully integrated into a theory of crime (that was not the intention of either book). However, in his collaborative work with Robert Sampson, such a theory began to emerge. While on faculty together at University of Chicago in 1995, Sampson and Wilson wrote an important book chapter, "Toward a Theory of Race, Crime, and Urban Inequality." This chapter was discussed in Chapter 4 in relation to its importance to the image of the community as the truly disadvantaged. However, here its importance for helping shape and revitalize cultural theories is considered.

Sampson and Wilson outline a community disorganization model that integrates both social structural and cultural disorganization. Many of their theoretical ideas overlapped with those proposed earlier by Kornhauser, Hannerz, Anderson, and others. However, Sampson and Wilson combined the notions of structural and cultural disorganization to explain higher rates of crime in African American communities most specifically. Further, they firmly situated the emergence of both structural and cultural disorganization not only within community-level ecological characteristics but also within broader, extracommunity, political-economic forces. The resulting framework that they outlined nicely integrates Sampson's previous work in the systemic tradition with Wilson's previous work on the macro-social forces behind urban inequality and resulting "ghetto-related behaviors."

Their perspective posits the interactive influence of extracommunity forces (e.g., structural transformation of the economy in the form of deindustrialization, out-migration of Whites and middle-class Blacks, and discriminatory and segregationist decisions about housing) and community-level characteristics (e.g., extreme poverty, social isolation, residential instability). More specifically, Sampson and Wilson suggest that these forces interact to create both structural and cultural disorganization. In terms of structural disorganization, Sampson and Wilson emphasize that, in disadvantaged contexts, systems of private and parochial network linkages are fractured and/or ineffective in terms of providing collective supervision. In terms of cultural disorganization, Sampson and Wilson (1995, p. 50) argue that norms regarding appropriate standards, expectations of conduct, and tolerances of behavior—what they term "cognitive landscapes"—are shaped such that "crime, disorder, and drug use are less than fervently condemned and hence expected as a part of everyday life." It is not that crime, disorder, and drug use are valued, but they are tolerated and accepted because mainstream behaviors, in extremely disadvantaged contexts, become "existentially irrelevant" (p. 51). They emphasize that these cognitive landscapes are *ecologically structured norms*. Hence, they make a point that they are norms that stem from a disadvantaged context rather than representing a monolithic subculture. Still, Sampson and Wilson do not shy away from delineating their importance in community rates of crime. They attribute causal significance to cultural disorganization by advocating the view, much like Wilson had done in his earlier work, that the tolerance of unconventional behaviors creates a context in which these behaviors can flourish to an even greater extent. When unconventional behavior is tolerated, it is seen with greater frequency. When it is seen with greater frequency, "the transmission of these modes of behavior by precept, as in role modeling, is more easily facilitated" (Sampson and Wilson, 1995, p. 51).

Sampson and Wilson argued that their framework is helpful for understanding the relationship between race and crime in the United States. In their view, communities are key in understanding the race-crime relationship. They suggest that the causes for Black rates of crime versus White rates of crime are not different. Instead, the structural-cultural integrative framework they offer is the presumed explanation for both rates. However, Blacks are disproportionately embedded in community contexts characterized by structural and cultural disorganization. As outlined in Wilson's earlier work on the "truly disadvantaged," deindustrialization, out-migration, and segregated housing had created a concentration of extremely poor, *predominantly minority*, inner-city residents. Thus, race is intertwined with the whole notions of "concentrated disadvantage" and "social isolation." Given that these factors are precursors to structural and cultural disorganization, it is no wonder that rates of crime among Black Americans greatly exceed rates for White Americans. In what has been referred to as the "racial invariance hypothesis," Sampson and Wilson argue that if Whites and Blacks experienced equivalent levels of community disadvantage and isolation, then racial differences in cultural attenuation and crime would disappear.

Some research supports their thesis of racial invariance (see Chapter 4 for more detail on this point). For example, in Lauren Krivo and Ruth Peterson's analysis of Columbus, Ohio, neighborhoods, structural disadvantage had a much stronger effect on community crime than did racial composition (percent Black). In addition, although Black neighborhoods were much more likely than White neighborhoods to be extremely disadvantaged, the effects of extreme disadvantage on crime were not worse in Black neighborhoods (Krivo and Peterson, 1996; see also Peterson and Krivo, 2005, 2012). However, when cultural attenuation is included along with structural disadvantage in tests of racial invariance, the findings are more nuanced. Sampson and Dawn Jeglum Bartusch analyzed data from the Project on Human Development in Chicago Neighborhoods (PHDCN, discussed more fully in Chapter 8), and found, first, that neighborhood-level concentrated disadvantage was positively related to tolerance for deviance (or, negatively related to cultural attenuation). Once levels of disadvantage were held constant across neighborhoods, racial differences in tolerance for deviance were still evident, though African Americans and Latino Americans were *less tolerant* of deviance than Whites (Sampson and Bartusch, 1998).

Code of the Street and Beyond

Anderson's Code of the Street: Decent and Street Families

While Sampson and Wilson were articulating their ideas about structurally rooted cognitive landscapes and the implications for racial difference in crime, Elijah Anderson was involved in intense ethnographic study of Philadelphia neighborhoods. Most prominently featured in this work was the extremely disadvantaged, predominantly Black, North Philadelphia. His research on North Philadelphia was reported in several articles and two books—*Streetwise* in 1990 and in 1999 *Code of the Street*. The latter work is arguably his most famous in terms of discussing cultural influences on community crime and is the focus of the discussion that follows.

Anderson's work is most notable for its delineation of a "street code," or set of informal rules that govern public interaction in disadvantaged, socially isolated neighborhoods like North Philadelphia. Anderson offered that an emergent cultural code—the code of the street—establishes a new set of standards for status and respect in contexts where obtaining such respect through conventional channels (i.e., educational and occupational achievement) seems out of reach.

The code counters mainstream values in that it promotes the use of violence as an avenue for obtaining respect. In particular, public displays of physical toughness are expected, and violent retaliation to insults and other forms of disrespect is prescribed. Displays of toughness and violence are important not only for respect purposes, however. As Anderson describes it, they are essential for social control and self-protection in severely disadvantaged communities that are distrustful of police. In fact, as alluded to above, it is that isolation from mainstream life—including isolation from public agencies such as the police—that is part of the reason for the emergence of the code in the first place. According to Anderson (1999, p. 10), "The code of the street emerges where the influence of the police ends and personal responsibility for one's safety is felt to begin."

The code of the street is thought to pervade public life in the inner city. However, Anderson is clear that not all those who reside in the inner city actually *believe in* the morality expressed in the code. Instead, Anderson (1999, p. 35) describes two competing value orientations characterizing families in the inner city, which he termed "decent" and "street": "Almost everyone residing in poor inner-city neighborhoods is struggling financially and therefore feels a certain distance from the rest of America, but there are degrees of alienation, captured by the terms 'decent' and 'street' or 'ghetto,' suggesting social types. The decent family and the street family in a real sense represent two poles of value orientation, two contrasting conceptual categories."

Street individuals have typically been born into "street families" characterized by a number of dysfunctional qualities, including the following: (1) sporadic and/or superficial parenting (i.e., children are often unsupervised, without parental contact); (2) aggressive parenting (i.e., yelling and hitting); (3) chronic unemployment; (4) a limited understanding of financial priorities and consequences, leading to mounting bills and insufficiently fed and clothed children; (5) a tendency toward self-destructive behavior (i.e., heavy substance use/addiction); and (6) a deep-seated bitterness toward "the system" that seems stacked against them. Youths raised in such street families are taught to fight at an early age and to respond with violence when crossed. More generally, from a young age, street individuals are socialized according to the code of the street and thus come to believe that violence and other displays of toughness are acceptable and, in fact, valued. As Anderson (1990, pp. 69–70) illustrates:

> At an early age, often before they start school and without much adult supervision, children from street-oriented families gravitate toward the streets, where they must be ready to "hang," to socialize competitively with peers. These children have a great deal of latitude and are allowed to rip and run up and down the streets. . . . The social meaning of fighting [for respect] becomes clarified as these children come to appreciate the real consequences of winning and losing. And the child's understanding of the code becomes more refined but also an increasingly important part of his or her working conception of the world.

In contrast, Anderson describes decent individuals as typically raised in families that value hard work, self-reliance, and education. Parents within these "decent families" are often among the working poor as opposed to dealing with chronic unemployment. They display concern about, yet have a real hope for, the future. Decent families place more confidence in societal institutions, such as schools and churches. In fact, decent families often raise their children "within the church" and utilize strict (yet not overly aggressive) child-rearing practices. In short, youths from decent families are socialized to reject the values of the code and accept mainstream values instead.

Although decent individuals are socialized against internalizing the values of the code of the street (prescribing violence, toughness), Anderson suggests that decent individuals must know and use the code situationally to achieve status and, sometimes, in order to survive. In public, decent youths inevitably will confront street youths whose interactions with others are shaped by the code. Decent youths must be able to "act street" even if they do not "believe street" if they want to be viewed as strong, as having "juice," and commanding respect—all of which helps define their self-worth. Anderson (1990, pp. 99–100) describes this "dilemma of the decent kid" as follows:

> Even the most decent child in the neighborhood must at some point display a degree of commitment to the street. Life under the code might be considered a kind of game played by rules that are partly specified but partly emergent. The young person is encouraged to be familiar with the rules of the game and even to use them as a metaphor for life—or else feel left out, become marginalized, and, ultimately, risk being rolled on. So the young person is inclined to enact his own particular role, to show his familiarity with the game, and more specifically his street knowledge, so as to gain points with others.

Anderson refers to the performance of the street code among decent individuals as "code-switching." Thus, code-switching is the process whereby decent individuals who adhere to mainstream values act, in particular situations, in a manner that suggests they are "street." Again, Anderson claims it is a necessary tool among decent individuals for surviving the tough streets of a community in which respect is hard fought and easily lost and where "young people who project decency are generally not given much respect" (1999, p. 100). Thus, through this process of code-switching, the presence of the street code in disadvantaged neighborhoods can lead decent individuals to sometimes act in ways that are quite different from their individual value orientations but that are essential for "saving face" in public. For example, if "disrespected," decent youths must be willing to display toughness and a willingness to fight, lest they be seen as weak and vulnerable to victimization. Anderson (1990, p. 105) describes this ability to code-switch as "crucial to solving the dilemma of being decent in a street-oriented environment." Unlike street-oriented individuals, for whom "the street is in the person," decent youths who can code-switch have a broader behavioral repertoire—"a wide array of styles from which to choose how to act" (Anderson, 1990, p. 105).

Culture as Values, Culture in Action, and the Cultural Frame of Legal Cynicism

The various ways that street codes affect behavior in street versus decent individuals, as implied by Anderson, has been echoed in other recent work yet framed as a distinction between "culture as values" versus "culture in action" (e.g., Berg and Stewart 2013; Kirk and Papachristos, 2015; Lamont and Small, 2008; Matsueda, 2015; Sampson and Bean, 2006; Swidler, 1986). In many ways, these terms represent a contemporary update of the "cultural deviance" versus "attenuated culture" perspectives. From a culture-as-values perspective, cultural effects are exerted through internalized values that have been transmitted and learned through social interaction. Values prescribed by a neighborhood culture are thus internalized by residents, with the individual values, in turn, affecting behavior. Hence, there really is no effect of "community culture" on behavior that is distinct from the effects of individual values from the culture-as-values perspective. The culture-as-values perspective is apparent in Anderson's (1999) description of street-oriented individuals. As described above, Anderson argued that those with a street orientation internalize the code of the street at an early age. Their actions in accordance with the code thus represent their deeply held values and constrain their behavioral repertoire.

On the other hand, the culture-in-action perspective proposes that culture is not deeply embedded within individuals—that is, as internalized values—but rather it is something people perform situationally in the process of social interaction. The culture-in-action perspective refers to culture as a tool kit of sorts, providing approval for the use of a repertoire of behaviors appropriate for use in specific situations. Thus, rather than culture reflecting a value orientation, the culture in action perspective views culture as providing behavioral tools for navigating social interactions in situationally appropriate ways. The culture-in-action perspective aligns with Sampson and Wilson's (1995) discussion of cognitive landscapes, whereby behaviors that are not valued are tolerated nonetheless in situations where they are deemed useful. The culture-in-action perspective is also quite consistent with Anderson's (1990) description of the code-switching among decent youths. Again, though decent youths do not value the code of the street, they often choose to "act street" (via code-switching) in certain public encounters, where maintaining an image of toughness and respect is necessary for respect and personal safety. In such situations, acting street is a cultural survival tool.

One very recent and still unfolding line of inquiry focused on community culture centers around the concept of "legal cynicism." Legal cynicism theory is grounded in aspects of Anderson's treatment of culture, Sampson and Wilson's notion of cognitive landscapes, and contemporary notions of culture in action. It is playing a more prominent role in contemporary work on community culture and crime, led in large part by the efforts of Sampson and Dawn Jeglum Bartusch and David Kirk and Andrew Papachristos.

Sampson and Bartusch (1998, p. 778) first introduced the concept of legal cynicism as "anomie about law" and claimed that it was a cognitive landscape—an ecologically structured normative orientation regarding the legitimacy of law and its norms; it was presented as contextual in nature, distinct from individual values regarding antisocial behavior. They state, "In the classic Durkheimian sense, anomie refers to a state of normlessness in which the rules of the dominant society (and hence the legal system) are no longer binding in a community . . . anomie in this sense is conceived as part of a social system and not merely a property of the individual" (p. 782; see also Bartusch, 2010). Sampson and Bartusch (1998) presented analyses illustrating that legal cynicism emerged from community-level structural disadvantage and residential instability rather than from individual characteristics such as race.

Kirk and Papachristos (2011, p. 1197) develop the concept of legal cynicism beyond the "anomie about law" definition provided by Sampson and Bartusch. In the process, Kirk and Papachristos also more fully root legal cynicism in processes of social interaction. They stress that legal cynicism is a cultural frame "through which individuals interpret the functioning and viability of the law and its agents." More specifically, *legal cynicism* refers to a view among citizens that the police are illegitimate, nonresponsive to residents' needs and calls for assistance, and unable to adequately provide public safety (Kirk and Papachristos, 2011, 2015). Cynicism as a cultural frame has two major sources: neighborhood-level concentrated disadvantage and neighborhood-wide experiences with police. First, concentrated disadvantage breeds a general alienation from society—a feeling that "the dominant societal institutions (of which the police and the justice system are emblematic) will offer them little in the way of security, either economic or personal" (2011, p. 1198). Second, in terms of cynicism emerging from neighborhood-wide experiences with police, Kirk and Papachristos point to literature suggesting that police are less likely to file incident reports in high-crime neighborhoods and are more likely to harass and use force (or threats thereof) against suspects in minority neighborhoods, racially mixed neighborhoods, and economically disadvantaged neighborhoods.

The cynicism that some residents feel becomes a more pervasive cultural frame through cultural transmission, according to Kirk and Papachristos (2011, pp. 1201–1202):

Direct experiences with harassing police may influence an individual's cynicism, but this cynicism becomes cultural through social

interaction. In this sense, individuals' own experiential-based perception of the law becomes solidified through a collective process
whereby residents develop a shared meaning of the behavior of the
law and the viability of the law to ensure their safety. . . . In this
sense, perceptions and injustices of the past become part of a legacy
that is transmitted to new generations.

Therefore, Kirk and Papachristos stress that individuals in the same neighborhood might have different views of law (variable in the extent to which
such views are cynical), legal cynicism is the *collective view of law* that emerges
from social interaction and that exists independent of individual views.

Legal cynicism has consequences for neighborhood rates of violence in
that it serves to constrain perceived courses of action for resolving disputes
(much like the street-code-constrained behavioral choices for Anderson's street
youths). In brief, legal cynicism increases the likelihood that residents will
take law into their own hands in order to address grievances. Consistent
with a culture-in-action perspective, Kirk and Papachristos contend that any
dispute resolution through violence that emerges from legal cynicism is not
viewed as a representation of internalized values defining violence as favorable action. Rather, it is representative of appropriate action in a situation in
which reliance on police is considered unviable (for further discussion of
legal cynicism, see Chapter 8).

Empirical Support

A number of empirical studies have examined Anderson's suggestions
regarding effects of individual adherence to the code of the street and/or
effects of a neighborhood-level street culture, net of individual values. Eric
Stewart and his colleagues have been at the forefront of this research with a
series of high-profile studies using data on more than seven hundred African
American youths from both Georgia and Iowa (as part of the Family and
Community Health Study [FCHS]). For example, analysis of these by Stewart
and Simons (2006) indicated that neighborhood disadvantage positively
affected individual-level street-code beliefs. In turn, street code beliefs were
significantly and positively related to violent behavior, controlling for neighborhood disadvantage (see also Brezina et al., 2004; Stewart, Simons, and
Conger, 2002).

A subsequent study by Stewart and Simons (2010) provides perhaps the
most rigorous test of the various ways in which street codes might function
to affect violence according to Anderson's work. This more recent study
extended the earlier Stewart and Simons work by analyzing the FCHS
data using multilevel models, allowing them to examine the effect of a

neighborhood-level street culture, alongside with but independent of individual-level street-code beliefs. Such an approach is closely aligned with Anderson's discussion of the street code as functioning through both individual-level adherence to it values and through an emergent property of a collective that might affect behavior even among individuals who do not internalize street values (i.e., decent youths). This latter study by Stewart and Simons showed that neighborhood-level street culture did, indeed, affect violent behavior above and beyond the effect of individual-level street-code beliefs. Furthermore, neighborhood-level street culture magnified the positive effects of individual-level street-code beliefs on violence.

Jody Miller's qualitative research on adolescents in disadvantaged inner-city Saint Louis neighborhoods also illustrates how the street code can affect community crime. However, Miller explores the code-crime linkage through women's victimization experiences. Miller emphasizes that the toughness and masculinity stressed in the code serve to validate the mistreatment of women, thus placing young women in communities with a pervasive street culture at heightened risk for sexual harassment and sexual assault. In fact, twenty-five of the thirty-five young women (71 percent) interviewed by Miller reported that young men had made sexual comments that made them (the women) feel uncomfortable. Seventeen of the thirty-five women (49 percent) stated that young men had grabbed or touched them in a way that made them feel uncomfortable. Miller's male subjects indicated that such actions were fun and status enhancing. They typically defined the actions as "play." In contrast, Miller's female subjects saw such actions as "playin' *too much*" (2008, pp. 82–83).

Other community crime studies focus less on the individual versus contextual influence of street code effects and more on the simultaneous effects of structural and cultural disorganization. Barbara Warner's research, appearing in *Criminology* in 2003, is one of the best examples of such work to date. Her analysis of sixty-six high-drug-use neighborhoods examined the effects on informal social control of structural organization, in the form of social ties, and cultural organization, in the form of a collective perception of widespread conventional values. She measured this latter concept by asking respondents within the studied neighborhoods about their perceptions of their *neighbors'* belief in conventional values such as "it is important to get a good education," "it is important to be honest," and "selling drugs is always wrong." In other words, her measure of cultural organization—or what she termed cultural strength—was based on the aggregated perceived values of *neighbors' values*. The effect of this measure of cultural organization was estimated net of the residents own reported conventional values. Warner's results indicated that both neighborhood-level cultural strength and neighborhood-level social ties were positively related to informal social control, net of collective conventional values. A subsequent study by Warner and Burchfield (2011) found that weak community culture in the form of pluralistic ignorance, or the underestimation of the level of conventional values among neighbors, was negatively related to neighborhood-level informal social control. This effect was found alongside a positive effect of community social ties and a negative effect of community-level faith in police on informal social control. In another important study that integrated structural and cultural disorganization, Kirk and Papachristos (2011) found that both structural disorganization and legal cynicism were related to community homicides.

Conclusion

The study of culture remains one of the most popular approaches to understanding variable community rates of crime in the United States. However, this tradition has arrived at this historical place after an intellectual journey that has taken many twists and turns. That journey largely began with the foundational work of Shaw and McKay, who had originally indicated that subcultures transmitting criminal values emerged in disorganized communities. Subsequent theorizing by Cohen and then by Cloward and Ohlin elaborated that subcultures emerged in communities in which access to legitimate opportunities for success were unavailable. Cloward and Ohlin also emphasized the importance of access to illegitimate opportunities, noting that the type of crime engaged in by subcultures was a function of neighborhood organization and criminal opportunities.

The perspective of community subcultures rooted in strain gave way to purer cultural perspectives in which it was posited that nearly all lower-class community members held values supportive of crime. By the late 1960s, however, these perspectives became seen as overly conservative and divisive. Perspectives that emphasized value consensus were thus more palatable in this era. The decade spanning the late 1960s to the late 1970s, in fact, was marked by Kornhauser's theoretical articulation of "cultural attenuation," as well as several important ethnographies that supported the idea. From this perspective, "ghetto-related behaviors" were recognized but not valued, even by those participating in them. Instead, all were presumed to value conventional or "middle-class" values. However, behavior inconsistent with those values was *tolerated* (but not valued) in disadvantaged contexts where conventional values were not particularly relevant—where conventional values were impractical given the community circumstances.

After Kornhauser's articulation of "cultural attenuation," alongside ethnographies in support of the idea, the concept sat largely idle in community-crime theory for a decade. However, since the late 1980s, spearheaded by the work of Wilson, Sampson, and Anderson, the prevailing paradigm for understanding community crime has been one that recognizes both structural and cultural disorganization, with much of this work assuming that cultural influences are due to situational culture in action as opposed to an enduring, value-based opposition to mainstream values.

6

Community as a Broken Window

Social psychologist Philip Zimbardo achieved widespread prominence—inside and outside academia—when he conducted the "Stanford Prison Experiment" (SPE) (Kulig, Pratt, and Cullen, 2017). In 1971, Zimbardo and his collaborators created a mock prison in the basement of the basement of Jordan Hall, which housed the psychology department at Stanford University. Selected from seventy-five potential volunteers, twenty-four college students, who were determined to be psychologically normal, were randomly assigned to the role of either a guard or a prisoner. Intended to last two weeks, the study had to be terminated prematurely after six days because the students-turned-guards soon treated their captives in a coercive and demeaning way, eliciting conflict and distress. Zimbardo (2007, p. 3) called this the "Lucifer Effect," after the "metamorphosis of Lucifer into Satan." Indeed, the SPE seemed to confirm that prisons were inherently inhumane—that the nature of the institutional situation inevitably trumped personality and caused otherwise good kids to act badly (Zimbardo, 2007; Zimbardo et al., 1973). Although this conclusion has been questioned (Griggs, 2014; Kulig, Pratt, and Cullen, 2017), it remains a powerful and popular view, so much so that the study was celebrated in a 2015 movie, *The Stanford Prison Experiment*, with Zimbardo played by actor Billy Crudup.

The SPE thus ranks as one of the most famous social science experiments ever undertaken—and, again, ensured Zimbardo's national notoriety. What is less well known, however, is that he conducted another study that also would have a major impact, this time on the policing of America's inner cities. Although designed for other purposes, Zimbardo's research on the fate of abandoned cars would be used by James Q. Wilson and George Kelling (1982) as the conceptual hook to introduce their now-classic "broken windows" theory. Zimbardo's study was reported in a 1969 article in *Time*, which was called "Diary of a Vandalized Car" and apparently caught the eye of Wilson and Kelling (see also Zimbardo, 2007).

Zimbardo and his fellow researchers wondered what would happen if a car was made to look as though it was abandoned and whether the fate of the vehicle would vary across social contexts. To achieve the experimental condition of abandonment, they parked a "good-looking" vehicle alongside a curb and then took off the license plates, slightly raised its hood, and moved out of sight where they could record any vandalism. Indeed, the lack of plates and a raised hood were intended to serve as "sure 'releaser' signals to lure citizens into becoming vandals" (Zimbardo, 2007, p. 24). To vary the context, the researchers conducted the experiment in two separate middle-class residential neighborhoods—one in the Bronx across from New York University's branch campus and one in Palo Alto across from Stanford University's campus. For the researchers monitoring the vehicle's fate in the Bronx—in what Zimbardo (2007, p. 24) calls a *"Candid Camera–*type field study"—the results soon proved stunning.

Within ten minutes, a car carrying what appeared to be a middle-class family of three stopped by the experimental automobile. With his eight-year-old son by his side, the father retrieved a hacksaw from the trunk of his vehicle and then proceeded to remove the battery and radiator. The mother, observed to be "well-dressed" and carrying a "Saks Fifth Avenue shopping bag," stood by the vehicle "keeping watch" ("Diary of a Vandalized Car," 1969, p. 68). This willingness to strip the car did not prove to be an idiosyncratic incident. Operating in broad daylight with passersby ignoring or even talking to them, in a little over a day (twenty-six hours) "a parade of vandals" absconded with the "air cleaner, radio antenna, windshield wipers, right-hand-side chrome strip, hubcaps, a set of jumper cables, a gas can, a can or car wax, and the left rear tire" ("Diary of a Vandalized Car," 1969, p. 68). A middle-aged man reached into the car, pilfered a part, and then placed it in the baby carriage he was pushing. The vehicle's final destruction was left to two teenagers, who threw the auto's rearview mirror at the headlights and windshield, and to two five-year-olds, who used the "car as their private playground, crawling in and out of it and smashing the windows" (1969, p. 68).

In Palo Alto, a different story unfolded. A comparable car stood untouched for a full week. One rainy day, a man even shut the hood to protect the engine. And when Zimbardo retrieved the car and drove it back to the Stanford University campus, three neighbors contacted the police to report the possible theft of the abandoned vehicle (Zimbardo, 2007, p. 25).

As a social psychologist, Zimbardo attributed the differential results to the situation—and not to the possibility that New York contains more people than California with criminal dispositions. Thus, even though the car was parked in a residential Bronx neighborhood, the context of a large urban area fostered "ambient anonymity"—the belief that "others do not know us or care to" (p. 25). Such anonymity, claims Zimbardo (2007, p. 25), "reduces their sense of personal accountability and civic responsibility" and can lead to "antisocial, self-interested behavior." By contrast, Palo Alto was a vastly different community, marked not by ambient anonymity but by "reciprocal altruism"—that is, the assumption that neighbors have mutual regard and, when necessary, would act to protect one another's person or property. This kind of trust and fairness, asserts Zimbardo (2007, p. 25), "thrives in a quiet, orderly way in places such as Palo Alto where people care about the physical and social quality of their lives and have the resources to work at improving both." In short, reciprocal altruism flourishes in organized communities that have close ties and collective efficacy—conditions outlined in the social disorganization/systemic model tradition (see Kornhauser, 1978; Sampson, 2012; Shaw and McKay, 1942).

Notably, in developing their broken windows theory, James Q. Wilson and George Kelling highlighted a specific conclusion from the vandalized car experiment. They were in agreement with Zimbardo that the situation and not individual dispositions triggered the vandalism. "Window-breaking," observed Wilson and Kelling (1982, p. 31), "does not necessarily occur on a large scale because some areas are inhabited by determined window-breakers whereas others are populated by window-lovers." Neighborhood context perhaps matters in how quickly vandalism might occur—almost immediately in the Bronx because of its "anonymity, the frequency with which cars are abandoned and things are stolen or broken, the past experience of no one caring" and only after a while in Palo Alto, "where people have come to believe that private possessions are cared for, and that mischievous behavior is costly" (p. 31). Indeed, "vandalism can occur anywhere once communal barriers—the sense of mutual regard and the obligations of civility—are lowered by actions that seem to signal that 'no one cares'" (p. 31). Even in Palo Alto? Although not discussed by Zimbardo in his account of the experiment, Wilson and Kelling (1982, p. 31) reported that shortly after Zimbardo hit the abandoned car with a sledgehammer, "passersby were joining in. Within hours, the car had been turned upside down and utterly destroyed. Again, the 'vandals' appeared to be primarily respectable whites" (p. 31).

So, if vandalism is not due to the concentration of bad people within bad neighborhoods, what is the key causal factor? For Wilson and Kelling, it is "broken windows" or, to use more academic language, social disorder. "Social psychologists and police officers," they noted, "tend to agree that if a window in a building is broken *and is left unrepaired*, all of the rest of the windows will soon be broken. This is as true in nice neighborhoods and in run-down ones" (1982, p. 31, emphasis in the original). The study thus assumed importance because it provided empirical support for this claim (Zimbardo, 2007, p. 25). In essence, the releaser signals of an elevated hood and lack of license plates on the experimental car were the functional equivalent of a broken window in a building; they invited more acts of vandalism.

As will be seen in more detail, Wilson and Kelling were not interested in vandalism but with applying the metaphor of broken windows to the problem of inner-city crime. For them, "at the community level, disorder and crime are usually inextricably linked, in a kind of developmental sequence" (1982, p. 31). Disorder involves minor breaches of community standards, such as displays of public drunkenness, the homeless sleeping in doorways, and rowdy teenagers congregating on street corners who harass passersby. Other manifestations of disorder are more physical than social—graffiti despoiling building walls, dilapidated buildings, and litter strewn about the sidewalks and street gutters. They argued that signs of disorder operate like broken windows—they invite more disorderly conduct and convey the message that nobody in the community can prevent waywardness. Disorder is the context out of which crime arises and flourishes. Thus, the "developmental sequence" of Wilson and Kelling's broken windows theory is as follows: disorder → crime.

As a political scientist, Wilson (1975) had criticized criminologists for searching for root causes of crime that could not be changed—short of a revolution occurring. Perhaps not surprisingly, he and his collaborator Kelling did not blame crime on deindustrialization, economic inequality, or cultures of violence nourished by concentrated disadvantage. Rather, the underlying cause of crime, especially in inner-city neighborhoods, was the *tolerance of disorder*, which in turn created conditions ripe for widespread criminality. In their view, however, crime was not an intractable problem beyond the reach of governmental intervention. No, they did not call for the expansion of jobs and other social welfare programs. Instead, Wilson and Kelling argued that the state already had at its disposal the resources it needed to eradicate disorder: the police. By using "order maintenance" techniques, officers could fix the broken windows of disorder. Once order was restored, crime would fall.

Wilson and Kelling (1982) set forth these ideas not in an academic journal article or full-length book but in a nine-page essay published in the *Atlantic Monthly* titled "Broken Windows: The Police and Neighborhood Safety." In most instances, writings such as this slip into obscurity, ignored by professors, police chiefs, and politicians alike. But this work appeared at a propitious time. It resonated with many observers of urban life who increasingly saw the nation's cities, especially its inner cities, as wildly out of control. When such views prevail, theories offering social order as the solution to crime generated by disorder make sense (see Rothman, 1971). Beyond this diagnosis, Wilson and Kelling rejected the prevailing view that "nothing works" to reduce crime, whether the intervention is undertaken by the police or correctional officials (Cullen and Gendreau, 2001; Sherman, 1993a). In fact, their diagnosis—that disorder leads to crime—offered a ready cure: get rid of disorder. Again, they argued, optimistically, that the police were up to this challenge.

This chapter begins with a discussion of the prevailing social context in which urban America was portrayed as increasingly gripped by social and physical disorder. This context lent credence to the image of the city as a broken window. Wilson and Kelling's broken windows theory is then reviewed in detail and, in the following section, their thesis that disorder leads to crime is evaluated. Finally, the role of policing strategy in reducing crime, including broken windows or zero-tolerance policing, is examined. The dispute over which type of policing will achieve the greatest public safety remains a vibrant policy issue today.

Disorder and Decline

Wilson and Kelling's "broken windows" *Atlantic Monthly* essay appeared at a time—extending from before to after its publication in 1982—when violent crime was an increasingly salient social and political issue (Beckett and Sasson, 2000; Garland, 2001; Simon, 2007). Starting in the mid-1960s, the homicide rate per 100,000 began a steady upward trend, doubling from 5.1 in 1965 to 10.2 in 1980. This rate fell to 7.9 in 1984 and 1985, but then swung upward again, exceeding 9.0 per 100,000 in the first half of the 1990s. In 1994 alone, more than 23,330 Americans were murdered (Disastercenter.com, 2016). Cities were particularly hard hit by this crime trend. In 1991, the homicide rate for cities with more than one million residents was 35.5; those living in small cities (100,000 to 249,999) fared better but still faced a murder rate of 15.0 (Cooper and Smith, 2011).

These statistics evoked a sense of true peril. In their book *Body Count*, Bennett, DiIulio, and Walters (1996, p. 13) lamented, "Late twentieth-century America has the distinction of being history's most violent 'civilized' nation." Our "shining city on the hill"—as America was once termed—"now leads the industrialized world in rates of murder, rape, and violent crime" (p. 13). They then cautioned, "We may be experiencing the lull before the coming crime storm" (see also DiIulio, 1995). In fact, crime in the United States took a sudden, largely inexplicable turn downward, leading to what Zimring (2007) calls "the Great American crime decline" (see also Blumstein and Wallman, 2000; Tonry, 2014). One temporary exception was juvenile violence that shot up in the latter part of the 1990s, but then followed the overall downward trend (Zimring, 2013). Remarkably, in 2014 the nation's homicide rate per 100,000 residents was 4.5 or 14,249 victims—statistics not seen since the 1960s (Disastercenter.com, 2016). In New York City, to cite but one example, the homicide rate in 2009 was only 18 percent of its 1990 total (Zimring, 2012).

Thus, broken windows theory appeared in the midst of a prolonged crime boom—bracketed by fifteen-year periods of escalating and/or high offense rates. The reality of crime, which hit urban America the hardest, lent credence to the image of the city as a broken window that could not be fixed even by the wars on drugs and crime various presidents initiated (Beckett and Sasson, 2000). During this era, however, cities seemed to be suffering from more than an intractable crime rate. They appeared to lose the capacity to enforce not only law but also order. They were portrayed as places to flee, as many White residents did to the suburbs. Old neighborhoods increasingly appeared to be plagued by run-down if not abandoned buildings and by public spaces populated by troubled if not troubling people. In short, disorder had set in.

In 1990, Wesley Skogan documented the extent and consequences of these conditions in his acclaimed book, *Disorder and Decline: Crime and the Spiral of Decay in American Neighborhoods*. Skogan based his conclusions on surveys from six cities, covering forty areas, between 1977 and 1983. He was careful to measure both social disorder—"loitering, drugs, vandalism, gangs, public drinking and street harassment"—and physical disorder—"noise, abandoned buildings, litter, and trash" (1990, p. 191). Although conceptually distinct, Skogan found that social and physical disorder were intercorrelated; that is, where one type was present so was the other type, a toxic brew. He cautioned that social disorder had wide-ranging impacts that could contribute to the further decline of neighborhoods. As he noted:

> Disorder not only sparks concern and fear of crime among neighborhood residents; it may actually increase the level of serious crime. Disorder erodes what control neighborhood residents can maintain over local events and conditions. It drives out those for whom stable community life is important, and discourages people with similar values from moving in. It threatens house prices and discourages investment. In short, disorder is an instrument of destabilization and neighborhood decline. (1990, p. 3)

Most of all, observed Skogan, communities marked by disorder "can no longer expect people to act in civil fashion in public places. They can no longer expect landlords to respect the character of their neighborhood" (1990, p. 3). Why did this deterioration in public rules occur in urban areas? For George Kelling and Catherine Coles (1997), two causal factors are clear, and they are not factors such as the deindustrialization of the urban core or concentrated disadvantage. First, they indict the growth of individual rights trumped by the civil rights movement, which led to the decriminalization of drunkenness, the deinstitutionalization of the mentally ill, and the limits on the enforcement of loitering and other public order laws. Although perhaps well intentioned, observe Kelling and Coles, these initiatives led to the increasing amount and ultimately tolerance of deviance and disorder in city streets. Second, at the same time, modern policing had moved away from its traditional role of order maintenance and prevention. In its place, law enforcement has embraced a "warrior strategy" that focuses on crime fighting and responding rapidly to 911 calls. Thus, at the time that police were needed to enforce order, they instead became isolated and lost their connection to the citizens in urban neighborhoods. For Kelling and Coles (1997, p. 194), the solution lay in "taking back the streets" by "restoring order." Broken windows policing was the key to doing so.

Wilson and Kelling's Classic Essay: Police as Window Fixers

In their classic essay, Wilson and Kelling (1982) had a simple message that resonated with Americans in the 1980s: people were fearful to go into the city because things were out of control. Once upon a time, police officers on foot patrol walked the streets, talked to the residents, and used their discretion—perhaps including a touch of aggression—to maintain order. But those idyllic days had passed, with officers now cruising around in police vehicles. They might occasionally roll down the window to yell at a rowdy teen or bothersome alcoholic to behave themselves, but otherwise they had little interest in minor forms of urban incivility. They had moved from maintaining order to supposedly fighting crime, a task that research showed they did poorly. Police officials and their officers simply did not understand that however important crime was, those living in and traveling to inner-city neighborhoods were immediately confronted each day with a social and physical environment rich with clues about the prevailing level of social order and of their safety. "But we tend to overlook or forget," observed Wilson and Kelling (1982, pp. 29–30), "another source of fear—the fear of being bothered by disorderly people." These were not "violent people, nor, necessarily, criminals, but disreputable or obstreperous or unpredictable people: panhandlers, drunks, addicts, rowdy teenagers, prostitutes, loiterers, the mentally disturbed" (p. 30).

Police had erred in not addressing these small things, not understanding that they produced fear and, said Wilson and Kelling, a fertile ground for the concentration of crime in the area. The prototypical inner-city community had become like a dilapidated, vandalized building with all its windows broken. At one point in time, this structure was in full repair. But at some point, one window was shattered and nobody cared enough to fix it. This single broken window was a sitting invitation for passersby to consider this building as untended and thus as an attractive target to vandalize further. As more windows were smashed—and again not fixed—the signal strengthened that this was a property that could be vandalized at will. Eventually, the building would be ruined and unfit for human settlement.

Again, the single empirical study cited by Wilson and Kelling to lend credence to this broken windows thesis was Zimbardo's experiment reported in "Diary of a Vandalized Car" (1969). They described the findings in detail, showing how, especially in the Bronx, a car that was arranged to look abandoned soon suffered vandalism, with one act encouraging future acts until the vehicle was virtually destroyed. Wilson and Kelling thus argued that there are grave consequences to sending the message that "no one cares" (p. 31). "Untended property," they warned, becomes fair game for people out for fun or plunder, and even for people who ordinarily would not dream of doing such things and who probably consider themselves law-abiding" (p. 31). In a similar way, they argued that "untended behavior" in cities leads to a spiral of social decline, marked by the "breakdown of community controls" (p. 31):

A stable neighborhood of families who care for their homes, mind each other's children, and confidently frown on unwanted intruders can change, in a few years or even months, to an inhospitable and frightening jungle. A piece of property is abandoned, weeds grow up, a window is smashed. Adults stop scolding rowdy children; the children, emboldened, become more rowdy. Families move out, unattached adults move in. Teenagers gather in front of the corner store. The merchant asks them to move; they refuse. Fights occur. Litter accumulates. People start drinking in front of the grocery; in time, an inebriate slumps to the sidewalk and is allowed to sleep it off. Pedestrians are approached by panhandlers. (1982, pp. 31–32)

According to Wilson and Kelling (1982, p. 31), "at the community level, disorder and crime are usually inextricably linked, in a kind of developmental sequence." Disorder does not spark a crime wave immediately. Rather, as residents become wary of their environment and fear that crime might be rising, "they will modify their behavior accordingly. They will use the streets less often, and when on the streets will stay apart from their fellows, moving with averted eyes, silent lips, and hurried steps" (p. 32). They will start to live by the dictum of "don't get involved" (p. 32). In the language of criminologists, informal social control and the capacity to enforce shared values of civility will attenuate. It is at this stage, argue Wilson and Kelling (1982, p. 32), that "such an area is vulnerable to a criminal invasion":

> Though it is not inevitable, it is more likely that here, rather than in places where people are confident that they can regulate public behavior by informal controls, drugs will change hands, prostitutes will solicit, and cars will be stripped. That the drunks will be robbed by boys who do it as a lark, and prostitutes' customers will be robbed by men who do it purposefully and perhaps violently. That muggings will occur.

This disquieting image of the city as a broken window spiraling into decline, however, was pregnant with optimism. The broken window thesis contained a clear solution to reverse urban decay: fix the broken windows. The key to this policy prescription was understanding the causal sequence underlying inner-city crime. Social disorder, by leading to weakening informal social control, created a place that attracted crime and made it easy to commit.

For Wilson and Kelling, the police would have to be the agents of social reform. They would have to fix the windows. Wilson and Kelling thus rejected the prevailing notion that law enforcement could not be used to reduce crime (Sherman, 1993a). As noted, however, they argued that officers were focusing on the wrong intervention target: crime itself and usually after the incident had occurred. Wilson and Kelling thus urged that police return to their traditional function of order maintenance. Concretely, this would mean their being in the neighborhood, often on foot, where they would put a stop to bothersome incivilities. They would tell loiterers to move along, drunks sleeping in doorways to go elsewhere, rowdy teenagers to quiet down and leave people alone, and prostitutes to ply their trade on someone else's beat. If need be, they would use their discretion to arrest recalcitrant deviants. Once order was being restored, the good people of the neighborhood would take to the streets, informal controls would strengthen, and criminals would realize that they need to seek out other places to do their handiwork.

As public policy analysts, Wilson and Kelling were interested in using available government resources in the most effective way to solve the problem of urban disorder, crime, and decline. They were not interested in so-called root causes of crime, such as poverty, which they saw as either causally unimportant or beyond the reach of public policy. Still, it is puzzling that

Wilson and Kelling never pondered the question of the origins of all the criminals, prostitutes, alcoholics, homeless, and loiterers that were prepared to invade a neighborhood showings signs of social disorder. They were confident, it seems, that this diverse wayward crowd could be displaced elsewhere or perhaps have their behavior suppressed by the police. But they never seemed to probe how the conditions of the neighborhoods they were studying might have created these troubled souls in the first place.

Do Broken Windows Cause Crime?

The causal connection between disorder and crime in urban America is undoubtedly complex (Sampson, 2012; Sampson and Raudenbush, 1999, 2001, 2004). For example, signs of physical and social disorder could cause a neighborhood to be stigmatized as a "bad area" and thus lose investment in homeownership and business development. If concentrated in minority areas, this disinvestment could contribute to racial inequality, increased economic barriers, and impoverished conditions inhospitable to healthy human development. Wilson and Kelling, however, ignore these potential criminogenic pathways, instead proposing that such "broken windows" lead to crime in a single way: by prompting decent citizens, increasingly fearful for their safety, to withdraw from public spaces and to diminish their willingness to activate informal social control. Into this vacuum, the disreputable and deviant find comfort and feel empowered to socially spoil the neighborhood.

But is there a direct link between disorder and crime—or, as Taylor (2001, p. 372) asks, between "grime" and crime? This is not some esoteric criminological question. For interventions to be effective, they must target known criminogenic risk factors with "treatments" that are responsive to— that is, capable of changing—the underlying condition (see Bonta and Andrews, 2017). Belief in the thesis that minor incivilities lead ultimately to major crimes is a powerful justification for using available police resources to show zero tolerance for any form of disorder. On balance, the research has not been supportive of all aspects of the broken windows theory (Taylor, 2001). Three critiques have surfaced: the no-effect critique, the spuriousness critique, and the perceptual critique.

The No-Effect Critique

First, in *Illusions of Order: The False Promise of Broken Windows Policing*, Bernard Harcourt (2001) provides the most comprehensive critical examination of Wilson and Kelling's ideas. As part of this assessment, he revisited the empirical results presented by Skogan (1990) in *Disorder and Decline*. In his data analysis, Skogan reported that residents' perception of disorder (as measured by his combined social and physical disorder scale) was related to self-reports of robbery victimization. In replicating this study, Harcourt challenged the robbery finding on methodological grounds, noting in particular that it was produced largely by neighborhoods in only one of the six cities studied (Newark). More instructive, he broadened the analysis to consider a range of other crimes. Importantly, Harcourt (2001, p. 78, emphasis in the original) concluded that "there are *no* statistically significant relationships between disorder and purse-snatching, physical assault, burglary, or rape when other explanatory variables are held constant. . . . In the end, the data do not support the broken windows hypothesis." Harcourt is thus articulating the *no-effect critique*.

A salient result in Skogan's (1990, p. 75) research should not be overlooked. Although the focus was on his examination of disorder, he found as well that "poverty, instability, and the racial composition of neighborhoods are strongly linked to crime" (see also Harcourt, 2001; Pratt and Cullen, 2005). Thus, while he favored, with reservations, the policing of disorder, his policy prescription for reducing inner-city crime was broad based. For example, his analysis of the "political economy of disorder" led him to recommend making "key investments" in job creation and housing (Skogan, 1990, pp. 172, 174). In contrast, by singling out only broken windows for fixing, Wilson and Kelling ignored any discussion of these empirical realities—these "root causes" of crime—boldly suggesting that the police could be relied on to solve the urban crime problem through order maintenance (see Wilson, 1975).

The Spuriousness Critique

Second, Sampson and Raudenbush (1999, 2001) provide the leading example of the *spuriousness critique*. For them, disorder is very real and "fundamental to understanding urban neighborhoods" (2001, p. 1). Disorder is important because it "can be observed, while crime, by contrast, is largely unobserved" (p. 1). Disorder and crime also co-occur, which might lead to the assumption that broken windows are criminogenic. Alas, they caution that the "contention that disorder is an essential cause in the pathway to predatory crime is open to question" (p. 1).

Their critical insight is that the association between disorder and crime is more apparent than real. Sampson (2012, p. 126) starts with the important observation that the line between incivilities and crime is not as clear-cut as Wilson and Kelling suggest:

> Consider items commonly used to define social disorder, such as solicitation for prostitution, loitering, and public use of alcohol or

drugs. Or consider "incivilities" such as graffiti, smashed windows, and drug raids in the streets. All these are evidence either of crimes themselves or ordinance violations, meaning that in one sense the broken windows theory is saying that crime causes crime. When cast in this light, broken windows theory takes on a different and, in my view, less compelling explanation of crime.

Put another way, Sampson sees many incivilities as part of what has been called the "generality of deviance," where such actions either are crimes or are analogous to them (see Gottfredson and Hirschi, 1990). If so, then they might have a common origin. "It may be, then," notes Sampson (2012, p. 137), "that public disorder and predatory crimes are manifestations of the same process at different ends of a seriousness continuum." They may have a common cause that causes both disorder and crime to occur in the same place—inner-city neighborhoods. Their association is thus spurious.

To test this possibility, Sampson and Raudenbush used data from the Project on Human Development in Chicago Neighborhoods (PHDCN). This massive undertaking surveyed thousands of residents, community leaders, and adolescents across 343 Chicago neighborhoods. They wanted to see if disorder predicted crime across neighborhoods. To do so, they made two important methodological choices.

First, as is explained in more detail in Chapter 8, Sampson developed "collective efficacy theory" to explain community variations in crime rates (Sampson, 2006, 2012; Sampson, Raudenbush, and Earls, 1997). In this analysis, he was betting that both disorder and crime would be explained by the core factors in his theory. These included measures of factors such as concentrated disadvantage, immigrant concentration, residential stability, population density, mixed land use, and—most important—collective efficacy. The construct of collective efficacy was measured by a scale that assessed residents' social cohesion and their willingness to exercise informal social control. When residents are cohesive, they are a collective; when they have "shared expectations for control," they can be said to have the potential for efficacy (Sampson, 2012, p. 152). Most important, collective efficacy implies the capacity to activate neighbors to come together to solve a problem that violates their values—such as a drug market or a rash of burglaries—should one arise.

Second, Sampson and Raudenbush (1999, 2001) wanted to develop an objective measure of disorder that did not have to rely on how individuals perceived their urban world. Perceptions are used in studies because they can be obtained simply by having respondents complete a survey and express their views (e.g., whether graffiti is a "problem" in the area). Sampson and Raudenbush, however, took the road less traveled: they used "systematic social observation" (SSO) to methodically record the level of disorder. In their words:

> To measure disorder, trained observers videotaped what was hap-
> pening on the face blocks of 23,000 streets in 196 neighborhoods that
> varied by race/ethnicity and social class. As the observers drove and
> filmed, they produced a permanent visual record that would be
> accessible at any time. They also logged the observations they made
> on each face block. Counted as signs of physical disorder were such
> items as garbage on the streets, litter, graffiti, abandoned cars, and
> needles and syringes. Counted as signs of social disorder were such
> activities as loitering, public consumption of alcohol, public intoxica-
> tion, presumed drug sales, and the presence of groups of young
> people manifesting signs of gang membership. (2001, p. 4)

Thus equipped with a strong theoretical framework and strong measure of disorder, they were prepared to assess the broken windows thesis. Their findings proved striking. The SSO measure of disorder was initially related to predatory crime. But once collective efficacy and the other independent variables were controlled, "the connection between disorder and crime vanished in 4 out of 5 tests—including homicide, arguably our best measure of violence" (Sampson and Raudenbush, 1999, p. 637). The only exception was robbery. "The implication," they noted, "is that disorder and crime have similar roots. The forces that generate disorder also generate crime" (2001, p. 4). The spuriousness critique thus seems to be substantially supported.

These finding have policy implications. According to Sampson and Raudenbush (1999, p. 638), "the active ingredients in crime seem to be structural disadvantage and attenuated collective efficacy more so than disorder." It is thus not clear how police suppression of incivilities will make communities safer. The wrong cause is being targeted for change. As they caution, "attacking public disorder through tough police tactics may thus be a politically popular but perhaps analytically weak strategy to reduce crime because such a strategy leaves the common origin of both, but especially the last, untouched" (1999, p. 638).

Sampson and Raudenbush (2004) add one final insight regarding disorder and crime. Broken windows theory would predict a close relationship between objective and perceived disorder. In fact, Wilson and Kelling imply that residents are acute observers of social and physical disorder, knowing when to retreat from public spaces (when incivilities rise) and when to return to public spaces (when, aided by the police, incivilities diminish). And, in fact, Sampson and Raudenbush's analysis of the PHDCN data show a relationship. But the key finding is that perceptions of disorder are increased even more by a high concentration of Blacks and the poor. These effects were found not only among residents but also in a sample of leaders who worked in the communities but did not live there (Sampson and Raudenbush, 2004). Thus, it appears that perceptions of disorder cannot be understood apart from their racial and economic context. Who is in the neighborhoods, not just loitering and littering, matters most in the meaning observers ascribe to an area.

Sampson (2012, p. 144) reports that neighborhood reputations are "durable and hard to overcome." In essence, areas become stigmatized—labeled as "disorderly." Most disquieting, he discovered that perceived community disorder was related to a measure of "later poverty"; objective disorder was unrelated to this outcome. Sampson (2012, p. 147) notes the implication of this finding:

> I suggest that collectively shaped perceptions of disorder may be one of the underappreciated causes of continued racial and economic segregation in the United States and perhaps cities elsewhere. At the very least, shared perceptions of disorder appear to matter for reasons that extend far beyond the presence of broken windows or the physical structure of the built environment.

The Perceptual Critique

Published in the *Atlantic Monthly*, Wilson and Kelling's (1982) classic article was remarkable in its straightforward thinking: fix broken windows. It is difficult to imagine anyone who would argue to the contrary—that a broken window should be left unrepaired. It offered a compelling, optimistic solution to an urban problem, crime and decay, that heretofore seemed intractable: get the police to rid communities of bothersome incivilities. If the neighborhood is spruced up and the wayward who externalize the costs of their deviance are removed, then the good urban villages of a past era will reappear. So, stop worrying about root causes of crime and empower the police to walk the beat, enforce social rules in a no-nonsense way, and let the decent people know they have a defender close by.

As Sampson and Raudenbush's work painfully discloses, urban life is more complicated than can be portrayed in a nine-page article written a quarter century ago for a general audience. They have shown that objective and perceived disorder are different phenomena that may have different effects. More than this, they have suggested that community stigma, similar to individual stigma, is sticky and not easily shed. Once an area becomes publicly labeled as a "bad neighborhood," it is not clear what it would take—police action included—to persuade residents, let alone local criminals and nonresidents, that community redemption has been achieved. The challenge is particularly difficult if, as Sampson and Raudenbush suggest, perceived disorder is inextricably mixed with how many African Americans live in an area. If being Black is the "incivility" that triggers perceptions of disorder, then "fixing" this "broken window" is far beyond the police's reach. The point is that Wilson and Kelling undertheorized perceptions of fear and risk, treating them as malleable and responsive to changes in objective conditions. Perceptions are more complicated than portrayed, thus calling the broken windows thesis into question. This is the *perceptual critique* (see Kubrin, 2008).

In this regard, Gau and Pratt (2008, p. 163) note that Wilson and Kelling's model is rooted in claims about perceptions: that residents' perceptions of disorder "cause fear and social withdrawal, which thereby opens the streets for serious predatory crime." In an innovative strategy, they used data in which respondents in a 2003 survey in Eastern Washington rated seventeen different crime and disorder items on the extent to which they were a problem in their neighborhood. If crime and disorder were distinct constructs, then they should load on separate factors. Alas, they did not, loading instead on a single factor. This finding poses problems for broken windows theory, which:

> insists that people observe disorder as a visible indicator of a breakdown in local social control. However, if people view disorder and crime as the same thing, then crime itself could serve as the visible indicator of the lack of informal social control in a community. If this is so, then broken window theory is untenable because it is tautological—crime cannot logically be asserted to cause itself. (2008, p. 181)

Gau and Pratt also point out that disorder, while a source of fear, is not the only factor that predicts this emotion (see, e.g., Ross and Jang, 2000). A voluminous literature now exists linking fear to a host of factors, including actual and vicarious victimization, perceived vulnerability and sensitivity to risk, type of crime (e.g., rape for women), situational contingencies, and media exposure (Fisher, Reyns, and Sloan, 2016). This empirical reality is consequential because it means that even if disorder is reduced, many other sources of fear of crime may remain untouched, and, in turn, residents will still be reluctant to take to the streets. "Thus, if disorder is not alone in causing fear," note Gau and Pratt (2008, p. 181), "then a key assumption that underlies the broken windows process is undermined."

Link and his colleagues (2017) raise another concern: the causal ordering between disorder and the perception that the risk of crime in the local environment is high. Again, broken windows theory contends that incivilities increase residents' perception of crime risk, which in turn leads them to withdraw from public spaces. Using data from Baltimore collected in 1987 and 1988, they examined this thesis longitudinally over the one-year period. Notably, they found evidence favoring the reverse causal model (crime risk → incivilities). As they concluded, the "results support an alternative view that crime risk perceptions themselves may shape how problematic the locale is seen to be" (2017, p. 676).

Yet another concern is knowing which incivilities matter more to which residents. It may be that some types of disorder are more likely than others to cause social withdrawal from public spaces. For example, having to negotiate rowdy, harassing teens or witness an open-air drug market might lead to more fear than seeing litter in the gutter or people jaywalking. Further, although some residents might stay home to avoid disorder (e.g., the elderly), others might find such street life attractive (e.g., young adult males).

Finally, Harcourt (2001) alerts us that the very notion of "order" is a social construction of reality that privileges a particular implicit normative theory of what is good and bad conduct in a specific public location—the inner city. The power to define matters as we draw a sharp distinction between "street disorder and other disorder" (2001, p. 130). As he notes:

> Paying a housekeeper under the table is a crime. So is avoiding sales tax by paying with cash or getting a false out-of-state residence, underestimating taxes, or taking office supplies home. Tax evasion, insider trading, insurance or loan misrepresentation, noncompliance with environmental or waste disposal regulations and police brutality—these are all disorderly acts and yet they figure nowhere in the theory or order maintenance policing. Who gets to define disorder for purposes of order maintenance and or what basis? (2001, p. 130)

Even with street disorder, observes Harcourt (2001, p. 130, emphasis in the original), we must ask, "Who drew the line between order and disorder in the first place? . . . Why is it, exactly, that *loitering* is disorderly? Or *littering*?" Many of us, it seems, may have thrown a wrapper on the ground, drunk alcohol in public, or even urinated in a bush or in a dark alley when no bathroom was available. As Harcourt cautions, creating a false moral university is blinding. "The truth is," he notes, "it is often hard to distinguish between the law abider and the disorderly" (p. 132). Indeed, it is ironic that the vandals in the very scenario used by Wilson and Kelling to demonstrate the broken windows principle—the stripping of the abandoned car—were mostly respectable adults and not disreputable "drunks, addicts, rowdy teenagers, or unattached adults" (Harcourt, 2001, p. 132). For Harcourt, dividing the world into the orderly and the disorderly, the decent and the street folks, the respectable and the disreputable is fraught with conceptual weakness and, ultimately, with policy misadventure:

> The point is, of course, that these may be the wrong questions. The proper question may be, why use these categories in the first place— particularly since the category of the disorderly is so unstable. It triggers an aggressive response to the disorderly—reflected in the idea of "cracking down" on disorderly people—even in the absence of any empirical evidence. (2001, p. 132)

Do the Police Reduce Crime?

As scholars of law enforcement, it is perhaps understandable that Wilson and Kelling proposed that police officers are best positioned to rid declining inner-city neighborhoods of their broken windows. But this choice is hardly the only one that might have been suggested (Harcourt, 2001; Kubrin, 2008). In fact, in the early 1980s, little confidence existed that the police could do much to reduce crime, let alone fix the disorder that might underlie it (Sherman, 1993a). Evidence-based policing was yet to be invented (Sherman, 1998), and a sustained era in police innovation was in its initial stages (Weisburd and Braga, 2006). In any event, even with a modicum of imagination, it is possible to envision a range of methods to reduce disorder. On the physical side, building owners could be sued to obey city ordinances and repair their property; abandoned buildings could be demolished; more trash cans and street cleaning could keep litter to a minimum; city investment in newly paved streets and fancy brick inlays on sidewalks could mirror the "look" found in middle-class enclaves; and beautification campaigns could bring flowers, trees, and green space to the area. On the social side, homes might be found for the homeless, treatment for the drug addicted and the mentally ill, and recreation and jobs for the "rowdy" teens with nothing to do but congregate on street corners. More generally, efforts could be made to bolster the collective efficacy of local residents. "A more palatable bottom-up approach," Kubrin (2008, p. 209) reminds us, "would be to enlist the efforts of neighborhood residents by, for example, informally mobilizing neighborhood cleanups or creating neighborhood watches." In fact, such efforts are under way in inner-city communities across the nation (Kubrin, 2008).

The research is clear that the size of a police force—simply having more officers on staff—is, at best, weakly related to crime (Lee, Eck, and Corsaro, 2016). The key issue is how the police are deployed and what enforcement tactics they employ. Much debate still exists on the effectiveness of such crime-reduction strategies (Cullen and Pratt, 2016; Weisburd and Braga, 2006). Importantly, Wilson and Kelling were shrewd enough to know that simply throwing more officers at the problem of disorder was a foolish idea. Instead, they proposed that officers walk the beat, see their function as order maintenance, not fighting crime, and use their discretion to stop public displays of incivility. This approach came to be known as "zero-tolerance" policing because of the mandate to crack down on minor forms of disorder. It was not clear how this approach would do much to dent physical cues of disorder that were built into the environment, such as abandoned or dilapidated buildings, streets marked by potholes, or the lack of community beautification. It also was not clear where the homeless sleeping in doorways, teens hanging on the corners, and drug addicts in need of a fix would go when rousted by police officers intolerant of their presence. Perhaps they could move on and become some other neighborhood's concern.

Notably, Wilson and Kelling's approach gained considerable legitimacy when the city of New York experienced a dramatic drop in crime, so much so that Franklin Zimring (2012) could title his book *The City That Became Safe*. When William Bratton became the city's police commissioner in 1994, he led a dramatic reform of the department, which included elements of zero-tolerance policing suggested by broken windows theory. The subsequent marked decline in crime rates seemed to provide convincing evidence that order maintenance enforcement aimed at suppressing minor incivilities was an effective strategy for blunting serious crime (Kelling and Coles, 1997).

Two central difficulties, however, make the accuracy of this claim unclear (Braga, Welsh, and Schnell, 2015). First, serous crime declined in other cities and areas that did not embark on broken windows policing. For example, Eck and Maguire (2000) analyzed homicide rates before and after the implementation of police reform in New York. They noted that the homicide rate had already peaked in the city and started to decline prior to the initiation of the reform. More instructive, in the next three years, the decrease in homicide rates was greater in Connecticut and in areas of New York outside the city.

Second and more complicated, the centerpiece of New York's reform was the CompStat system. In brief, statistics on the distribution of offenses across the city were used by officials to map emerging crime hot spots and to target personnel for rapid deployment. Regular meetings were held to review the data, to plan strategy, and to hold precinct and operational commanders accountable for addressing the identified crime problems. As Zimring (2012, p. 129) explains, "strategic features in the 1990s program include (1) crime reduction as a central priority, (2) sustained resources allocated to hot spot identification and control, and (3) very aggressive street police behavior in target areas, including stop and frisk and minor offenses targeted at suspicious street behavior or persons." To the extent that law enforcement contributed to the city's crime drop, it is not clear whether it was hot spots policing, the use of minor violations to stop and frisk potential "bad guys" (e.g., carrying guns), or cracking down on incivilities. Zimring (2012, p. 130) points out the "rather frequent conflation of the order maintenance focus of 'broken windows' with the crime-centered crusade of CompStat." He goes on to question whether "the department ever tried to enforce 'quality of life' offenses as a consistent priority" (p. 146). For example, noting that prostitution is a classic broken windows offense, he shows that "the rate of prostitution arrests never went up in the CompStat era" (p. 146).

Where does this all leave us? It is fairly clear that carefully planned, focused police interventions reduce crime (Braga and Weisburd, 2012; Braga, Papachristos, and Hureau, 2014; Lee, Eck, and Corsaro, 2016; cf. Gill et al., 2014). The debate over broken windows or zero-tolerance policing, however, has been less settled, with scholars lining up on both sides of the effectiveness debate (cf. Harcourt, 2001; Kelling and Sousa, 2001). A recent meta-analysis by Braga, Welsh, and Schnell (2015) does much to define the status of the empirical literature.

Their search "identified 30 randomized experimental and quasi-experimental tests of disorder policing" (2015, p. 567). Overall, they found that the strategy of policing disorder had a significant and meaningful crime-decreasing effect ($d = .210$). Probing further, they then analyzed the data by two different types of disorder policing: "(1) increased use of aggressive order maintenance techniques to reduce disorderly behavior by individuals and (2) community problem-solving approaches that seek to change social and physical disorder at particular places" (p. 573). And here their findings take on much importance. The effect size for the community approach remained stable ($d = .271$), but for aggressive policing fell markedly ($d = .058$). "When considering a policing disorder approach," Braga, Welsh, and Schnell (2015, p. 581), conclude, "police departments should adopt a 'community coproduction model' rather than drift toward a zero-tolerance policing model" (see also Carr, 2003, 2012).

Conclusion

In the 1980s, it appeared to many Americans that the urban core was in serious difficulty. Violent crime was intractably high, and signs of social and physical disorder were ubiquitous. The image of the city as a broken window thus seemed empirically accurate, and, equally important, it resonated with the nation's sense that the ghetto was a lost cause. The genius of Wilson and Kelling was their abiding confidence that at least some urban neighborhoods could be saved from the spiral of decline. For them, the police were the one representative of the larger society who had the capacity and moral obligation to stand beside the decent residents trapped in communities that the rest of us feared to tread (see also Anderson, 1999). They were to be instruments of what Rengert (1989) once called "spatial justice"—using the state to protect the community from those who do not care who they hurt or inconvenienced. In a very real way, saving the city meant taking sides, an uncomfortable but necessary choice.

As discussed, their classic essay could not anticipate the many criticisms that subsequent scholarship would articulate. In a way, however, Wilson and Kelling were perhaps guilty of excessive hubris—having no qualms about differentiating the disorderly form the orderly or the crime-reducing powers of order maintenance policing. The world ultimately proved more complicated than they admitted.

Still, Wilson and Kelling played an instrumental role in reinvigorating American policing, calling on officers to do their jobs and make cities safer again. Although not the only voice calling for police reform, they were among the loudest in a chorus that persuaded many police officials to experiment with a range of policing strategies aimed at decreasing crime (see Weisburd and Braga, 2006). Ironically, while the field of "corrections" fell prey to nothing-works thinking and mass imprisonment, the field of policing embraced accountability and effectiveness.

The image of the city as a broken window, however, faded as the United States turned into the current century. To be sure, pockets of entrenched concentrated disadvantage and deteriorated neighborhoods persist. But cities seemed to rebound in the public mind, many of which grew much safer, more gentrified, and more culturally appealing. A spiral of advancement was replacing the spiral of decline. The time soon would come for a new, more optimistic image of the city.

7

Community as Criminal Opportunity

T he vast majority of criminologists explore why it is that some people—whether as individuals or as groups located in an ecological area—are more likely to break the law than others. This likelihood or propensity to break the law is typically called *criminality*. In turn, it is assumed that where criminality is stronger, crime will be higher. A growing number of scholars, however, have questioned this way of explaining crime. They note that for a *criminal event* to take place, offenders must have more than criminality or the willingness to break the law. They must also have the *opportunity* to act on their desires. Thus, burglars will be thwarted from a break-in by bars on a window or by an activated alarm system; robbers will forgo a shakedown if a police officer is present or a potential target is joined by a group of friends. Further, writ large, this means that some communities are going to be organized in a way as to make crime harder to commit. If so, then crime across areas is going to be determined not only by *criminality* (how many motivated offenders are present) but also by *criminal opportunity*—how hard or easy is it to commit a crime.

The criminal opportunity perspective is actually a unification of various, compatible theoretical ideas produced in piecemeal fashion in the 1970s and 1980s, including "lifestyle-routine activities theory," "environmental design

Parts of this chapter previously appeared in Wilcox (2015). Reprinted with permission from Elsevier. Other parts of this chapter previously appeared in Cullen, Agnew, and Wilcox (2014). Reprinted with permission from Oxford University Press.

theory," "rational choice theory," and "offender search theory." As will be discussed in detail below, these crime opportunity theories emerged in an era when crime was on the rise and cities were seemingly in decline. We were searching for answers. However, unlike many of the perspectives discussed in previous chapters, the answer that opportunity theories provided looked beyond the identification of community conditions that fostered criminal motivation. They set offender motivation aside and focused instead on the various ways the environment provided opportunity for the enactment of crime events. This chapter elaborates on the development of the various pieces constituting the criminal opportunity perspective, and in the process elucidates how each piece adds to our understanding of community-level crime patterns. We begin this description with an explanation of routine activities theory, posited initially by a group of scholars working together in the mid to late 1970s at University of Illinois's Department of Sociology.

Importantly, this perspective challenges the idea that inner-city communities are what Shaw and McKay (1942, 1969) called "delinquency areas"—that is, neighborhoods so in the throes of culture conflict and criminogenic influences that much of their youthful populations are at risk of criminal careers. Rather, the argument is made that inner-city communities are less safe because they are more susceptible to the presence of attractive criminal opportunities. Over the years, commentators have revealed how "urban renewal" policies that replaced supposed "old houses" with dense, high-rise public housing buildings created such opportunities. Land use policies also have allowed the creation of establishments, such as bars, that facilitate crime events. Even those motivated to offend in these areas do not do so indiscriminately. Rather, with a measure of rationality, they search to victimize targets—property, people, and places—that are attractive and lack guardianship. Within inner-city neighborhoods, crime thus tends not to be randomly distributed but concentrated on certain blocks and, within those locations, at certain places (Sherman, Gartin, and Beurger, 1989; Weisburd, Groff, and Yang, 2012).

The image of the community as a criminal opportunity might seem to offer a troubling future for urban America. To be sure, broader contextual factors, such as social disorganization and poverty, combined with existing environmental designs, such as dense housing projects and variegated land use, obviate against simple solutions to reducing criminal opportunities. The silver lining, however, is that in many instances, preventing a crime event from taking place is a less daunting task than reforming a career offender with deeply entrenched criminal propensity. Once crime opportunities can be mapped, they can be targeted for intervention—whether by the police (as "broken windows" advocates have suggested), by property owners and their place managers, or by residents themselves. The task is how best to transform an opportunity into a nonopportunity. Many scholars committed to making high-crime places safer spend considerable time thinking about this problem (e.g., Smith and Clarke, 2012; Madensen and Eck, 2013).

Routine Activities and Crime Opportunity

Throughout this book, we have depicted the various concerning images of communities and crime—images that, in turn, generated new thought on community-based origins of crime. Public and scholarly concern over the crime problem was clearly justified in the 1970s and 1980s. Historical trends of national crime data show that there were unprecedented increases between 1960 and 1970, in particular, with rates still climbing, albeit less dramatically, up to 1980. But what were the social changes behind these trends? Accounting for the striking rise in crime, nationally, was the starting point for a series of articles published by University of Illinois colleagues Lawrence Cohen, Marcus Felson, and Kenneth Land during the late 1970s and through the 1980s. Routine activities theory emerged from this work (for other reviews, see Wilcox, 2010, 2015).

The Origins of Routine Activities Theory

Cohen, Felson, and Land were together in the Department of Sociology at Illinois during the 1970s, in the early stages of their academic careers. Cohen joined the faculty at Illinois upon receiving his Ph.D. in sociology from the University of Washington. Felson went to Illinois, after receiving his Ph.D. in sociology from University of Michigan. Land had received his Ph.D. in sociology, with a minor in mathematics, in 1969 from University of Texas. He joined the faculty at Illinois as an associate professor in 1973, after completing a postdoc in mathematical statistics at Columbia University and working as a research associate and mathematical sociologist for the Russell Sage Foundation.

The collaborative work of the Cohen-Felson-Land trio began when Land and Felson joined forces in the mid-1970s on a grant from the National Science Foundation to explore aggregate over-time social-behavioral trends in the United States. As part of that larger study, they examined crime trends in post–World War II United States, largely focusing on the period between the late 1940s and the mid-1970s. Figure 7.1 displays two examples of the sorts of crime trends they considered in their work.

In an initial study of such crime trends, Land and Felson (1976) analyzed the longitudinal crime pattern vis-à-vis annual levels of police expenditures. Land and Felson presumed flows in annual police expenditures to be good examples in the realm of public safety of "changes in social indicators in terms of social forces that affect the opportunities of individuals to accomplish

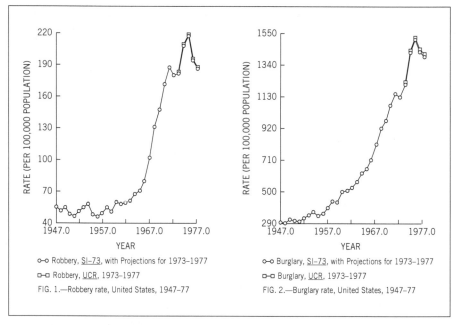

Figure 7.1 Crime Trends in the United States as Seen by Those Developing Routine Activities Theory in the Late 1970s
Reprinted from L. E. Cohen, M. Felson, and K. C. Land, "Property Crime Rates in the United States: A Macro-dynamic Analysis, 1947–1977; with *ex ante* Forecasts for the Mid-1980s," *American Journal of Sociology* 86 (1980), pp. 93–94.

whatever objectives their 'free wills' establish" (p. 576). Their findings indicated that police expenditures in any given year *t* were positively related to crime rates in year *t-1*, yet negatively related to crime in year *t*. Hence, the findings supported the notion that opportunity for crime appeared structured (at a macro level) by spending on law enforcement efforts. Thus, they offered initial support for what they called an "opportunity structures" perspective of changes in crime.

This "opportunity structures" perspective would evolve into their now-famous routine activities theory through additional analyses of the historical macro-level crime patterns in the post–World War II United States. Consistent with Felson's overall persona as a self-proclaimed nonconformist and "outsider," Felson encouraged the research team to move in a direction that more strongly rejected the prevailing theories of the day as possible explanations for the historical, national-level trends they were observing (Clarke and Felson, 2011).

Consistent with Felson's wishes, the group's subsequent work much more clearly separated itself from those prevailing explanations and offered a more concrete opportunity-based routine activities theory as an alternative. The group explicitly eschewed the then-popular notion that the dramatic increases in crime, especially starting around 1960, could be attributed to economic deprivation. In fact, they identified a "sociological paradox" in comparing trends in economic conditions in the United States with trends in crime. During the 1960s household income increased, and the disparity between White and Black household incomes declined; the percentage of urban residents living in poverty decreased; unemployment decreased; and median education level increased, especially among Blacks (Cohen and Felson, 1979). However, between 1960 and 1975, robbery rates increased by 263 percent; aggravated assault, rape, and homicide increased between 164 percent and 188 percent; and burglary increased by 200 percent (Cohen and Felson, 1979).

The group's efforts at highlighting the sociological paradox and offering a competing explanation for crime culminated in a series of studies, reflected most famously in an article published in 1979 by Cohen and Felson in the *American Sociological Review*, "Social Change and Crime Rate Trends: A Routine Activity Approach." In that article, Cohen and Felson addressed the paradox as follows: "Why, we must ask, have urban violent crime rates increased substantially during the past decade when the conditions that are supposed to cause violent crime have not worsened—have, indeed, generally improved? . . . we consider these paradoxical trends in crime rates in terms of the changes in the 'routine activities' of everyday life. We believe the structure of such activities affects criminal opportunity" (pp. 588–589).

The Minimal Elements of Crime

As a starting point for explaining how routine activities structure opportunity for criminal activity, Cohen, Felson, Land, and their colleagues enumerated three minimal elements for a crime event—a simple yet profound point that served as the backbone of their collaborative body of work (e.g., Cohen and Felson, 1979; Cohen, Felson, and Land, 1980; Cohen, Kluegel, and Land, 1981; Felson and Cohen, 1980). At minimum, they argued that for a crime event to occur, the following three elements must converge:

1. A *motivated offender*—someone inclined, willing, and able to commit the crime
2. A *suitable victim or target*—a person or thing that allows the offender to fulfill criminal objectives
3. A *lack of capable guardianship*—an absence of any persons or things that can discourage or prevent the crime (i.e., third parties, security devices, self-protective devices)

Note that the inclination to offend—the focus of traditional criminological approaches—is the first of the three minimal elements of crime listed. However, the inventors of routine activities theory stressed that the mere presence of a motivated offender, while required, is not sufficient for the enactment of crime. Instead, a motivated offender must encounter a suitable, inadequately guarded target in order for a crime event to occur. Cohen, Felson, Land, and colleagues added one more key stipulation to their theoretical model: a crime event cannot take place unless these three minimal elements converge in time and space—in what can be called a *spatiotemporal setting*. As such, crime involves an *interdependence* or *symbiosis* among offenders, victims, potential guardians, and the time-place contexts in which they meet.

The Role of Routine Activities

Cohen, Felson, Land, and colleagues presumed that the convergence in time and space of the three necessary ingredients for crime was affected by the patterns of activity composing everyday life. Activities outside the home were seen as particularly opportunistic. Going to school, to work, to shop, to dine out, or to be entertained—these are all legitimate, public activities. Yet these legal, routine activities were said to structure opportunities for illegal activities. More specifically, these activities affect both the supply of suitable victims or targets available to motivated offenders and the level of guardianship provided to the potential victims/targets.

As an example of how legitimate activities feed illegitimate activities, Cohen, Felson, Land, and colleagues posited that the dramatic rise in crime witnessed in the United States between 1960 and 1970 was a result of profound changes in the routine, daily activities of its residents. But how, specifically, were American activities changing, beginning in 1960, so as to affect criminal opportunity? The short answer to the question was that Americans were engaging in many more *nonhousehold activities*. Substantial growth in women's labor force participation between 1960 and 1970 was responsible for a large share of the increase in Americans' non-household activities. Women's public exposure grew significantly, thus increasing the pool of suitable targets for predatory street crimes like robbery. At the same time, women provided less guardianship to American households during the daytime, thereby increasing opportunity for crimes such as burglary. For example, in 1960 about 30 percent of households were unoccupied by someone fourteen years or older between the hours of 8:00 a.m. and 3:00 p.m.; by 1971 that figure exceeded 40 percent (e.g., Cohen and Felson, 1979).

The time period between 1960 and 1970 saw shifts in activities beyond the realm of work (and women's labor-force participation, in particular). In fact, the changing work-related routines generated more disposable income for American households—income that was channeled toward more leisure pursuits outside the home (i.e., attending sporting events, movies, restaurants, or vacation destinations) and the purchase of more household durable goods (i.e., televisions, stereos, cars, bicycles). The proliferation of public leisure activities and household items—especially valuable but lightweight items that were easy to steal in a concealed fashion—also increased opportunities for crime. Overall, the crux of the explanation offered by routine activities theory for the large upswing in crime after 1960 (especially between 1960 and 1970) was that motivated offenders were increasingly likely to encounter people in public with money and other valuables on their person and/or encounter an empty house with plentiful goods for the taking.

Cohen and Felson provided the first test of routine activities theory in their 1979 article by examining whether a "household activity ratio" was related to the changing rates of predatory crime in the United States between the years 1947 and 1974. They measured the household activity ratio as the proportion of total U.S. households that were either "non-husband-wife" households or households that could be classified as "married, husband-present, with a female labor-force participant" (Cohen and Felson, 1979, p. 600). They surmised that these types of households were likely to engage in public activities that would increase exposure to motivated offenders, increase target suitability, and decrease guardianship. They found that the household activity ratio (the proportion of presumably "active" households) was, in fact, positively and significantly associated with five different types of predatory crime rates. In a follow-up article the next year, Cohen, Felson, and Land (1980) also found that a measure of consumer expenditures on durable goods (nonautomobile) was positively related to twenty-five-year trends in U.S. burglary rates.

Cohen, Felson, and Land thus put forth and tested a theory that challenged conventional ways of thinking about crime—that it was a pathology that emerged from other pathological conditions. This challenge was particularly significant given the social and political context of the 1970s. It was not just that crime was rising during this time; there were riots in the inner cities and protests seemingly everywhere. In response, presidential crime commissions were formed, and there were conservative calls for law and order (e.g., Wilson, 1975). As alluded to in previous chapters, it was natural that many were worried about the "bad things" happening in society, and they looked for pathological roots to understanding crime, in particular. But Cohen and Felson took a step back and boldly presented an alternative view—that "good things" were causing fluctuations in crime.

Lifestyle, Exposure, and Criminal Victimization

Around the same time that Cohen, Felson, Land, and colleagues began publishing numerous works on opportunity structures and the influence of routine activities on U.S. crime, a similar idea was set forth as an explanation for variation in victimization risk across demographic subgroups by a group of criminal justice scholars at State University of New York at Albany. In the 1970s and 1980s, the Criminal Justice Research Center at Albany, under the founding directorship of Michael Hindelang, was engaged in analysis of national victimization survey data. The data came from the annual National Crime Survey, now called the National Crime Victimization Survey. The analyses they provided of victimization data were transformative for a field that had historically relied upon official police reports for the measurement of "crime" (see, e.g., Gottfredson and Hindelang, 1981). Yet the National Crime Survey data did more than provide an alternative aggregate measure of crime in the United States. It also provided the opportunity for understanding the victim's role in crime occurrences.

One particularly influential product of the Albany analysis of the National Crime Survey was the 1978 book *Victims of Personal Crime: An Empirical Foundation for a Theory of Personal Victimization* by Michael Hindelang, Michael Gottfredson, and James Garofalo. The book suggested that victimization risk was a function of lifestyle. Their argument was that demographic groups experiencing relatively higher rates of victimization—men, younger adults, and African Americans—tended to have lifestyles associated with work, school, and leisure that exposed them to victimization opportunities. In particular, the lifestyles of these high-risk groups relative to low-risk groups (i.e., women, the elderly, Whites) were posited to involve more time in public (especially at night), more time away from family or household members, and greater proximity to and/or association with high-offending groups. This idea was termed the "lifestyle-exposure theory" of victimization.

Thus, lifestyle-exposure theory was originally developed to understand variation in *victimization risk* across different demographic groups in the United States, while routine activities theory was provided to understand *temporal patterns in national-level crime rates*. Although they developed independently, and within the context of very different academic departments and research programs, the theoretical overlap between the theories was evident. Given the similarity and compatibility among these perspectives, they were eventually merged into a more general "lifestyle-routine activities theory" or L-RAT (e.g., Cohen, Kluegel, and Land, 1981; Miethe, Stafford, and Long, 1987). And by the late 1980s and into the 1990s, L-RAT had become a popular approach for understanding *individual variation in victimization risk*, in particular (e.g., Cohen, Kluegel, and Land, 1981; Miethe and Meier, 1990; Miethe, Stafford, and Long, 1987; Fisher et al., 1998; Fisher, Daigle, and Cullen, 2010; Mustaine and Tewksbury, 1998). Other scholars, however, utilized the perspective for understanding spatial patterns of crime, including *community-level patterns*—the topic of the section that follows.

Community Life, Routine Activities, and Crime Patterns

As originally conceptualized, routine activities theory draws heavily on the work of human ecologist Amos Hawley, and thus views "community" as an essential unit in defining routine activities and the criminal opportunities that they create. Felson and Cohen (1980, p. 391), for example, describe "community" as "the structure of relationships through which a localized population provides its daily requirements," thus establishing the rhythm, timing, and tempo of activities that occur within. How a community organizes work, school, leisure, and other activities will affect the convergence of motivated offenders and suitable targets, and the levels of guardianship within the community.

Community life has changed throughout history, with daily activities having been transformed and new opportunities for crime created in the process. Marcus Felson (1994) details the evolution of "community life" as consisting of four major historical stages: (1) agrarian village, (2) town, (3) urban village within a convergent city, and (4) suburb within a divergent metropolis (Felson, 1987, 1994; see also Felson and Eckert, 2016). In describing the evolution from stages one through three—from agrarian village to urban village—he offers the following summary (Felson, 1994, pp. 55–56):

> It would be nice to say that there is a simple progression, that the growth of crime is directly related to the growth of cities. But the reality is not that simple. At the first stage, the development of towns reduces rural crime by offering security from bandits. As towns develop into cities, local security begins to decline. The central districts and transportation corridors of the city provide anonymity to the offender, who can emerge from the crowd, commit a crime, and then lose himself in the crowd. The transportation corridors extend the range of potential offenders while exposing people to additional risks away from home. Yet, the urban village, based on row houses, high fertility, pedestrian traffic, and women close to home, maintains a modicum of control.

Thus, Felson described shifting patterns in both the volume and nature of crime as dependent on the opportunities provided by community life in agrarian villages, versus small towns, versus urban villages. Felson (1994) goes further to suggest that, when community life takes the form of a divergent metropolis (stage four), local crime becomes "endemic," as it becomes ever easier for offenders to find victims or targets free of guardianship. "The divergent metropolis serves to unpack human activities. It disperses people over more households, households and construction over more metropolitan space, travelers over more vehicles, and activities away from household and family settings. . . . the divergent metropolis [also] weakens localism, with the loss of control producing even higher levels of crime" (p. 70). The subsections to follow provide more discussion about how features of community life affect activity patterns and social control, with implications for the structuring of crime opportunity at the community level.

Community Density and Crime Opportunity

Important work by Robert Sampson in the 1980s highlighted how community density can influence residential activity and, in turn, opportunities for crime. Although Sampson is typically associated with the systemic model (Chapter 3), the notion of cognitive landscapes (Chapter 5), and collective efficacy theory (Chapter 8)—all implicitly addressing community levels of *criminality*—his early work was often framed using the concept of community-based criminal opportunity. This orientation is not altogether surprising given that Sampson's training at Albany (see Chapter 3) involved work at their Criminal Justice Research Center with Hindelang, Gottfredson, and Garofalo. Furthermore, shortly after finishing graduate school, he was an assistant professor of sociology at University of Illinois for a time, where Cohen, Felson, and Land had worked together on the original statements of routine activities theory (he and Felson actually overlapped there for one year). Thus, Sampson was undoubtedly influenced by the work on lifestyles, routine activities, and criminal opportunity established by mentors and colleagues within these contexts. His early work examining the influence of neighborhood density on rates of victimization is reflective of that influence (Sampson, 1983, 1985; Sampson and Wooldredge, 1987).

Sampson theorized that neighborhood density should increase criminal opportunity because of its impact on the convergence of offenders, suitable targets, and absence of guardianship. The denser the population in a community, the more likely it is that criminals can encounter inadequately guarded victims or targets. Surveillance is often impeded in dense areas, which tend to have less open and less visible spaces. Further, community members in high-density areas have greater difficulty recognizing strangers and suspicious activity—people and things are less likely to stick out as "unusual" in increasingly dense contexts. Even in instances where suspicious individuals and their activity are viewable and recognized as potentially troublesome, neighborhood density impedes intervention because it has the effect of diffusing responsibility for guardianship. In dense areas, it is easy to presume that "someone else will take care of it." This assumption can lead to no one intervening when problems arise. Sampson's seminal work on the community density-crime linkage found support for the notion that density creates crime opportunity (Sampson, 1983, 1985; Sampson and Groves, 1989; Sampson and Wooldredge, 1987). Beyond Sampson's work, other researchers using an opportunity framework provide empirical support for the positive impact of neighborhood density on crime (Greenberg, Rohe, and Williams, 1982; Smith, Frazee, and Davison, 2000; Rice and Smith, 2002).

Community Land Use and Crime Opportunity

Communities can also structure activity and subsequent criminal opportunity through their various land uses. Nonresidential land uses are thought to be particularly opportunistic because they are high-density spaces within neighborhoods and they support a high level of public activity. Beginning in the 1980s, Dennis Roncek and his colleagues published a series of studies showing that certain facilities—especially bars and high schools—were positively related to crime on street blocks (Roncek and Bell, 1981; Roncek and Faggiani, 1985; Roncek and LoBosco, 1983; Roncek and Maier, 1991; Roncek and Pravatiner, 1989). These establishments were presumed to generate crime by increasing "ephemeral density"—that is, by drawing concentrations of adolescents or young adults (prime age-groups for offending and victimization) at particular times of day. And, in the case of bars, many of the young adult patrons become under the influence of alcohol. Thus, nonresidential land uses such as bars and schools create large supplies of potential offenders and potential victims converging in contexts where guardianship is compromised (owing to both the density of users and the activities supported by such places). Contemporary research since Roncek's pathbreaking work continues to support the idea that neighborhoods with more nonresidential land uses of various types experience higher rates of crime. Beyond schools and bars, studies have shown that crime rates are higher in neighborhoods with land uses allocated to liquor stores, malls, businesses, and payday lending operations, among others (Bernasco and Block, 2011; Deryol et al., 2016; Duru, 2010; Kubrin et al., 2011; Kurtz, Koons, and Taylor, 1998; LaGrange, 1999; Lockwood, 2007; Rice and Smith, 2002; Smith, Frazee, and Davison, 2000; Stucky and Ottensmann, 2009; Wilcox et al., 2004).

Community Activity and Crime Opportunity

A number of other studies examine community-level routine activities more directly as opposed to relying on density or land use as a proxy measure. For example, research has more directly tapped community supplies of suitable targets by measuring the average numbers of goods owned by residents, the average amount of cash carried in public by residents, and the average number of nights residents spend outside, on foot. Research has more directly assessed community-level guardianship by measuring the percentage of empty households, as reported by residents. In general, this research has supported the conclusion that aggregate patterns of routine activities among a community's residents help structure opportunity for crime and victimization events within the community (Kennedy and Forde, 1990; Sampson and Wooldredge, 1987; Smith and Jarjoura, 1989; Wilcox, Madensen, and Tillyer, 2007).

Community-Based Control and Crime Opportunity

A good deal of work suggests that community-level informal social control influences opportunity for crime. This is an important connection to discuss more fully because, traditionally, theories of opportunity and control have been viewed as competing. As stated at the beginning of this chapter, "criminal opportunity" is a concept aimed at understanding why *crime events* actually occur. Social control, on the other hand, is a concept that has historically been treated as one aimed at understanding *criminality*—why some people are more inclined to commit crime than others (Hirschi, 1986). The social control perspective assumes that individuals who have weak constraints, or controls, are more likely to offend.

Marcus Felson has been instrumental in establishing that weak control not only fosters criminality but also crime events. More specifically, Felson explicates a view of "social and situational control" that accounts for its effects on both criminality and crime events, with this view premised on the notion that control is a two-stage process (see, e.g., Felson 1994, 1995). In the first stage, bonds are created—strongly or weakly—between an individual and society. For example, individuals may bond in the form of developing attachments to others (e.g., parents, teachers) or developing commitments to conventional ideals (e.g., education, employment). Felson describes the establishment of bonds as akin to attaching a social "handle" to individuals (1995, p. 54). The relative strength versus weakness of these handles establishes criminality, or an individual's likelihood of being an offender. Weaker handles are presumed to cause greater criminality. In contrast, a second stage of social control involves the identification of people violating the rules. It is control that takes place—or not—at the time of a crime event and deals with supervision and intervention behavior on the part of bystanders or onlookers. Stage-two control essentially refers to the idea that opportunity for crime can be reduced through effective *guardianship.* As such, stage-two control overlaps substantially with L-RAT.

Drawing on this distinction between stage-one and stage-two control, community control theories—such as Ruth Kornhauser's version of social disorganization theory, the systemic model, and cultural disorganization theories—can be viewed as community-level theories of criminality *and* crime events (Wilcox and Land, 2015; Wilcox and Swartz, in press; see also Chapter 8). Weak community-level stage-one control, in the form of attenuated aggregate attachments and commitments, can create contexts in which *criminality* can flourish. For example, collectively speaking, the social handles are quite weak in disorganized communities with weak systems of ties and/ or attenuated culture. Because such communities fail to "provide routes to valued goals" and to "exact instrumental and affectively based conformity," they create "defective socialization" (Kornhauser, 1978, p. 73). Thus, they are likely to develop a greater-than-average number of delinquents.

However, weak community-level stage-two control affects whether *crime events* actually transpire in these same communities (Wilcox and Land, 2015; Wilcox and Swartz, in press). In the second stage, the issue is whether communities "discover and enforce" common standards (Kornhauser, 1978, p. 73). The control in this second stage is not related to social development but is situational instead—it deals with interrupting the ability of offenders to access targets in the community through effective guardianship. In the absence of strong stage-two (situational) control, communities will produce a large share of crime events (e.g., the *locations of crime incidents* cluster in these neighborhoods).

A good deal of research has, in fact, supported the idea that community-level informal social control is related to the numbers of crime and victimization incidents experienced by different neighborhoods (e.g., Sampson and Groves, 1989; Sampson and Wooldredge, 1987; Sampson, Raudenbush, and Earls, 1997). Such findings suggest that there is likely a stage-two, guardianship-like quality to informal social control. In sum, much of the literature in the social disorganization tradition that has been the focus of preceding chapters (and Chapter 8) has relevance for understanding community-level criminality as well as community-level opportunity for crime events.

Environmental Design and Community Crime

Alongside the development of theory centered on lifestyles and routine activities in the 1970s and 1980s was a theoretical and empirical line of inquiry stressing the idea that a community's physical design—its "built environment"—played a major role in the opportunities for crime therein. The origins of the focus on the relationship between environmental design and crime can be traced to two influential works: Jane Jacobs's 1961 book, *The Death and Life of Great American Cities*, and the 1972 book by Oscar Newman, *Defensible Space: Crime Prevention through Urban Design*.

Eyes on the Street

Jane Jacobs had no formal training as an urban planner, but she became a most influential voice on the subject.[1] After growing up in Scranton, Pennsylvania, Jacobs moved to New York City in 1934, during the middle of the Great Depression. She and her sister initially shared an apartment in Brooklyn Heights, though they eventually settled in an apartment in Greenwich Village. While living in Greenwich Village, she took courses at Columbia and held several successive secretarial and editorial/journalistic posts. She met her husband, architect Robert Jacobs, in 1944, and she became an associate editor of *Architectural Forum* in 1952.

While she had addressed urban housing issues in some of her previous journalistic work, it was largely through her position at *Architectural Forum* that she was most fully exposed to the conventional theory about urban renewal. The "modernist" urban renewal planning of the 1950s was dominated in New York by Robert Moses. Moses and other modernists advocated a movement away from high-density, mixed-use neighborhoods in favor of a separation of residential, industrial, and commercial uses, with interstate highways linking these separate areas. The modernist approach also advocated demolishing dense, low-rise housing in poor neighborhoods in favor of "sleek" high-rise towers surrounded by open spaces—such as those being designed by the likes of Le Corbusier. She became very critical of modernist planning and architecture, and she actively sought to change thinking on urban renewal. More concretely, she fiercely opposed the bulldozing of poor urban neighborhoods and the building of high-rises and highways throughout such areas. For example, she deplored the way community life in East Harlem had been changed by rehousing low-income residents from low-rise tenement housing to high-rise projects (e.g., the George Washington Houses). She claimed that in that process, East Harlem had lost thousands of storefronts—butchers, delicatessens, bars, diners—as well as the community churches, social clubs, and political clubs

---

1. Much of the biographical information on Jane Jacobs provided here is drawn from three sources: (1) Project for Public Spaces website (http://www.pps.org/jjacobs-2/); (2) Douglas Martin's (2006) article "Jane Jacobs, Urban Activist, Is Dead at 89," and (3) Robert Kanigel's 2016 book, *Eyes on the Street: The Life of Jane Jacobs*.

that sometimes fill vacancies in these low-rent "hole-in-the-wall" storefronts. As a result, there was no real place for community residents to meet except in the laundry room of a basement of one of the high-rises. In short, her position was that the hole-in-the-wall storefronts that had been razed in East Harlem were where meaningful and effective *community* had actually happened (Kanigel, 2016, p. 148). She devoted many years of her life fighting to make sure what happened in East Harlem did not happen in West Village.

Her feisty activism against the modernist approach to urban renewal led to several run-ins with police; she was removed from a City Planning Commission meeting after rushing the podium as a protestor, and she was charged with rioting and criminal mischief in 1968 while protesting at a public meeting regarding the construction of a highway that would have divided Lower Manhattan. Her speech denouncing modernist urban renewal—sometimes invited, oftentimes not—caught the attention of William H. Whyte, editor of *Fortune* magazine. Whyte invited Jacobs to write an article on urban downtown neighborhoods in 1958. Ultimately, the reputation she developed through her speeches and writings on urban life culminated in grants that would help her produce *The Death and Life of Great American Cities*, published in 1961.

In *Death and Life of Great American Cities*, Jacobs espoused the view that high-density, mixed-use neighborhoods (i.e., with many little storefronts) were the most vibrant and natural of communities. In contrast to the work that touted high-density neighborhoods as dangerous, Jacobs argued that such places fostered both a sense of community as well as safety. They did so by providing, in Jacob's words, many "eyes on the street"—a positive depiction of busy neighborhoods for which she would become famous. Instead of drawing on formal theoretical or empirical training to inform her view, she drew on her previous journalistic experience and, especially, her own experiences living above a store in Greenwich Village. *New York Times* columnist Douglas Martin (2006) summarizes Jacobs's lived experience, which she conveyed so vividly in *Death and Life,* as follows:

> She puts out her garbage, children go to school, the drycleaner and barber open their shops, housewives come out to chat, longshoremen visit the local bar, teenagers return from school and change to go out on dates, and another day is played out. Sometimes odd things happen: a bagpiper shows up on a February night, and delighted listeners gather around. Whether neighbors or strangers, people are safer because they are almost never alone.

In short, she saw high-density, mixed-use urban neighborhoods as places where people could live and work, as magnets for stimulating culture, and as strong sources of local identity. They were places that were interesting enough to stay busy at all hours of the day and night. Jacobs also felt that design principles could help counter criminal opportunities and enhance, instead, sociability and informal social control within urban, high-density, mixed-use communities. For example, she recommended that blocks be short and that buildings be variable in use and oriented vis-à-vis the street so as to maximize the ability of residents to provide surveillance—to provide those all-important "eyes on the street." She also recommended that neighborhoods be designed so as to clearly distinguish public and private spaces, and that public spaces be positioned in such a way that, once again, surveillance could be more easily provided. Although her ideas were dismissed as nonacademic by many, they were and still are revered by others. As Martin suggests in his tribute at the time of her death in 2006:

> The battles she ignited are still being fought, and the criticism was perhaps inevitable, given that such an ambitious work was produced by somebody who had not finished college, much less become an established professional in the field. Indisputably, the book was as radically challenging to conventional thinking as Rachel Carson's "Silent Spring," which helped engender the environmental movement, would be the next year, and Betty Friedan's "The Feminine Mystique," which deeply affected perceptions of relations between the sexes, would be in 1963. Like these two writers, Ms. Jacobs was able to summon a freshness of perspective. Some dismissed it as amateurism, but to many other it was a point of view that made new ideas not only thinkable but suddenly and eminently reasonable.

Defensible Space

While Jacobs's ideas are still being discussed today, Oscar Newman was among the first to formally elaborate them, framing her insights more explicitly as components of a theory of defensible space. Newman was an architect and urban planner. He received his training at McGill in Canada, with postgraduate study in the Netherlands. His famous work, *Defensible Space*, was a study of urban residential housing communities, the various physical forms they take, and the implications of those forms on crime rates within. Although he mainly analyzed New York City communities for the book, related work took him to inner-city residential neighborhoods throughout the United States. In fact, he attributes the creation of the term *defensible space* to his study of the Pruitt-Igoe public housing community in Saint Louis, while he was on faculty at Washington University in the 1960s (Newman, 1996).

The study described in *Defensible Space* highlighted that some urban housing communities were less crime ridden than others, though they often contained similar residents, socio-demographically speaking. This empirical fact implied that such crime variation had less to do with the residents and more to do with the spaces in which they lived. Equipped with this insight, Newman observed that urban residential communities that consisted of multiple high-rise buildings tended to be particularly crime prone. Examples of such communities were abundant in the 1940s, 1950s, and 1960s, with the proliferation of communities like Pruitt-Igoe in Saint Louis; the Robert Taylor Homes and Cabrini-Green in Chicago; Van Dyke and Red Hook Houses in Brooklyn; and the Queensbridge Houses in Queens, just to name a few. In fact, with more than four thousand units in its heyday (with three to four bedrooms each), Robert Taylor Homes was once the largest public housing project in the world. The high-rise developments resulted from the exact sort of urban planning that Jane Jacobs had fought so hard to discourage. These often were (and some still are) massive developments, consisting of twenty to forty high-rise buildings, housing tens of thousands of residents each. They were intended to remove low-income residents from urban "tenement housing" and pave the way for urban renewal. But most of these developments became notorious for murder, drug dealing, and gang activity, as well as for deplorable maintenance and physical decay. In fact, the social problems associated with them led to the eventual demise of most, as urban high-rise public housing communities became viewed as a social experiment gone terribly bad (e.g., Belluck, 1998; O'Neil, 2010).

In contrast to the high-rise public housing developments, Newman (1972) noted that low-income residential communities that were designed using low-rise-style housing (i.e., townhouse-style buildings) tended to have few problems. He claimed that the high-rise versus low-rise building designs were behind the differences in crime and other social problems across public housing communities. According to Newman, the physical layout of low-rise housing allowed space to be more easily defended or controlled by its residents. In short, low-rise-style housing was *defensible space*. Newman (1972) elaborated that defensible space was related to four principles: (1) territoriality, (2) natural surveillance, (3), image, and (4) milieu.

First, he defined *territoriality* as "the capacity of the physical environment to create perceived zones of territorial influences" (1972, p. 51). In other words, territoriality is the extent to which a space, through its design, conveys a sense of being "private" or "owned" and that there are norms regarding its use—so people observing the space have a clear sense that it is under someone's care and that there are expectations about acceptable and unacceptable behavior within the space. Examples of physical features of spaces that convey territoriality include boundary markers such as fencing, walls, sidewalks, and landscape borders, as well as signs indicating the appropriate (or inappropriate) use of space (e.g., "No Parking," "Park Closes at Dusk"). In Newman's view, public housing communities designed with high-rise buildings had little territoriality, as hundreds of residents shared common doorways, lobbies, and outdoor "yard" space. In contrast, public housing communities with low-rise apartment buildings offered a design that allowed residents to more readily define space as their own and to there-fore have control over the space (i.e., it was space that was much more clearly within their individual sphere of influence). For example, low-rise apart-ments provided direct access to each of the residences through individual doorways, and apartments typically had front yard and/or backyard space that was uniquely associated with individual units.

Newman defined *natural surveillance* as "the capacity of physical design to provide surveillance opportunities for residents and their agents" (1972, p. 78). Specific design features that affect the potential for resident-based surveillance include the height of buildings; the placement of buildings vis-à-vis the street and other buildings; the number of access routes to the build-ings; the height and placement of landscaping materials; and the presence or absence of alcoves, niches, or alleyways. In Newman's view, developments that consisted of dozens of high-rise buildings clustered together, as was typical in large public housing communities, simply did not provide strong natural surveillance. Many units within such developments provided no view of street activity. In addition, each of the high-rise buildings themselves were notorious for having many areas within that provided limited oppor-tunity for surveillance (i.e., enclosed lobbies, elevators, and stairways).

According to Newman, *image* refers to the "capacity of design to influ-ence the perception of an area as unique, well-maintained, and non-isolated" (1972, p. 102). The use of unique designs and distinctive materials in the building of a space, as well as the upkeep and maintenance of the space, conveys the message that the area is being cared for, thus deterring incivility and making the space more easily defended. Alternatively, poorly maintained spaces generate a negative type of distinctiveness—one that is stigmatizing, easily perceived as vulnerable, and thus attractive to offenders. Newman felt that high-rise projects had much more of a stigma associated with them than low-rise public-housing communities. The high-rise project—with dozens of unattractive towers clustered together—sticks out as "different" from sur-rounding areas. At the same time, the generic, indistinctive finishes and furnishings often characterizing the buildings lend an institutional feel, lacking in character and positive image.

Related to image is Newman's concept of *milieu*, or the location of the space within the broader urban locale. Thus, with the concept of milieu, Newman considers the juxtaposition or adjacency of a particular space in relation to other spaces. Physical spaces are differentially "risky" versus "safe" in that they offer different levels of criminal opportunity. As a result, spaces near risky places can experience "spillover." A housing project adjacent to a high school, for example, is likely to suffer problems in part simply because the project is proximal to a large collection of individuals (high school students) who are of prime age in terms of offender motivation and target suitability and yet who are relatively free of controls once class lets out each afternoon (Newman, 1972). The juxtaposition of such a project makes it less defensible in comparison to a project adjacent to, for example, a business office housing adults engaged in employment practices.

Overall, Newman (1972) suggested that spaces which provided territoriality, natural surveillance, positive image, and "safe" adjacency would be more easily defended by residents. His theory, therefore, assumed that the *physical* environment was important because of how it affected the *social* control exerted within. Newman, in fact, defined defensible space as "a model for residential environments which inhibits crime by creating the physical expression of a social fabric that defends itself" (p. 3). He viewed defense of space as a latent characteristic of small communities, like public housing projects. This latent territorial behavior only needed to be fostered through smart physical design.

Beyond Newman: Crime Prevention through Environmental Design (CPTED)

Newman's idea that physical design affected crime through prompting resident-based territorial attitudes and behavior was influential yet unpopular among some commentators. His critics thought Newman was overly obsessed with building height as an indicator of criminogenic space, and many also disagreed with his presumption of latent territorial inclinations among community residents (see, e.g., Brantingham and Brantingham, 1993; Donnelly and Kimble, 1997; Merry, 1981). However, many aspects of Newman's work proved long-lasting. In particular, his work fostered a movement that focused on the idea that physical design of spaces can affect the opportunity for crime, *regardless of whether community-wide, resident-based territorial attitudes or behavior are affected*. Therefore, physical design of places could be manipulated for prevention purposes. This alternative conceptualization of the role of physical design is typically referred to as Crime Prevention through Environmental Design (CPTED), and it is popular in a variety of settings today beyond residential environments (see, e.g., Crowe, 2000).

The term *CPTED* was actually coined by C. Ray Jeffery in his 1971 book, *Crime Prevention through Environmental Design*. Although Jeffery's work antedated Newman's *Defensible Space*, it largely stood in the latter's shadows. This was probably due to Jeffery's heavy emphasis on theory, in contrast to the practical guidelines and applications that characterized Newman's work (Paulsen and Robinson, 2004). Nonetheless, Jeffery's term "stuck," and contemporary discussions of the role of physical design in crime is likely to involve the reference to CPTED as opposed to "defensible space." Contemporary discussions of the role of environmental design in community crime typically stress the mechanism of criminal opportunity. That is, aspects of environmental design are thought to affect the extent to which offenders can easily access rewarding targets/victims with little risk of detection.

While Newman's original four concepts are still implicitly a part of contemporary discussion of environmental design and crime, they also have evolved. For example, the concept of "territoriality" is largely discussed today in terms of *access control* and *target hardening*. As Reynald (2015, p. 78) suggests, Newman's *territoriality* is broadly focused on the control of and responsibility for space by its owners, whereas *access control* hinges specifically on the regulation of access to targets in an area through the regulation of movement into, out of, and within the area. Then, at the level of a specific property within an area, the related concept of *target hardening* comes into play. Target hardening is "the mechanism through which access to individual property targets can be restricted for all but legitimate owners and users" (Reynald, 2015, p. 79). And beyond the evolution of the concept of territoriality, Newman's concept of *natural surveillance* has also evolved. Contemporary discussions focus on the potential within areas for both natural and mechanical surveillance. In other words, *surveillance* is presumed to be affected not only by the type, design, and layout of buildings, streets, and walkways but also by the presence or absence of mechanistic devices such as security cameras. Finally, most contemporary discussions of environmental design and crime emphasize the concept of *activity support*. This concept borrows from Newman the importance of design in encouraging a particular intended use for space.

A number of community-based studies over the past three decades have shown support for the importance of physical design features related to access control and surveillance potential, in particular. For example, studies show that accessibility, traffic volume, presence of escape routes (i.e., proximity to highway), inadequate street lighting, and obstacles to surveillance within neighborhoods are positively related to crime (Bernasco and Luykx, 2003; Donnelly and Kimble, 1997; Greenberg, Rohe, and Williams, 1982; Sidebottom et al., in press; Taylor and Harrell, 1996; Welsh and Farrington, 2009; White, 1990; for a recent review, see also Reynald, 2015).

Offender Decision-Making and Community Crime Patterns

The routine activities and environmental design perspectives discussed in the two preceding sections are both based on an assumption of offender rationality—the idea that behavior, including criminal behavior, is chosen in utilitarian fashion. The key concepts within these theories imply that "crime opportunity" involves assessment of effort, risk, and reward on the part of offenders. For example, a "suitable target" is one the offender finds accessible and deems rewarding. "Absence of capable guardianship" connotes low risk to the offender. This section explores theory that further specifies the processes behind offender choices, with a particular focus on how community plays into crime decisions. These perspectives address more specifically how motivated offenders find opportunities to offend—how they search for and select attractive targets that lack capable guardianship.

Crime as a Rational Choice

The field of criminology was founded on the notion that crime is a choice in which offenders weigh risks versus rewards. The Classical School of criminology emerged in the 1700s, led by "enlightened" thinkers such as Cesare Beccaria and Jeremy Bentham. They touted the idea that crime was a result of voluntary, hedonistic action that could be deterred through a legal system that provided certain, severe, swift, yet fair, punishment. In such a system, potential offenders would be unlikely to perceive the benefits of crime as outweighing the costs and would thus *choose* not to offend. However, classical thinking gave way to positivist thinking, which presumed that crime was *not* a choice, but caused instead. In particular, the Positivist School of criminology claims that criminal behavior is determined by distinct biological, psychological, or social characteristics beyond an individual's control. Positivist thinking has essentially dominated criminology since the late 1800s.

That said, a rational choice framework reemerged around 1980, challenging the stronghold of positivist approaches on the field. The work of Ronald Clarke, often in collaboration with Derek Cornish, was particularly instrumental in defining contemporary ideas about "reasoning offenders" (Clarke and Cornish, 1985; Cornish and Clarke, 1986). Clarke was trained as a behavioral psychologist in the United Kingdom. Early in his career, he held a research position within the United Kingdom's system of training schools for delinquent boys (Clarke and Felson, 2011). As part of that work, Clarke was asked to predict absconding behavior among the training-school boys. His research revealed "few usable results—those who ran away from the schools turned out to be little different from other residents in terms of their scores on a wide range of psychological tests and background variables" (Clarke and Felson, 2011, p. 251). However, the research did reveal substantial variation across training schools in rates of absconding. Thus, Clarke concluded that criminal motivation (propensity) did not vary across absconders and non-absconders since differences in individual background factors were not substantial. Instead, he concluded that opportunity explained differences in absconding behavior across the boys—some training schools provided environmental conditions that produced ample opportunities for absconding (i.e., lax supervision) while others did not.

In another study, Clarke and Cornish compared reconviction rates conducted across boys randomly assigned to a therapeutic treatment program as opposed to a control group at one particular training school. They found no differences in reconviction rates, thus cementing Clarke's earlier frustration with behavioral-clinical psychology and its focus on modifying dispositional characteristics presumed to cause offending. Clarke thus left the training school and took another position—this time with the Home Office Research Unit. This was the federal research department in the United Kingdom. There, he was asked to head a section of the unit tasked with developing a crime-reduction program. In his new professional role, Clarke recalled the lessons learned from his days of doing research in training schools: individual-level dispositional differences in offenders and non-offenders were minimal, but environmental opportunities for offending were highly variable. Thus, Clarke headed the crime-reduction unit under the assumption that crime could be prevented by reducing opportunities within the environment. This environmentally based approach to crime prevention—which Clarke refers to as situational crime prevention—went hand in hand with a view that offenders were rational actors responding to opportunity structures within their environments.

Clarke and Cornish put forth a theoretical framework supporting situational crime prevention in a seminal book chapter by Clarke and Cornish, "Modeling Offenders' Decisions: A Framework for Research and Policy." This essay was published in the 1985 edition of *Crime and Justice: An Annual Review of Research*. In this work, Clarke and Cornish essentially provided a modern-day rational choice perspective on crime. This work suggested that offenders make active decisions to commit crime, though their choices might not be characterized by the same degree of free will as assumed in classical criminology.

According to Clarke and Cornish, offender decisions are based on "bounded rationality." In other words, cost-benefit decision making occurs among offenders, though there is clear recognition that biological, psychological, and social "background" factors constrain or put boundaries around the assessment of alternative lines of action (e.g., to commit a crime or do something else). For example, those afflicted with impulsivity or poverty will probably evaluate criminal options as more rewarding than those with high self-control or a middle-class existence. Additionally, foreground characteristics, such as the immediate presence of a criminal opportunity or an immediate need, can shape decision making. Thus, an individual might not generally view the benefits of crime as outweighing the rewards, but that view might change if presented with an opportunity that he or she just cannot refuse. A pressing need for drugs to feed an addiction might serve as another factor affecting an individual's assessment of the costs versus benefits associated with a criminal line of action, thus bounding rationality. In short, individuals faced with circumstances such as impulsivity, poverty, situational opportunities, or an immediate need for cash will likely reach decisions regarding the costs versus benefits of criminal action that differ from the decisions reached by individuals experiencing different background and foreground circumstances. Regardless, rationality can be viewed as characterizing the decisions of all in the sense that decisions are ultimately based in the utilitarian pursuit of pleasure over pain. The evaluation of perceived pleasure versus perceived pain is simply bounded by myriad distal and proximal influences.

It is also important to note that "pleasure" or "benefit" does not have to be financial, nor does it have to be long term. Research has indicated that many decisions about offending are made within a cultural context emphasizing a party lifestyle and living in the moment (Wright, Brookman, and Bennett, 2006; Wright and Decker, 1994, 1997; Shover, 1996). Although the lack of long-range planning seems to defy the notion of rationality, Clarke and Cornish's modern-day rational choice perspective allows for decisions to be based on short-run hedonism. Overall, the contemporary approach to rational choice, with its emphasis on bounded rationality, "widens" the rather-narrow classical criminology. According to Clarke and Cornish (1985, pp. 163–164; see also Shover, 1996), "rationality must be conceived of in broad terms. For example, even if the choices made or the decision processes themselves are not ideal, they make sense to the offender and represent his best efforts at optimizing outcomes."

Beyond describing crime as a choice within bounded rationality, Clarke and Cornish contend that there are two major types of decisions made by offenders: *involvement decisions* and *event decisions*. Involvement decisions surround the offender's "readiness" to engage in crime and include three subtypes: (1) first-time decisions to be involved in crime (initial involvement); (2) decisions to continue involvement in crime (persistence or continuance); and (3) decisions to stop involvement in crime (desistance). By contrast, event decisions consist of the choices that are made in actually carrying out an offense. Some examples include decisions about where to offend (area selection), against whom or what to offend (target selection), and how to offend (modus operandi). Clarke and Cornish stress that the specific decisions involved in an event depend upon the crime. For example, a decision about how to convert stolen goods to cash is relevant to a burglar but not to a drug dealer.

Offender Searches

Offender decisions regarding target selection—part of "event" decision making in the rational choice framework described above—are particularly relevant to understanding community-level crime. Beginning with their 1981 book, *Environmental Criminology*, Paul and Patricia Brantingham have been at the forefront of scholarship that describes the offender search process and the resulting non-random patterning of crime across and within communities.

Their work suggested that targets are chosen through a purposeful search—one that attempts to balance issues of effort, risk, and profit. As such, offenders more often seek targets that are easily accessible, vulnerable, and valuable. The Brantinghams recognized, however, that the offenders' target-selection decision is also *hierarchical*, or *multistaged* (Brantingham and Brantingham, 1981, 1993, 2013; see also Taylor and Gottfredson, 1986). Thus, before certain targets are selected, offenders choose a general area in which to operate, usually a place or community that is close by and with which they are familiar. In fact, offenders have been described as foragers, who "must find a good hunting ground before starting to chase prey" (Bernasco and Block, 2009, p. 96; see also Bernasco, 2010; Bernasco and Nieuwbeerta, 2005; Coupe and Blake, 2006; Felson, 2006). Thus, environments in which specific targets are located—not just the specific targets themselves—are key in providing criminal opportunity to offenders. Simply put, places vary in terms of their suitability for offenders' searches for crime.

What sorts of places are perceived by offenders as advantageous hunting grounds? As noted above, the Brantinghams suggest that offenders do not roam widely and randomly but find their targets within the geographic space where they carry out their routine activities. They refer to this area as an offender's "activity space" (see, e.g., Brantingham and Brantingham, 1981, 2013; Brantingham and Brantingham, 1993, 1995). Specifically, offenders are likely to search for and then choose attractive targets at or near the places where they conduct their routine activity. These activity nodes include schools, workplaces, shopping or entertainment areas, and, more generally, areas near offenders' residences. Motivated offenders can readily come into contact with suitable targets at such nodes. Hence, activity nodes generate plentiful opportunities for crime. Major routes that surround and connect various nodes, such as streets and walkways, also provide numerous targets for offenders searching for crime. These major routes, which the Branting-hams refer to as "paths," are therefore likely to host higher than average crime events. Some central nodes and pathways will generate so much opportunity that they might actually become "crime attractors"—places that offenders travel to specifically for crime purposes.

The Brantinghams have also suggested that offenders find targets in their search for crime not only at major nodes and paths within their activity spaces but also at "edge space." They describe edge space as a boundary area that forms the transition from one distinct physical space to another. Given their transitional nature, there are sometimes multiple users of edge spaces; those who use adjacent spaces often converge at the edges, creating a "cross-over" of users. Such crossover provides an abundance of targets for offenders. At the same time, there is often ambiguity in terms of who "owns" and controls edge space, thus diminishing guardianship.

In fact, a good deal of research has examined in more detail the characteristics of communities that make them seem as "advantageous hunting grounds" from offender vantage points—the sorts of communities that are likely to be chosen by offenders as locations in which they will search for a specific target. Findings from this body of work supports both Clarke and Cornish's rational choice perspective on crime events and the Brantinghams' ideas about offender searches. Specifically, research suggests that offenders choose communities according to qualities such as: (1) proximity of an area to an offender's home; (2) similarity in racial/ethnic composition of the area to that of the offender's home; (3) number/supply of suitable targets in the area; (4) intensiveness of other vice or crime in the area; and (5) amount/density of non-residential land uses (Bernasco, 2010; Bernasco and Block, 2009; Bernasco and Nieuwbeerta, 2005; Clarke and Cornish, 1985; Cornish and Clarke, 1986; Rengert and Wasilchick, 2000; Reynald et al., 2008; Wright and Decker, 1994, 1997).

Seminal ethnographic research on active street robbers by Richard Wright and Scott Decker provides particularly rich detail regarding the through processes of offenders in their search for targets, particularly as it relates to community-level influence on such decision making. For example, one of the active street robbers they interviewed in Saint Louis said, "You stay close to your home. You don't go too far past your boundaries because you don't know about everything" (Wright and Decker, 1997, p. 74). Robbers indicated that staying close to home was preferred because, in those areas, they had familiarity with patrol practices and the layouts of streets and alleys, which was particularly crucial for the purposes of escaping police or others trying to intervene. Others indicated that they chose areas close to home because transportation options were limited: "We can't go burning up our mother's or father's car to go way out in the county to do a jack; we walk around the neighborhood looking for someone" (p. 73). Overall, proximity as a criterion for neighborhood selection in the offender search process was strongly supported in Wright and Decker's research and that finding has been corroborated in a good number of other studies (e.g., Bernasco and Block, 2009; Bernasco and Luykx, 2003; Bernasco and Nieuwbeerta, 2005).

Robbers interviewed by Wright and Decker also indicated that neighborhood racial composition was important because it was presumed to be related to the likelihood that they would arouse suspicion. One respondent said, for example, "I can go in a Black neighborhood . . . and I don't stand out." More recent research has supported Wright and Decker's research, though there is some evidence that racial or ethnic composition of a neighborhood is especially important among African American and Hispanic robbers but less so among White robbers (Bernasco and Block, 2009; Bernasco and Nieuwbeerta, 2005; Reynald et al., 2008).

Various robbers interviewed by Wright and Decker pointed to selecting neighborhoods that contained shopping centers, stadium areas, parks, entertainment/bar districts, and business districts, as such places were thought to provide large supplies of targets. As one active robber indicated, "I . . . try to go to an area, gaming events, sporting events where people are going . . . where you assume [they] are going to take money . . . they gonna buy tickets, have refreshments, you know" (Wright and Decker, 1997, p. 76). Areas with ATMs, check-cashing stores, and drug markets were also named as providing abundant supplies of suitable targets. Beyond Wright and Decker's work, other research supports the idea that offenders search for crime in neighborhoods with land uses perceived to have plentiful targets (e.g., Deakin et al., 2007; Hart and Miethe, 2014; Weisburd, Groff, and Yang, 2012).

In sum, there is both theoretical and empirical support for the idea that community characteristics play an important role in offender decision making—particularly decisions related to offender searches for targets. Furthermore, the community characteristics highlighted by the offender decision-making literature overlap substantially with that in the routine activities and environmental design traditions. That is, they are community characteristics that speak to opportunity in terms of supplies of targets, levels of guardianship, accessibility, and so forth.

The Criminology of Place

From the outset, this book has avoided use of a specific definition of "community" (or, "neighborhood"). Arbitrating between different conceptual and operational definitions is simply beyond the focus of our enterprise (though we revisit the issue in Chapter 9 as we look ahead to future issues). That said, it is useful to note that the empirical research on community influences that has been cited throughout uses a variety of units for the approximation of community—including census tracts, census block groups, police districts, political wards, or locally demarcated areas defined on the basis of within-area homogeneity and/or natural barriers. In part, scholars choose such units for convenience, not necessarily because they represent "real" neighborhood boundaries. Thus, researchers will often select a unit for analysis because data (e.g., arrest statistics, demographic information) exist for this kind of ecological area. Although these "convenient" units may not precisely align with neighborhood boundaries, there is general agreement that they are acceptable approximations of the notion of "urban villages" (Boessen and Hipp, 2015). Importantly, "community" or "neighborhood" is thus a *mesolevel* spatial unit—smaller than a city or town, yet larger than a street. In fact, it is the sort of geographic unit that dominated our understanding of communities in the study of crime until the past several decades.

However, since approximately 1990, a different approach to understanding community crime has taken hold—an approach increasingly referred to as the *criminology of place* (Weisburd, Groff, and Yang, 2012). This contemporary approach emphasizes variation in crime events at small geographic units of analysis, thus making it *microlevel* as opposed to mesolevel in focus. Scholars advocating for a criminology of place point to discernible *within-neighborhood* clusters of crime. In particular, they suggest that most locations within "high-crime neighborhoods" experience little to no crime. Instead, there are a relatively small number of places that experience an unusually high amount of crime, and it is these problem places that drive neighborhood crime rates.

In short, crime is seen as a problem specific to "hot spots" within a community rather than integral to the community as a whole. This observation has had the effect of shifting focus away from the traditional analysis of neighborhood conditions (e.g., concentrated disadvantage social disorganization) and toward the analysis of criminal opportunity in the *immediate locations* where crime events occur. Simply put, neighborhoods are considered "too big" a unit of analysis, and subneighborhood "places" such as street segments or specific addresses are deemed more appropriate for accurately understanding community crime problems (e.g., Braga, 2012; Sherman, Gartin, and Buerger, 1989; Weisburd, Groff, and Yang, 2012). The focus on specific problem places is said to offer greater crime prevention precision and efficiency than neighborhood-based interventions.

A criminology of place served as the foundation of many of the crime prevention strategies, centered on opportunity-reduction, pursued by the Home Office in the United Kingdom under the leadership efforts of Ronald Clarke. In the United States, however, the perspective arguably arrived on the scene with the publication of a famous study on crime in Minneapolis by Lawrence Sherman and colleagues, published in 1989. Sherman, Gartin, and Buerger analyzed all calls for service for one-year in Minneapolis. These crimes could have potentially occurred at 115,000 different "places" (i.e., addresses or intersections) within the city. However, their analysis of the calls revealed that most places experienced no crime. Instead, crime tended to cluster nonrandomly in just a few places with repeat crime problems—places Sherman et al. famously termed "hot spots." The key finding to come out of the study was that 50 percent of all crime in the city occurred at just 3 percent of the places throughout the city, thus highlighting the extent of *crime concentration* that existed at a *micro-spatial level*.

Sherman, Gartin, and Buerger (1989) attribute their findings to the idea that there is substantial variation in opportunities for crime across places within communities. Places within communities structure activity and behavior differently as a result of their social organizational properties—they have variable "customary rules of interaction, financial wealth, forbidden and encouraged activities, prestige rank, moral value, patterns of recruitment and expulsion, legal rights and duties, and even language spoken" (Sherman, Gartin, and Buerger, 1989, p. 32). The researchers claimed that such criminogenic properties of places are missed if the focus is on community-level differences. Thus, their findings highlighted the importance of micro-ecological crime patterns within neighborhoods (i.e., clustering at specific addresses or intersections) as opposed to focusing on between-neighborhood differences in crime.

Subsequent work by David Weisburd and his colleagues showed similar patterns of hot-spot concentration in Seattle at the street segment level. More specifically, a series of studies by Weisburd and colleagues showed that crime clustered nonrandomly on certain street segments, and this pattern of clustering largely remained stable over the course of several decades (Groff, Weisburd, and Yang, 2010; Weisburd et al., 2004; Weisburd, Groff, and Yang, 2012; see also Weisburd, 2015). Recent work by other scholars reveals similar street-level and place-level crime clustering in other cities (e.g., Andresen, Linning, and Malleson, 2017; Bernasco and Block, 2011; Braga, Hureau, and Papachristos, 2011). The empirical evidence of within-neighborhood hot spots has had the effect of transforming the way in which police go about their work in inner-city communities. Specifically, police agencies are increasingly encouraged to engage in crime analysis (through intensive mapping of crime locations) and to embrace "hot-spots patrol" and "directed patrol" as opposed to traditional routine patrol of police beats (see Chapter 6). The thinking is that police can make the most efficient gains in terms of crime reduction by focusing on specific crime problems and particularly problematic places within crime-ridden areas of the city (Telep and Weisburd, 2012).

However, the empirical evidence in support of hot spots of crime has implications beyond the realm of policing. It has led to analyzing problem places within neighborhoods and applying a whole host of problem-solving

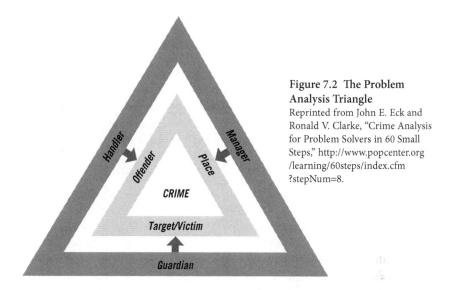

Figure 7.2 The Problem Analysis Triangle
Reprinted from John E. Eck and Ronald V. Clarke, "Crime Analysis for Problem Solvers in 60 Small Steps," http://www.popcenter.org/learning/60steps/index.cfm?stepNum=8.

strategies aimed at opportunity reduction—strategies that may or may not involve criminal justice agents. John Eck—one of Sherman's former Ph.D. students—has been particularly influential in this regard (for recent reviews, see Eck and Guerette, 2012; Madensen and Eck, 2013). Eck has been at the forefront of outlining a criminology of place in conceptual terms and providing an associated agenda for place-based crime prevention. The framework advocated by Eck is perhaps most famously illustrated in figure form as the "Problem Analysis Triangle" (see Figure 7.2).

The inner layer of Figure 7.2 depicts the fundamental tenet of the criminology of place—that crime occurs at the intersection of an offender, a target, and a place. Importantly, "places" are intended to refer to small-scale, microlevel geographic units such as addresses, intersections, or street segments that are thought to offer variable levels of crime opportunity. The outer layer of Figure 7.2 depicts the posited mechanisms for preventing crime. In particular, the Problem Analysis Triangle suggests that crime opportunity can be blocked by three types of controllers: offender handlers, target guardians, and place managers (see also Felson, 1987, 1995). Handlers prevent crime by exerting control on potentially motivated offenders. For example, parents enforcing a curfew on their teenage child or a parole officer checking up on a client could both be considered offender handling. Guardians disrupt crime by controlling potential victims. Friends walking together while downtown at night serve as bystanders, helping guard one another against assailants, as one simple example. Finally, managers discourage crime by effectively controlling places that are potential settings for crime. Place management can occur through actions such as effective rule enforcement by a business owner (e.g., no serving to intoxicated patrons) or appropriate surveillance (e.g., hiring a security officer).

Overall, the criminology of place examines criminal opportunity and community crime in a fresh light. Instead of treating communities as homogenous spatial units, it recognizes instead within-neighborhood heterogeneity regarding criminal opportunity and crime incidents—with some particularly opportunistic areas within any one neighborhood experiencing a good deal of crime while most other areas experience little or none. This way of thinking has spurred prevention initiatives that focus on problem-solving (centered around opportunity reduction) at a very localized level—at the immediate hot spot of crime. Prevention efforts aimed at disrupting the opportunity for crime at hot spots certainly include more focused law enforcement practice, but such efforts need not involve formal criminal justice intervention. In fact, much of the appeal of place-based problem-solving is that it encourages opportunity reduction efforts by "ordinary" citizens acting as handlers, guardians, and place managers.

Multilevel Crime Opportunity

Crime opportunity has traditionally been considered at one spatial unit of analysis. Opportunity at the community level has been the focus of this chapter, though the previous section highlighted a recent trend at considering opportunity at hot spots of crime within communities, and still other work mentioned earlier in the chapter addressed individual-level opportunity as key in understanding victimization risk. Currently, there is much scholarly debate regarding the most important unit for the structuring of opportunity. Some favor a focus on individuals (as potential victims), others a focus on micro-scale places or streets (as potential hot spots), and still others favoring a focus on broader-scale neighborhoods (as potential high-crime communities). But do we need to choose a winner? A multilevel opportunity perspective suggests not. It suggests that crime opportunity is structured at multiple, embedded units of analysis. With respect to the focus of this chapter, multilevel opportunity is important because it illuminates the interplay between communities and the individuals and smaller-scale places that constitute them in the production of crime opportunity.

Preference for a single-level focus among many scholars interested in the concept of crime opportunity is puzzling given that implicit support for a multilevel approach to opportunity has been around for decades. As mentioned previously, offenders appear to search for crime in a multilevel, sequential process whereby they assess crime opportunities at progressively smaller units of analysis. For example, offenders first select neighborhoods in which to operate and then select places or people within neighborhoods as the targets of their crime (e.g., Brantingham and Brantingham, 1993; Taylor and Gottfredson, 1986; Wright and Decker, 1994, 1997). Hence, offenders seem to provide evidence that opportunity structures for crime exist at multiple levels of analysis.

There is other evidence that crime clusters at small-scale "micro places" (e.g., specific addresses or streets), thus forming "hot spots" of crime, but that these hot spots, in turn, cluster within "meso or macro spaces" (e.g., neighborhoods or broader areas). For example, recent work by Weisburd and colleagues (2012; discussed above) emphasizes block-to-block variability in crime in Seattle, suggesting that there is clear and meaningful within-neighborhood, block-level clustering (i.e., evidence of hot blocks). At the same time, they also note some clustering of hot blocks: "We do find cases in our data where several adjacent street segments, one after another, evidence similar developmental trends of crime" (p. 173). They offer such evidence as support for the idea that higher geographic influences, such as neighborhoods, play some role in understanding crime on street blocks.

Multilevel criminal opportunity theory (also called multicontextual criminal opportunity theory) explicitly considers such evidence. It accounts for the fact that individuals or places characterized by certain levels of crime opportunity are nested within broader environmental units—like block groups or neighborhoods—which can also be characterized in terms of opportunity (e.g., see Taylor and Gottfredson, 1986; Wilcox, Land, and Hunt, 2003). Therefore, multilevel opportunity theory rejects the consideration of particular units of analysis in isolation. Instead, multiple embedded levels of analysis—and their corresponding opportunity structures—are considered simultaneously.

Wilcox, Land, and Hunt (2003) provide a detailed articulation of multilevel criminal opportunity theory that serves to integrate the various perspectives on opportunity discussed in previous sections of this chapter while also considering opportunity at multiple levels of analysis (see also Wilcox, Gialopsos, and Land, 2013). First, they state that criminal opportunity is affected by a multitude of factors such as lifestyles and routine activities, environmental design, and formal and informal social control. Second, they state that opportunity is present at multiple levels of analysis (Wilcox, Land, and Hunt, 2003; Wilcox et al., 2013). For example, opportunity characterizes individuals, places, streets (or street blocks), neighborhoods, and so on. Third, they posit that indicators of criminal opportunity at various levels of analysis might operate independently but also suggest that the interaction between micro levels and meso/macro levels of analysis is likely. More specifically, individual-level or place-level characteristics might affect opportunity for crime or victimization differently, depending on characteristics of the larger environmental context (such as the neighborhood) in which the individuals or places are situated. The "opportunity context" characterizing meso-level or macro-level environments can serve to accentuate or attenuate the opportunity-related characteristics of individuals and places. The specific interactions posited by this multilevel criminal opportunity theory are presented in Box 7.1.

There is mounting empirical evidence that the tenets of a general, multilevel opportunity theory—such as that posited by Wilcox, Land, and Hunt (2003)—have merit. For example, there are now a number of multilevel studies of victimization that, collectively, promote the idea that characteristics associated with routine activities, environmental design, and social control—at individual/household and neighborhood levels of analysis—impact victimization risk. These studies recognize that individual victims or place-specific targets are situated within broader contexts, such as neighborhoods. Again, such studies are grounded in work suggesting that offenders make decisions about crime events in a multistaged fashion—that characteristics of neighborhoods are important as offenders first choose general areas of a city/town in which to offend, but that characteristics of individual targets/victims are important too. Thus, multilevel victimization studies estimate both the effects of individual-level and neighborhood-level characteristics related to victimization.

Sampson and Wooldredge (1987) provided one of the first tests of a multilevel opportunity perspective to understand victimization risk. Using the British Crime Survey, they examined how risk of personal and property victimization was affected by both individual/household- and neighborhood-level indicators of opportunity. Their findings largely supported their hypotheses regarding multilevel opportunity. For example, Sampson and Wooldredge (1987) found that single-person households and households that were frequently left unoccupied were at greater risk for burglary victimization, thus supporting the idea that individual-level lifestyles and routine activities structure opportunities for criminal victimization. However, they also observed that community-level characteristics affected victimization risk. In particular, households in communities marked by high rates of family disruption (i.e., single-parent households), high rates of single-person households, low social cohesion, high rates of VCR ownership, high rates of unemployment, and high proportions of apartments were at greater risk for burglary. Such findings support for the idea that community context can structure opportunities for burglary.

In an especially telling example of the importance of community context in structuring opportunity, Sampson and Wooldredge (1987) found that the risk of burglary was affected by neighborhood-level percentage of households with VCRs but not affected by individual ownership of a VCR (an item considered to be a suitable target in the 1980s). This finding implied that the

BOX 7.1 CROSS-LEVEL INTERACTIONS POSITED BY WILCOX, LAND, AND HUNT'S (2003) MULTILEVEL OPPORTUNITY THEORY

How individual-level or place-level *exposure* is conditioned by opportunity in the broader environment:

- A large supply of offenders in the broader environment increases market demand for targets and makes individual-level or place-level exposure seemingly all the more risky.
- A large aggregate supply of suitable targets in the broader environment diminishes the value of any one target, making individual-level or place-level distinctions on the basis of exposure all the more important.
- Effective guardianship in the broader area increases the market cost of criminal acts, thus deterring crime and making individual-level exposure or place-level exposure less important.

How individual-level or place-level *target suitability* is conditioned by opportunity in the broader environment:

- A large supply of offenders in the broader environment increases market demand for targets and makes individual-level or place-level target suitability all the more important.
- A large aggregate supply of suitable targets in the broader environment diminishes the value of any one target, making individual-level or place-level distinctions on the basis of suitability less important.
- Effective guardianship in the broader area increases the market cost of criminal acts, thus deterring crime and making individual-level or place-level target suitability less important.

How individual-level or place-level *guardianship* is conditioned by opportunity in the broader environment:

- A large supply of offenders in the broader environment increases market demand for targets and makes costs associated with individuals and places (including costs of detection associated with guardianship) matter less.
- A large aggregate supply of suitable targets in the broader environment diminishes the value of any one target, making "costly" (e.g., well-guarded) individuals and places all the more avoidable.
- Effective guardianship in the broader area increases the market cost of criminal acts, thus deterring crime and making individual-level and place-level guardianship all the more effective.

neighborhood-level supply of suitable targets in the broader environment influenced burglary risk more so than the target suitability of individual households. Sampson and Wooldredge's analysis revealed additional findings that addressed the fact that indicators of opportunity existed at both individual and neighborhood levels. For example, the mean level of cash carried in public by neighborhood residents had a significant impact on whether an individual experienced larceny victimization, net of the individual's own level of carrying cash in public. Other findings showed that respondents' risks of personal victimization were heightened by a community-level measure of street activity (i.e., the percentage of residents who went out at night). This community-level effect was observed net of the number of nights that the individual respondents went out in the neighborhood. Thus, here again, the community-level opportunity structure impacted individual victimization risk above and beyond individual-level routine activities. Overall, Sampson and Wooldredge's 1987 study was groundbreaking because it highlighted the idea that opportunity could be structured at multiple levels of analysis and emphasized the potential for opportunity structure at the community level, in particular.

Analyses of data from the Seattle Victimization Survey, collected by Terance Miethe, also provide empirical evidence consistent with a multilevel opportunity perspective. These findings are particularly important because they highlight how individual-level and community-level opportunity structures can interact in affecting crime and victimization events. More specifically, studies of the victimization patterns of residents within Seattle neighborhoods have estimated *cross-level interactions* showing that individual lifestyles and routine activities do not uniformly influence risk for victimization across all settings. Instead, neighborhood characteristics sometimes condition or moderate these effects. For example, studies using the Seattle data indicate that safety precautions taken by residents (i.e., locking doors, installing alarms) had greater burglary-reduction effectiveness in orderly, affluent areas compared with less affluent areas (Miethe and McDowall, 1993; Miethe and Meier, 1994; Wilcox Rountree, Land, and Miethe, 1994). The effects of individual safety precautions also appeared stronger in neighborhoods with high levels of informal social control and in neighborhoods with overall physical design features that promoted natural surveillance (Wilcox, Madensen, and Tillyer, 2007). Thus, researchers examining the Seattle data conclude that burglary reduction cannot come from individual lifestyle changes alone; macro-level changes to the opportunity structure of the neighborhoods may be necessary. More recently, Deryol and colleagues (2016) provided evidence from Cincinnati to support such conclusions. Their multilevel analysis of crime locations nested within Cincinnati block groups found that the proximity of locations to drinking/liquor establishments and bus stops (opportunistic nodes and paths, respectively) was more strongly related to crime in neighborhoods with higher overall commercial density.

Conclusion

Although initially tested at the national level with time-series data on U.S. crime rates, routine activities theory was, in many ways, originally conceptualized as a theory about local community crime since routine activities were posited to be organized and structured by community life. In fact, as reviewed here, there is a rich tradition of community-level applications of the theory. These community-level applications have emphasized that communities suffering higher rates of crime have more criminal opportunity because they structure activities in such a way that offenders are likely to converge with suitable targets in the absence of capable guardianship and/or capable offender handling.

Beyond routine activities theory (which would become L-RAT), other theoretical perspectives address the role of community in structuring opportunity for crime. Building off the work of Jane Jacobs and Oscar Newman, there is now ample evidence that the physical design of community space can potentially impact crime—once again, by affecting the extent to which offenders and victims/targets can readily converge, unimpeded, within the space. Such evidence is complemented by scholarship on offender choice and decision-making, indicating that searches for targets during crime events does involve consideration of the broader area (community) in which specific targets are located.

Further, multilevel opportunity theory considers how community-level indicators of opportunity work in conjunction with opportunity at smaller levels of analysis. Work in this tradition has indicated that crime opportunity does exist at multiple embedded levels of analysis. Most important, cross-level interactions can occur whereby community-level opportunity moderates the effects of individual- or place-level opportunity, thus offering a more nuanced understanding of the role of community in the production of crime events.

Taken together, these various theoretical perspectives challenge how crime should be envisioned within communities, including inner-city neighborhoods. As seen in other chapters, the traditional criminological approach has been to uncover the community conditions—whether that is social disorganization and week ties, a criminal culture, or concentrated disadvantage—that create criminogenic propensities among area residents. This alternative group of scholars, however, have been less interested in why someone becomes a "motivated offender." They admit that a pool of wayward people must exist for crime to occur. But these scholars are concerned with the other essential ingredient of a crime: opportunity (see Clarke, 2010).

When they look (or have looked) into an environment, they do not see root causes of crime but rather how this space is designed—physically and socially—to produce criminal opportunities. A dense high-rise building is not a container of impoverished motivated offenders but a structure that exposes many attractive targets to little guardianship. When urban, ethnic neighborhoods are torn down and highways are built that run through them, they worry that eyes will be removed from the streets and residents will no longer know one another well enough to come to the rescue should the need arise. When zoning boards allow bars, check-cashing stores, and virtually any other business to set up shop, they worry about how this land use attracts offenders in search of easy targets.

As noted, the positive feature of seeing the community as a criminal opportunity is that the recipe for thwarting victimization seems obvious and within reach: remove the opportunity to offend. Sometimes the solution is large and dramatic, such as tearing down high-rise housing projects that have become too dangerous to save. But other times the solution is small and mundane: install a lock or burglar alarm; have someone escort you home at night; remove bushes to make an entryway visible; hire a security guard to monitor admission to a building; or perhaps take away the liquor license for a bar that is a hot spot for violent incidents. Because crime events are situational and occur in a particular time and in a particular place, it becomes possible to figure out ways to prevent them from occurring. Indeed, once the city is imagined as a criminal opportunity, it becomes virtually impossible not to seek practical ways to make targets less attractive and guardianship more plentiful.

8

Community as Collective Efficacy

A commercial for Chrysler entitled "Imported from Detroit" first aired during Super Bowl XLV in 2011. It featured famous rap artist and Detroit native Eminem. The text of the ad was as follows:

[Commentator]

I got a question for you. What does this city know about luxury? What does a town that's been to hell and back know about the finer things in life? I'll tell you, more than most!

You see, it's the hottest fires that make the hardest steel, add hard work and conviction. And the know-how that runs generations deep in every last one of us.

That's who we are.

That's our story.

Now it's probably not the one you've been reading in the papers. The one being written by folks who have never even been here. And don't know what we're capable of.

Because when it comes to luxury, it's as much about where it's from as who it's for.

Now we're from America—but this isn't New York City. Or the Windy City. Or Sin City. And we're certainly no one's Emerald City.

[Marshall Bruce Mathers III (Eminem)]

This is the Motor City. And this is what we do.

The advertisement hit on the tough times Detroit had experienced owing to the ravages of deindustrialization: dramatic job loss, population loss, concentrated disadvantage among those that remained—conditions that some characterized as "post-apocalyptic" (Austen, 2014). But the ad also suggested that "luxury" could rise from the ashes of such devastation. In short, the ad emphasized *community resilience*. This theme of community resilience resonated with those living in other older communities within American large cities.

Paralleling Detroit's resurgence in the wake of the devastation wrought by deindustrialization, a number of other large American "Rustbelt" cities are in the process of reinventing themselves as we settle into the twenty-first century—creating new identities as "post-post-apocalyptic cities" (Austen, 2014, p. 22). There is evidence of some rebound from the urban structural disadvantage that had racked these large, once-thriving industrial cities, especially their African American communities (see Chapter 4). This resilience has been noted even amid population "downsizing." For example, cities such as Detroit, Baltimore, Washington, DC, and Cleveland, which were built on strong manufacturing bases and among our nation's ten largest cities in 1970, have fallen in the ranks population-wise. They have been replaced by cities in southwestern border states. Phoenix, San Antonio, San Diego, and San Jose ranked as the sixth, seventh, eighth, and tenth largest cities in the country, respectively, as of the 2010 U.S. Census. Such a demographic shift is in part due to the rapid growth and settlement patterns of the immigrant Latino population, which grew by 43 percent between 2000 and 2010 (U.S. Census Bureau, 2010).

Rustbelt resilience is seen not only in the face of population decline but also despite the early twenty-first-century Great Recession that featured a stock market meltdown, a real estate boom that went bust, and the bankruptcy of major industries, including American motor companies. Despite those formidable challenges, today's once-manufacturing-dominant central cities are experiencing economic revitalization. Their downtowns are now headquarters of high-tech, globally positioned industries. Their once-empty industrial spaces are being transformed into lofts, bars, craft breweries, coffeehouses, and chic shops. Their population's young professionals are choosing residences in the urban core, and the baby boomers are following suit—often eschewing the once-cherished suburbs because of lifestyle preferences for downsized residential space, shorter commutes to work, and walkability. But cities are not experiencing a complete return to the idyllic urban village life of decade's past. Instead, the resilience in once-deteriorated inner cities is seen even amid growing anonymity, congestion, and continued urban sprawl, with rings of settlement still forming outward, sometimes one hundred miles from the urban core (e.g., see Austen, 2014; Conzen, 2005).

These developments suggest a revised vision of urban America. Yes, serious problems—such as concentrated disadvantage and concentrated crime—still exist (Weisburd, Groff, and Yang, 2012). What has changed, however, is the view that inner-city decline and disorder is an inevitable fate from which there is no escape. Whatever its limitations, the image of community as a broken window was pregnant with the possibility that crime could be reduced; all that was needed was for the windows to be fixed, albeit with strong assistance from the police (see Chapter 6). Likewise, the image of the community as criminal opportunity offered the possibility that crime could be confronted with attentive city planning or smarter environmental design (see Chapter 7). In a similar way, a growing sense of optimism emerged that residents in communities could, when necessary, come together collectively to address pressing problems effectively, including crime. Such "collective efficacy" is clearly present in more affluent neighborhoods where residents are intolerant of problems—whether potholes, a lack of speed bumps, excessive noise, or bad teachers. But the ability to rise up and solve problems is not limited to so-called good communities. Some inner-city neighborhoods also possess this capacity, which is one reason why they might experience lower rates of crime.

In this context, a new image of the community for criminologists has become increasingly possible—one that sees the community as resilient, crime as reducible, and residents as exerting human agency in a concerted effort to solve neighborhood problems. In 1997 Robert Sampson, in conjunction with Stephen Raudenbush and Felton Earls, set forth just such a theoretical framework, called "collective efficacy theory." Over the next two decades, Sampson and various colleagues have elucidated the theory further and tested it systematically. As noted in the book's previous chapters, Sampson—deeply influenced by Ruth Kornhauser—played a key role in revitalizing social disorganization theory and advancing the systematic model through his early work. But the evolving nature of the modern city led him to become increasingly dissatisfied with these aging ideas. "Social disorganization theory," Sampson (2011, p. 79) observed, "tended to assume that the ideal contextual setting for social control was one characterized by dense, intimate, and strong neighborhood ties (e.g., through friends or kin), even though the so-called 'urban village' is hard to achieve in modern cities."

Thus, Sampson searched for a more satisfying construct—one that could capture the fundamental nature of "modern cities." As will be explained in detail, with Raudenbush and Earls, his empirical investigation of crime rates across the modern city of Chicago would lead him to invent just such a construct—*collective efficacy*. Still harboring strong loyalty to control theory, Sampson wanted to illuminate the key factors that allow, in any given neighborhood, for the capacity for informal social control to grow strong and to be activated when a challenge to the social order occurred. Based on empirical data, he argued that one essential element was a sense of being part of a collective—that is, the presence of social cohesion or trust. The second essential element was the shared expectation that neighbors could be counted on to take action should the need arise—that is, the presence of the expectation of efficacy.

It is instructive that collective efficacy has become the dominant community-level paradigm in criminology (Chouhy, 2016). Part of its popularity can be traced to the scholarly genius of Sampson, who has conveyed the theory persuasively and provided substantial evidence in its support. But the other source of its prominence is that it offered an image of urban America—*the community as collective efficacy*—that resonated with scholars entering criminology in the twenty-first century, a time when urban realities departed from those that prevailed in previous eras. In short, Sampson's insights, not those of Clifford Shaw and Henry McKay, seemed to make more sense to contemporary scholars.

This chapter thus tells the story of the rise of collective efficacy theory. The section that follows describes the theory, with a focus on how it evolved from the systemic model of community attachment—a previous conceptualization of community that Sampson had also played a major role in developing (see Chapter 3). Next, we take a step back and discuss the origins of the theory in work emerging from the Project on Human Development in Chicago Neighborhoods, with special attention given to the seminal analysis provided by Sampson, Raudenbush, and Earls in 1997, as well as a key follow-up analysis published in 2001 led by Jeffrey Morenoff, a former student of Sampson's at University of Chicago. The findings of these initial empirical tests led to further elaboration of collective efficacy theory, and this chapter details such revisions. In a final major section of the chapter, recent challenges to collective efficacy theory are articulated.

Resident-Based Crime Control in the Contemporary Community: An Overview of Collective Efficacy Theory

Collective efficacy theory is a close cousin to the systemic model—the topic of Chapter 3. Similar to the systemic model, collective efficacy theory descends from Kornhauser's notion that residents' use of informal social control is key in explaining why disadvantaged and unstable communities often suffer high rates of crime. However, it departs from the systemic model by looking beyond networks of social ties as the source of effective control.

Largely led by the intellectual efforts of Sampson and colleagues, collective efficacy theory emerged in the late 1990s when empirical evidence was mounting against the idea that social ties (especially interpersonal ties) could consistently account for variation in neighborhood crime. The main dilemma was that strong intracommunity ties (private ties, in particular), which lay at the heart of the systemic notion of social control, did not always appear to produce lower rates of crime. In particular, research showed that poor, minority communities were contexts in which friendship and kinship ties were often quite extensive but where crime flourished. At the other end of the spectrum, middle-class American suburbs typically enjoyed low rates of crime despite fostering anonymity as opposed to dense social ties. For example, suburban life was characterized by an extensive reliance on cross-community automotive travel for purposes of daily activities, thus minimizing face-to-face encounters among neighbors—encounters that occur readily when local pedestrian travel is the norm instead. Moreover, the suburbs offered residents large, private lots, where they could effectively be cut off from their neighbors. In short, rather than forming close intracommunity private networks, many suburban dwellers were unlikely to even know, let alone associate with, their neighbors.

The disenchantment with the core tenet of the systemic model surrounding the importance of interpersonal ties led to several important new developments in the community crime literature around the turn of the twenty-first century. As already discussed in Chapter 3, some scholars (e.g., Maria Vélez, Patrick Carr) responded to this disenchantment by widening the focus of the systemic-control model to emphasize the importance of public ties and private/parochial-public partnerships above and beyond private ties. This broader focus helped alleviate some of the systemic model's problems. After all, disadvantaged crime-ridden communities might experience strong private ties, but they were often sorely lacking in parochial and public ties. Quite the opposite situation seemed to exist in middle-class communities. While suburban residents rarely formed strong friendships, their educational and occupational statuses created networks with longer reach and more organizational, political, and economic clout. Thus, elevating the stature of parochial and public ties has proven a worthwhile pursuit in attempts to address the shortcomings of the systemic model.

Another path to addressing the shortcomings of the systemic model involves the development of collective efficacy theory (Morenoff, Sampson, and Raudenbush, 2001; Sampson, 2002, 2006, 2012; Sampson, Raudenbush, and Earls, 1997). Collective efficacy theory accepts the systemic model's underlying premise suggesting that crime is a function of variation in community-level informal social control. However, it rejects "systems of ties" as the central construct and offers instead "collective efficacy." Sampson observes that collective efficacy, "draws together two fundamental mechanisms—*social cohesion* (the 'collectivity' part of the concept) and *shared expectations for control* (the 'efficacy' part of the concept)" (2012, p. 152; see also, Sampson et al., 1997; Sampson, 2002, 2006, 2012; Warner and Sampson, 2015). According to collective efficacy theory, communities need not have dense interpersonal ties for effective community control. Rather, strong resident-based social control emerges in contexts where (1) there is some level of social cohesion *rooted in working trust and mutual support* (rather than strong friendships); and (2) shared expectations for action when community well-being is at stake. Thus, the systemic model relied on the notion that informal social control of crime emerged from "the accumulation of stocks of social resources as found in ties and member-ships" (Sampson, 2006, p. 153). In contrast, collective efficacy theory suggests that crime control emerges from residents' willingness to work together and take action, regardless of friendship or other associational ties.

Collective efficacy theory was originally formulated in a seminal article by Sampson, Stephen Raudenbush, and Felton Earls, which appeared in *Science* in 1997. According to that original statement of the theory, collective efficacy should be stronger in communities experiencing economic advantage, few immigrant residents, and a stable resident population (Sampson, Raudenbush, and Earls, 1997). Conversely, the theory posited that neighborhoods characterized by concentrated disadvantage, large immigrant populations, and residential instability would suffer weak collective efficacy. In turn, communities with strong collective efficacy were expected to enjoy low rates of crime while neighborhoods with weak collective efficacy were theorized to experience higher levels of crime.

The Project on Human Development in Chicago Neighborhoods and the Birth of Collective Efficacy Theory

The emergence of collective efficacy theory cannot be understood apart from the data that yielded the first ever measure of this new construct. The data that served as the basis for Sampson, Raudenbush, and Earls's article in *Science*

were part of the larger Project on Human Development in Chicago Neighborhoods (PHDCN). The PHDCN was a large, interdisciplinary project with
a focus on understanding human development in community context
(Sampson, 2002). Felton Earls, a child psychiatrist from Harvard, was the
principal investigator on the project. Scientific directors included Sampson,
Raudenbush, Terrie Moffitt, and Albert Reiss. Since the overall objective
included an understanding of developmental pathways in and out of crime,
the project incorporated a longitudinal study of multiple cohorts of youths
(ranging in age from zero to eighteen) and their families. Further, since
the developmental pathways were intended to be understood "in context,"
the project necessitated the sampling of youths from a variety of community
contexts. Although the original plan of the study was to sample cohorts from
neighborhoods in multiple cities, budget restrictions necessitated a focus
on neighborhoods in just one city; Chicago was ultimately chosen as the site
(Sampson, 2012). In order to gain a full picture of the community contexts of
the Chicago youths sampled, a community survey was undertaken as part
of the larger project. The community survey consisted of home interviews of
8,782 residents across 343 "neighborhood clusters"—combinations of contigu-
ous census tracts, similar on key census characteristics (Sampson, Raudenbush, and Earls, 1997). As Sampson (2002, p. 218) describes:

> The *Community Survey* (CS) was a multi-dimensional assessment by
> Chicago residents of the structural and cultural organization of their
> neighborhoods. The idea was to use residents as informants about
> neighborhood context using a clustered survey approach, or what
> one might think of as contextual sampling. The design yielded a
> representative probability sample and a large enough within-cluster
> sample to create reliable between-neighborhood measures of social-
> organizational dynamics.

The community survey itself was a landmark study for community-level
research. At the time the PHDCN was starting, relatively few data sets
existed that offered scholars the ability to study, on a large sample of neighborhoods, community-level measures of the social and cultural processes
implicit in the social disorganization tradition. In fact, until the emergence
of the PHDCN, most studies of community crime relied on the British
Crime Survey, administered in more than two hundred electoral wards (e.g.,
Lowenkamp, Cullen, and Pratt, 2003; Sampson and Groves, 1989; Veysey
and Messner, 1999); the Police Services Study conducted across sixty Saint
Louis, Tampa/Saint Petersburg, and Rochester neighborhoods (Bellair, 1997;
Vélez, 2001; Wilcox Rountree and Land, 2000); and victimization survey
data from more than five thousand residents in three hundred block pairs

within one hundred Seattle census tracts (Markowitz et al., 2001; Warner and Wilcox Rountree, 1997; Wilcox Rountree and Warner, 1999; Wilcox Rountree, Land, and Miethe, 1994).

Although such surveys were cutting-edge at the time of their administration, they were nonetheless limited in terms of the measurement of social ties and social control. These concepts were simply not the primary focus. Therefore, the extent of private ties was typically measured by a few survey items asking about whether relatives lived nearby, the frequency with which respondents got together with their neighbors, or the extent to which neighbors borrowed things from one another or helped one another with problems. Informal social control, if measured at all, was typically assessed by asking respondents whether they watched neighbors' property or participated in crime prevention groups. The Community Survey as part of the PHDCN dramatically improved this situation, offering more detailed measurement of processes surrounding the informal social control of crime (discussed more fully below). Moreover, the Community Survey was not the only source of community-level data that were gathered as part of the PHDCN. The project also included a component that involved systematic social observation of 23,000 street segments in a subsample of 80 of the 343 Chicago neighborhood clusters mentioned above (see Chapter 6). Streets were videotaped and carefully coded for information pertaining to land uses; the physical condition of the streets, buildings, and vehicles; and social interactions (e.g., harassment, public intoxication).

Analysis of data from the various components of the PHDCN has become somewhat commonplace in the field of criminology today, but Sampson, Raudenbush, and Earls's 1997 publication in *Science* is widely recognized as the first major article on community crime using the data (but see also Sampson, 1997). The article, entitled "Neighborhoods and Violent Crime: A Multilevel Study of Collective Efficacy," set out to measure *social cohesion and trust* and *informal social control* based on aggregating (within neighborhoods) residents' responses to ten survey items from the Community Survey portion of the PHDCN. More specifically, *social cohesion and trust* was measured by five items, asking residents to rate the extent to which they thought (1) their neighbors were willing to help one another, (2) the neighborhood was close-knit, (3) neighbors were trustworthy, (4) neighbors got along with one another, and (5) neighbors shared the same values. The measurement of *informal social control*, on the other hand, was based on residents' assessments about the likelihood that their neighbors could be counted on to intervene in the face of a variety of different problems: (1) children skipping school, (2) children tagging a local building, (3) children disrespecting an adult, (4) public fighting, and (5) a budget cut threatening to close a local fire station.

These two measures of *social cohesion and trust* and *informal social control* were ultimately combined for both empirical and theoretical reasons. First, empirically speaking, the two measures were highly correlated ($r = 0.80$, $p < .001$). Thus, at the neighborhood level, social cohesion and trust and informal social control were closely associated. As such, the two measures appeared to be tapping into a single latent construct. Theoretically, such a single latent construct made sense to Sampson and colleagues, who explain, "We also expected that the willingness and intention to intervene on behalf of the neighborhood would be enhanced under conditions of mutual trust and cohesion" (1997, p. 920). Thus, the two scales were combined into a summary measure that was labeled *collective efficacy.*

Again, collective efficacy theory views this measure that combines trust in neighbors and a shared willingness to intervene on behalf of the community as the key mediating mechanism between community social structure and community rates of crime. This thesis is in contrast to the systemic model, which views density of social ties as the key intervening mechanism between community social structure and community rates of crime. Moving the focus away from social ties and toward collective efficacy instead "signifies an emphasis on shared beliefs in neighbors' conjoint capability for action to achieve an intended effect, and hence an active sense of engagement on the part of residents" (see Sampson, 2002, p. 220; see also Sampson, 2006, 2012; Warner and Sampson, 2015). In essence, collective efficacy builds on the work of Albert Bandura and "extends the idea of self-efficacy to a collectivity" (Hipp, 2016, p. 33; see also Wickes et al., 2013). Collective efficacy's emphasis on *an expected, active sense of engagement* among neighbors makes the concept more dynamic and tied to agency in comparison to the concept of social ties. At the same time, engagement or action need not be behaviorally concrete for it to have an impact. In fact, Sampson and colleagues claim that relying only on behavioral displays of control confounds norms regarding action/engagement with opportunities for enactment of such norms. Thus, *expectations for action* are considered key:

> Collective efficacy theory view[s] shared perceptions about the neighborhood, including expectations of informal control, as mattering in and of themselves. . . . Indeed, counting up actual acts of crime control may actually be biased since controls appear only under conditions of challenge. Incidents of informal social control may be infrequent in neighborhoods with low crime rates, for example, but only because of the lack of need for such intervention" (Warner and Sampson, 2015, p. 226).

Warner and Sampson's (2015) recent review of collective efficacy theory highlights the point that conceptualizing efficacy in terms of expectations regarding rules of behavior offers a cultural component to the theory that was absent from the systemic model (with its key concept of social ties). More fully, the idea that there is variation in expectations for action across communities implies difference in the strength of commitment to conventional norms. In this way, the concept of collective efficacy (in particular, the "efficacy" part of the concept) overlaps with Kornhauser's suggestion that cultural strength (as opposed to cultural attenuation) is an aspect of effective social control. But, importantly, a strong culture of upholding norms, as reflected in "efficacy," is rooted in social ties in the form of working trust and social interaction (the "collective" part of the concept). In this way, collective efficacy represents a theory that incorporates both structural and cultural dimensions into its key construct.

Overall, through its explicit recognition that friendship and kinship ties do not serve as the heart of contemporary community life perhaps the way they once did, collective efficacy theory is said to modernize the social disorganization tradition (the systemic model, most specifically). Collective efficacy implies that the essence of "community" is no longer a "complex system of friendship and kinship networks and formal and informal associational ties rooted in family life and on-going socialization processes" (Kasarda and Janowitz, 1974, p. 329). In short, communities are no longer the idyllic urban villages that they might have been in the twentieth century (Sampson, 2006). Instead, community life is relatively anonymous, with residents as likely to be e-connected to people half-way around the world as they are connected to their neighbors. Nonetheless, the modern community is still very much a system that residents rely on for social good, though focusing on collective efficacy rather than neighbor networks in order to understand community control of crime is likely more compatible with the realities of today's urban life.

Community listservs and message boards provide interesting illustrations about how community control has changed in this era of collective efficacy as opposed to thick private ties. In contrast to the inconvenience of building strong personal within-neighborhood networks in today's increasingly busy world, many residents find it quite easy (and preferable) to communicate with neighbors through online forums. Listservs and similar forums are used to provide recommendations regarding contracted work (i.e., plumbers, roofers, electricians), to spread news about neighborhood events (yard sales, block parties, club meetings), and to discuss problems and potential solutions to neighborhood problems.

Box 8.1 presents excerpts from a neighborhood listserv hosted by a greater Cincinnati community. The excerpts illustrate how collective efficacy was manifested to address an issue that had arisen and was disturbing to a number of residents—a neighborhood cat was observed to be stuck in a tree.

BOX 8.1 COLLECTIVE EFFICACY SAVES THE CAT

On July 5, 2012, at 11:13 a.m., "Angela" wrote:
This morning I became aware of a cat stuck up very high in a large tree in front of my house on Maple Ave. The cat is maybe 30 feet up. It is mostly white with a gray tail—looks malnourished. I can see that it does have a collar on though.

A neighbor said it's been up there for several days. Another neighbor put a few ladders together for it to climb down (with no luck). I put some food at the bottom as well. I also called the fire department to ask for their help. However, they said it was too dangerous for them to help in a situation like this.

So . . . is anyone missing a cat? Does anyone have any ideas on getting the cat down? Email me directly, as I'm not likely to be checking back here often-Thanks, Angela

A reply from a neighbor, "Erin," also of Maple Avenue:
This is a very sad situation. With the heat, this cat will not last too much longer. The nice guys from "The Painting Company" tried to get to her but the cat is afraid. It would be so nice if we could get some help from the city or fire department! Time is of the essence and this is sad to watch. We are at the end of the street if anyone can help! The cat is 30 ft up!—Erin

Another reply from someone on the neighborhood listserv, street of residence unknown:
Has anyone checked with animal control or the SPCA? They might be able to help.

Another reply from someone on the neighborhood listserv, street of residence unknown:
How high up is the critter, and is it mean, had its rabies shots?
I have a 40 foot ladder if someone would hold it, if it's not too close to the power lines.
You could call "Deckaid" they have a bucket truck and would love the publicity.
Does anyone know why cats do that? Where are all the animal Psychics when we need them?
I'm good with dogs and frogs, but not too good with cats(allergic).

A later reply from someone on the neighborhood listserv, street of residence unknown:
Does anyone have an update on the poor cat?

A reply to the listserv from a local district court judge:
The cat in the tree on Maple was rescued in quite a dramatic fashion this evening by the fire department. Afterward, a very kind Erin took him to a vet for an

(continued)

BOX 8.1 (continued)

assessment. The vet gave all the care for free! He was given an IV and some food to help him recover. It turns out he is friendly. The little guy just needed some luck and basic care!

Mostly white, he has a gray tail and one blue eye and one yellow eye. The vet thinks he's about 1½ years old, not neutered, and has claws. He was found with a faded collar that has two tiny bells attached.

We would obviously love to find his home. Erin will keep him for a day or two, but neither of us can take him in permanently. If anyone knows who he may belong to or has room for a new kitty (with a wonderfully dramatic story) please let me know.

Of course, a cat being stuck in a tree is a noncrime issue. However, the posts to the listserv regarding this issue illustrate well the way in which collective efforts to solve a problem can emerge among a group of people who seem to have working trust in one another and shared expectations about community well-being, including the safety of neighborhood pets! As is seen by the posts to the listserv (among people who may not be well acquainted with one another beyond the virtual world), many in the neighborhood were posing concern and potential solutions to this problem. Community action ultimately prompted a judge on the list to call on the local fire department to rescue the cat, with a local vet then offering free care, and "Erin" fostering the cat until a permanent home was located.

Assessing Collective Efficacy Theory: Initial Tests

Sampson, Raudenbush, and Earls (1997) used the concept of collective efficacy to help explain the link between neighborhood-level indicators of concentrated disadvantage, immigrant concentration, and residential stability (all from census data) and three different measures of crime: (1) perceptions of neighborhood violence (based on survey responses); (2) violent victimization (again, based on survey responses); and (3) officially recorded incidents of homicide. In an analysis of 343 Chicago neighborhood clusters (but controlling for individual respondent differences), collective efficacy proved a robust and strong negative correlate across measures of neighborhood crime. In short, as collective efficacy increased, neighborhood-level perceptions of violence, reports of victimization, and officially recorded homicides all decreased. Furthermore, collective efficacy mediated a substantial portion of the effects of concentrated disadvantage, immigrant concentration, and residential mobility on the various crime measures. As such, collective efficacy

helped explain the correlations between the neighborhood structural characteristics and the measures of crime. Supplemental analyses by Sampson,
Raudenbush, and Earls (1997) also showed that the effect of collective efficacy
was a stronger predictor of neighborhood crime in comparison to social processes emphasized in the systemic model—namely, friendship and kinship
ties (private ties), organizational ties (parochial ties), and neighborhood services (public ties).

Though this initial study indicated that collective efficacy's effects
appeared quite robust, subsequent research has provided evidence that such
effects can be bolstered or attenuated, depending on levels of collective efficacy and crime in spatially adjacent areas. Briefly, Morenoff, Sampson, and
Raudenbush (2001) found that crime was tied to not only collective efficacy
in that focal community but also to levels of collective efficacy and crime in
surrounding communities (i.e., "spatial proximity" effects). In addition to
highlighting the potential for spatial proximity to moderate the effects of
focal neighborhood collective efficacy on focal neighborhood crime, the
analysis provided by Morenoff and colleagues also clarified the relationships between private and parochial ties and collective efficacy, thus serving
to explicitly integrate systemic theory and collective efficacy theory. In particular, they found that social ties and organizational participation were
indirectly related to crime through collective efficacy. In other words, private
and parochial ties fostered the emergence of collective efficacy which, in
turn, reduced community rates of homicide. Finally, though also touched on
in Sampson and colleagues' original test of the theory, Morenoff and colleagues' subsequent study provided further and more explicit evidence that
collective efficacy and community crime are likely reciprocally related. Specifically, their analysis showed that prior levels of crime were negatively related
to collective efficacy, and in turn, collective efficacy was negatively related to
subsequent crime.

A Refined Conceptualization

The findings stemming from the research discussed above by Morenoff,
Sampson, and Raudenbush served as the basis for further refinement of the
initial conceptualization of collective efficacy theory put forth in the landmark Sampson, Raudenbush, and Earls (1997) work. In fact, in a 2006 chapter, Sampson was tasked with taking stock of collective efficacy theory to
date. His revised model is presented in Figure 8.1. It is possible to summarize
this model by listing the following propositions:

1. Concentrated disadvantage and residential instability reduce collective efficacy.

2. Dense social ties and organizational participation (i.e., private and parochial ties) increase collective efficacy.
3. Collective efficacy, in turn, decreases community crime.
4. A "feedback effect" exists whereby crime negatively affects subsequent levels of collective efficacy.
5. Characteristics of adjacent areas, including their levels of crime and collective efficacy, affect community crime.
6. Spatial location within the broader urban milieu also conditions the effects of collective efficacy on community crime. For instance, collective efficacy is expected to more strongly reduce community crime when the community in question is spatially proximal to low-crime, high-collective efficacy communities. In contrast, collective efficacy's crime-controlling function is expected to be attenuated when the community in question is spatially proximal to neighborhoods with high crime and/or low collective efficacy.

Thus, the core causal model of collective efficacy theory set forth in the original 1997 article remains in place today. Specifically, the theory proposes that in any community, the level of concentrated disadvantage and residen-

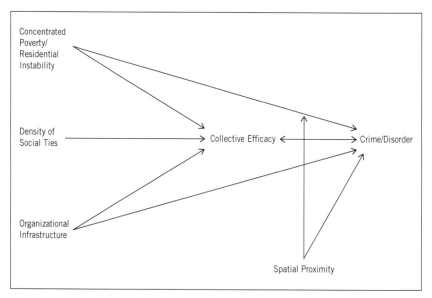

Figure 8.1 Collective Efficacy Theory
Copyright (c) 2006 from "Collective Efficacy Theory: Lessons Learned and Directions for Future Inquiry" by Robert J. Sampson in *Taking Stock: The Status of Criminological Theory* by F. T. Cullen, J. P. Wright, and K. R. Blevins (eds.). Reproduced by permission of Taylor and Francis Group, LLC, a division of Informa plc.

tial instability determines the level of collective efficacy. In turn, the level of collective efficacy determines the level of crime in that community. Still, Sampson's (2006) article—and the propositions presented above—suggest three important refinements. Additional important linkages are now specified more explicitly in the theory.

First, private and parochial ties are theorized to exert indirect effects on crime, thus integrating key concepts from the systemic model into collective efficacy theory. In particular, collective efficacy theory suggests that friendship networks and levels of organizational participation affect crime indirectly, through their more proximal effects on collective efficacy. Thus, private and institutional ties may foster the development of collective efficacy (which affects crime), but they themselves are not independently related to crime.

Second, the revised conceptualization of the theory explicitly recognizes the potential endogeneity of collective efficacy in relation to crime. In other words, while the theory is still primarily interested in the causal effect of collective efficacy on crime, it does specify that there is probable reciprocity regarding this relationship, with previous levels of crime likely influencing a community's level of collective efficacy (Sampson, Raudenbush, and Earls, 1997; Morenoff, Sampson, and Raudenbush, 2001).

Third, collective efficacy theory embraces the notion of neighborhood spatial interdependence—neighborhoods are viewed as functionally interwoven as opposed to islands unto themselves (see, in particular, Morenoff, Sampson, and Raudenbush, 2001). Therefore, collective efficacy and crime in adjacent neighborhoods are expected to affect crime in focal neighborhoods, net of focal neighborhood characteristics. Furthermore, crime and collective efficacy in adjacent neighborhoods are expected to moderate effects of focal neighborhood characteristics, including collective efficacy, on focal neighborhood crime.

Collective Efficacy Theory and the Immigrant Paradox

The propositions of collective efficacy theory reviewed in the section above largely represent an elaboration of Sampson, Raudenbush, and Earls's (1997) original statement of the theory, with several effects (i.e., model paths) being explicitly *added* to the theory based upon empirical findings that had emerged since. However, the revised version of the theory also differs in that it *subtracted* one of the original predicted effects from the model: the effect of immigration.

Dating back to the early work of the Chicago School, theories on communities and crime had often suggested that immigration might disrupt community organization (e.g., by increasing residential mobility and population heterogeneity), making neighborhoods more vulnerable to crime (Shaw and McKay, 1942). Similarly, Sampson, Raudenbush, and Earls (1997) originally posited that immigrant concentration should negatively affect collective efficacy, which in turn would foster greater levels of community violence. The analysis they presented provided initial support for those hypotheses, showing that Chicago neighborhoods with larger immigrant concentrations tended to have lower levels of collective efficacy and higher levels of violence. However, their subsequent multivariate analyses (in the same 1997 article) revealed a more mixed and complex picture of immigrant concentration effects on community measures of crime.

Specifically, once they controlled for collective efficacy, immigrant concentration had a positive effect on rates of violent victimization but a null effect on perceived neighborhood violence and homicide counts. On the one hand, such findings were somewhat unsurprising since collective efficacy was expected to mediate the effects of immigration. On the other hand, this "mixed evidence" regarding the effect of immigrant concentration on community crime, net of collective efficacy, was a precursor of sorts for the debate that would ensue over the coming decades regarding the immigration-community crime relationship.

At nearly the same time that Sampson and colleagues were developing their theory of collective efficacy, immigration to the United States (largely from Central and South America) began to escalate to levels not seen since the European migration of the early 1900s. Both lawmakers and the American public became increasingly concerned that rising levels of immigration would generate crime and social problems in U.S. communities. In response to these concerns, criminologists began to explore the relationships between immigration and crime for this newest wave of migration. This line of research began in the 1990s with a slow trickle of analyses from several early pioneers, which included Sampson and colleagues (Sampson, Raudenbush and Earls, 1997; Sampson, Morenoff, and Raudenbush, 2005; see also Hagan and Palloni, 1999; Lee, Martinez, and Rosenfeld, 2001; Martinez, 2002; Martinez and Lee, 2000), but would soon escalate into a flood of more than fifty empirical studies examining the immigration-crime nexus. Overall, this burgeoning body of work has led to a reversal of the relationship posited in collective efficacy theory's initial test—that immigrant concentration would be positively related to community crime via weakened collective efficacy.

Instead, and in contrast to widespread public concerns, research has overwhelmingly shown that immigration is *not* linked to increased levels of community crime and disorder (see reviews in Feldmeyer, Harris, and Scroggins, 2015; Feldmeyer et al., 2017; Kubrin, 2013; Ousey and Kubrin, 2009, in press). Rather, studies typically indicate that immigration has either null or crime-reducing effects. Perhaps more notably, immigrant neighborhoods have been shown to have remarkably low levels of crime, even in the face of severe poverty and structural disadvantage—a finding that has become known as the "immigrant paradox" (or Latino paradox). Furthermore, this paradox does not seem to be limited exclusively to crime. Public health literature shows that immigrant communities have surprisingly low rates of mental illness, physical illness, and substance use, despite having multiple disadvantages and risk factors (see Rumbaut and Ewing, 2007; Sam et al., 2006; Vaughn et al., 2014). Thus, there is now a growing consensus among scholars that immigration is not a key source of neighborhood offending and instead tends to have protective (or at worst neutral) effects on community levels of crime and social problems.

To explain this immigrant paradox, scholars, including Sampson and colleagues, argue that a process of "immigrant revitalization" has been occurring throughout many ethnic communities, in which immigration insulates neighborhoods from crime and disadvantage. Rather than destabilizing neighborhoods, disrupting social cohesion, and creating disorganization, immigration actually seems to bolster social networks and add to community stability. Researchers note that patterns of chain migration, in which new migrants settle near family and friends in established immigrant neighborhoods, have helped create strong sets of kinship ties and dense networks of social capital and social support in many immigrant enclaves (Feldmeyer, 2009; Martinez, 2002; Sampson, 2008). In addition, immigration has been shown to attract employers and businesses, reinforce traditional family structures, and foster connections to protective institutions (e.g., the Catholic Church), which may help strengthen communities and reduce social problems like crime (see reviews in Feldmeyer, Harris, and Scroggins, 2015; Feldmeyer et al., 2017; Ousey and Kubrin, 2009, in press; Sampson, 2008). In other words, research increasingly suggests that immigration is a source of community organization and social control, rather than a source of social disorganization and crime as once thought.

Sampson and colleagues were among those early scholars that helped identify the immigrant paradox and advance arguments about immigrant revitalization. Thus, it was through portions of this work that they began to reconsider the ways that immigration might intersect with collective efficacy and crime. By 2006, in his chapter taking stock of the current state of collective efficacy, Sampson had pulled immigration from the conceptual model of his theory and no longer included it as one of the sources of reduced collective efficacy as he had in 1997. Similarly, in a chapter published in Peterson, Krivo, and Hagan's book, *The Many Colors of Crime*, Sampson and Bean (2006, p. 21) began to more vocally suggest that immigration was a likely source of community organization rather than instability, noting that "in today's world it is no longer tenable to assume that immigration and diversity automatically lead to social disorganization and consequently crime." Perhaps the clearest indication of Sampson's changing thoughts on immigration, collective efficacy, and community stability was provided in his 2008 *Contexts* article, which has become one of the most highly cited articles on immigration and crime to date. Here he summarizes the protective effects of immigration on neighborhood violence observed in his earlier work using the PHDCN data (Sampson, Morenoff, and Raudenbush, 2005) and suggests that immigration may actually have contributed to the great crime decline of the early twenty-first century. He argues that immigration is no longer the engine for urban disorder and crime that scholars once portrayed it as being. Instead, Sampson (2008, p. 30) suggests that immigration is more likely a catalyst for community revitalization and increased social organization, ultimately leading him to conclude that, "Cities of concentrated immigration are some of the safest places around."

Collective Efficacy Theory: Potential Limitations and New Directions

Following the initial influential studies by Sampson, Morenoff, and colleagues, subsequent research using the PHDCN provides additional support for collective efficacy's effect on various community crime measures, particularly those tapping rates of neighborhood-based crime events (e.g., Browning, 2002; Kirk and Papachristos, 2011; Wright and Benson, 2011). Further, there is mounting evidence that collective efficacy affects neighborhood crime or victimization events in other countries, including Sweden (Sampson and Wikström, 2008), Australia (Mazerolle, Wickes, and McBroom, 2010), and China (Jiang, Land, and Wang, 2013; Zhang, Messner, and Liu, 2007). Yet despite substantial support for collective efficacy theory in explaining community crime in the modern era, there is also evidence that collective efficacy theory may not generalize completely to all cultural contexts (Bruinsma et al., 2013; Chouhy, 2016). Likewise, there is evidence that there are some limits to the theory's utility even within cultural contexts where it has found support. In this section, we discuss some of this evidence while also examining new theoretical developments paralleling collective efficacy theory that offer promise for a continually evolving perspective of community crime.

The Conditionality of the Collective Efficacy-Control Linkage

There is evidence that the effects of collective efficacy may be conditional on neighborhood-level social ties. For example, using the PHDCN data, Christopher Browning and colleagues found that collective efficacy's ability to reduce crime was attenuated in the presence of strong social ties (Browning, 2009; Browning, Dietz, and Feinberg, 2004). They attributed this conditional effect to "negotiated coexistence" between law-abiding and criminal residents. In contexts where the personal networks of law-abiding and law-violating citizens are intertwined, strong ties might actually provide social capital for the law violators, thereby compromising the expected effect of collective efficacy (see also the ethnographic work by Pattillo [1998] and Venkatesh [1997], discussed in Chapter 3). Social networks linking conventional and criminal residents, and accompanying social exchange, foster collective efficacy. But such networks also pose challenges for collective efforts to control crime. As Browning (2009, p. 1560) suggests, "strong social ties among constituents of collectivities are likely to contribute to the strength of shared norms but also limit the severity of sanctions when norms are violated." In other words, communities that otherwise exhibit a strong willingness to act on behalf of the social good might be unwilling to intervene in the illicit activities involving people to whom many residents are closely tied.

Thus, the evidence that Browning and colleagues present suggests that shared norms about control do not always translate into actual engagement in informal social control. In fact, several studies have more explicitly examined the link between collective efficacy and control actions, and they find that this linkage might be tenuous. For example, a recent Australian study by Rebecca Wickes and colleagues (2017) examined the effect of neighborhood collective efficacy on residents' actual engagement in informal social control when faced with significant neighborhood problems. The sorts of social control actions that they examined were classified as "parochial social control," and "public social control." Parochial control included actions such as direct intervention, discussing the problem with neighbors, and contacting a community group. Public control included behaviors such as contacting a local council or government agency and calling the police. Findings revealed that collective efficacy was unrelated to either parochial or public control actions on the part of residents faced with problems. Somewhat similarly, an earlier U.S.-based study by Barbara Warner (2007) indicated that a measure of neighborhood-level social cohesion and trust was unrelated to residents directly intervening (i.e., parochial control) when faced with a problem with a neighbor. Furthermore, "social cohesion and trust" was actually negatively associated with contacting formal authorities (i.e., public control) in cases of neighbor problems.

In sum, collective efficacy theory assumes that expectations for action among residents translate into engagement of control when problems arise, but that important linkage has not received full support. The recent findings that challenge that relationship have led some scholars to emphasize the process of negotiated coexistence, whereby the nature of social ties might condition the collective efficacy-control linkage (e.g., Browning, 2009; Browning,

Dietz, and Feinberg, 2004). However, others call for greater clarity in the concept of collective efficacy itself. In particular, some have suggested that the field needs to move toward conceptualizing collective efficacy as a task-specific process as opposed to a general perception of a neighborhood's ability and willingness to respond to social problems of any form. Quite simply, community action can take many different forms and can emerge in response to myriad problems. Thus, is a global concept regarding action sufficient? Rebecca Wickes and her colleagues (2013, p. 125) suggest not: "Scholarship focusing on collective efficacy needs to now consider the task at hand, the degree to which the task requires collective versus individual action, and the extent to which certain residents—and certain neighborhoods—may differ in their sense of a collective ability to engage in different tasks."

Effects on Offending versus Offenses: Is Collective Efficacy a Developmental or Situational Theory?

To date, much evidence has emerged to support the effect of collective efficacy on rates of crime events (or offense incidents), but there is limited corresponding evidence that collective efficacy is related to self-reported offending. More specifically, a careful review of the literature on collective efficacy theory indicates that most support to date stems from studies estimating its effects on neighborhood-based offense incidents (e.g., homicide counts, reports of victimization in the neighborhood, neighborhood perception of crime). In contrast, studies that examine the effects of collective efficacy on rates of offending behavior among neighborhood residents (e.g., arrests among residents, residents' self-reported criminal behavior) often find null effects (Kirk, 2008; Sampson, Morenoff, and Raudenbush, 2005; but see Maimon and Browning, 2010).

Such findings call into question whether collective efficacy is about controlling the development of criminality among neighborhood residents or, instead, is about the situational control of crime incidents within neighborhood space (see discussions in Kirk, 2009; McNeeley and Wilcox, 2015; Sampson, 2006; Wilcox and Land, 2015; Wilcox and Swartz, in press). If conceived as "criminality control," then collective efficacy is presumed to involve the collective pro-social development of residents, which should, in turn, affect residents' behavior even when they leave neighborhood boundaries—this is control akin to Felson's notion of "stage-one control," as discussed in Chapter 7. On the other hand, if collective efficacy is conceived as "crime-incident control," then it involves group-level intervention within neighborhood space, thereby reducing opportunities for offenses to be carried out successfully within the space, regardless of whether the would-be perpetrators actually reside there. This latter form of control is analogous to what Felson referred to as "stage-two control" (see Chapter 7).

In short, the question remains: Does collective efficacy involve control of criminality or control of crime events? As discussed in Chapter 7, theories addressing social control (such as collective efficacy theory), have historically been treated as theories of criminality. Such treatment dates back to Shaw and McKay's work correlating neighborhood conditions to rates of juvenile *offending behavior*, not community-specific rates of crime events (i.e., their maps of "delinquency" plotted home addresses of known delinquents rather than locations of crime incidents). However, contemporary tests of collective efficacy theory often implicitly allow for situational effects by using dependent variables measured as incident rates of crime or victimization. And, as reviewed above, the literature is quite supportive of such effects, while it is less supportive of collective efficacy's effects on offending. As such, collective efficacy may operate most effectively as a form of collective opportunity-reduction or problem-solving akin to situational crime prevention (e.g., Eck and Guerette, 2012; Smith and Clarke, 2012), though this issue is certainly not resolved.

It is worth noting that collective efficacy need not be viewed as *either* control of the development of criminality *or* situational control of crime incidents (Bursik, 1988; Felson, 1994). Instead, the answer to the question, "Is collective efficacy theory a theory of criminality or one of crime events?" could be: "Both." Adapting Wilcox and Land's (2015, p. 252) illustration of social disorganization theory as one of criminality and crime events, Figure 8.2 depicts a dual conceptualization of collective efficacy theory. As suggested above, this dual conceptualization of collective efficacy theory is rooted in Marcus Felson's explication of informal social control as a two-stage process (see also Chapter 7). In applying Felson's ideas about the two stages of control to collective efficacy theory, stage-one collective efficacy serves to provide communities with strong aggregate attachments and commitments and strong cultural beliefs. In such contexts, the development of criminality among community residents should be minimal. Next, second-stage collective efficacy provides effective collective guardianship and problem-solving, thus reducing the opportunity for crime events to occur locally. The dual role of collective efficacy depicted in Figure 8.2 thus views the concept as useful in explaining both community-level patterning of criminality and community-level opportunity for crime events. Despite the advantages of a theory being able to account for both processes, it is important to reiterate the point from Chapter 7 that scholars studying theories of criminality and theories of crime events have traditionally looked past one another. Those working in these respective camps have not universally embraced ideas and concepts from the other, so there is still important debate about the validity of suggesting that collective efficacy theory can be useful to both theoretical camps (e.g., Braga and Clarke, 2014).

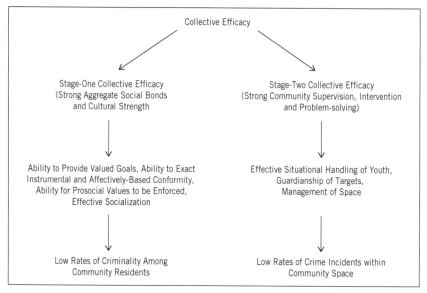

Figure 8.2 Collective Efficacy: A Theory of Criminality and Crime Events
Adapted from P. Wilcox and K. C. Land, "Social Disorganization and Criminal Opportunity," in
*Challenging Criminological Theory: The Legacy of Ruth Rosner Kornhauser, Advances in Criminological
Theory*, ed. F. T. Cullen, P. Wilcox, R. J. Sampson, and B. Dooley, vol. 17, *Advances in Criminological
Theory* (New Brunswick, NJ: Transaction, 2015), p. 252.

At What Time Scale Does Collective Efficacy Operate?

Overlapping with the debate surrounding whether collective efficacy affects
the opportunity for crime events versus the development of criminality is the
question about the time scale associated with collective efficacy's effects. John
Hipp and Rebecca Wickes (in press) raise this issue in a very recent study
using multiple waves of survey, census, and crime incident data from 148
Brisbane, Australia, neighborhoods. Using a crime event measure as an
outcome variable (i.e., violent crime incidents), they explore the "proper
causal time length" regarding the relationship between collective efficacy
and violent crime. Does collective efficacy work to disrupt crime incidents
in the very short term, or does collective efficacy have a longer-term effect on
crime? Hipp and Wickes examine this question through three different
specifications—each based on a unique set of assumptions about the appropriate time scale associated with collective efficacy's effect on crime incidents. One
model estimated a "simultaneous" effect of collective efficacy on violence, consistent with collective efficacy being a highly situational process. Two additional models specified collective efficacy as having two-year and five-year
lagged effects on violent crime, respectively. Both of these "lagged-effect"

models were intended to capture enduring effects of collective efficacy on violent incidents within a community, albeit at different time scales.

Interestingly, *none* of the models estimated by Hipp and Wickes supported a direct linkage between collective efficacy and lower crime. Instead, collective efficacy only seemed to lower violent crime through a complex dynamic process in which neighborhoods with lower collective efficacy experienced greater concentrated disadvantage over time, which, in turn, increased subsequent violence. In sum, in arguably the only test to date of the effects of collective efficacy at various time scales, Hipp and Wickes find no evidence of simultaneous effects. They also find no evidence of lagged effects in terms of direct effects of collective efficacy at one point in time on subsequent violent crime. However, they do find evidence of indirect lagged effects of collective efficacy on violent crime, working through concentrated disadvantage. As such, this work challenges earlier research indicating simultaneous or short-term lagged effects of collective efficacy on crime and suggests an alternative process—one in which collective efficacy affects neighborhood crime over time, largely through its impacts on neighborhood disadvantage. Clearly, scholarship examining the temporal nature of collective efficacy's effects (like that of Hipp and Wickes) is in its infancy. However, that which exists raises additional important questions about the precise nature of the role of collective efficacy in neighborhood crime.

Integrating the Cultural Frame of Legal Cynicism

As mentioned above, collective efficacy theory has had a cultural dimension to it since its inception. The notion of shared expectations for control implicitly recognizes potential variation in values and attenuation of expectations for behavioral proscriptions. A parallel line of inquiry emerging in recent years on legal cynicism has addressed cultural attenuation more explicitly (see Chapter 5). As will be discussed here, empirical research examining the causes and consequence of legal cynicism possibly represents a challenge to collective efficacy theory (i.e., a theoretical competitor). Alternatively, it might provide an additional component to be integrated into a still-evolving collective efficacy theory.

As described in Chapter 5, David Kirk and Andrew Papachristos have been at the forefront of fully explicating and testing a theory of legal cynicism (see, e.g., Kirk and Papachristos, 2011, 2015). To recap, they described legal cynicism as the community-level cultural frame (rather than an individual view) that the police are illegitimate, nonresponsive to residents' needs and calls for assistance, and unable to adequately provide public safety. Legal cynicism restrains residents' available responses in threatening situations, making it seem necessary to take the law into their own hands and to resolve disputes without police involvement, often resulting in use of violence. Thus, many individuals who do not personally condone violence still might resort to violence in the context of a cultural frame of legal cynicism.

The antecedents and effects of legal cynicism have been examined using data from the PHDCN (Kirk and Papachristos, 2011; Sampson and Bartusch, 1998). This work shows that neighborhood structural characteristics, including concentrated disadvantage and residential mobility, predict legal cynicism. In turn, legal cynicism is positively related to neighborhood violence, net of individual attitudes toward violence (in fact, individual attitudes were shown by Kirk and Papachristos to be unrelated to neighborhood homicide counts). Perhaps most important for the purposes of this chapter, the effect of legal cynicism on neighborhood rates of violence appears to be reduced or attenuated once collective efficacy is controlled, though it still exhibits a significant effect. This suggests that legal cynicism affects community crime both directly and indirectly through collective efficacy. The indirect effect of legal cynicism makes sense in that "negative cultural frames toward the law deter neighborhood residents from collectively working to control crime" (Kirk and Papachristos, 2011, p. 1222). As such, while legal cynicism has been shown to be a cultural frame distinct from collective efficacy, it has also been suggested that it (negatively) affects collective efficacy and should potentially be integrated more fully with collective efficacy theory.

Further, although structural conditions (most specifically, concentrated disadvantage) appear to be associated with legal cynicism, Kirk and Papachristos also propose that this cultural frame may persist despite shifts in disadvantage and other structural conditions. Patterns of mass incarceration and prisoner reentry in the United States are offered as one of the main reasons for the persistence of legal cynicism even in the face of changing structural conditions. In particular, an era of mass incarceration has created a situation whereby large numbers of prisoners are taken from and returned to disadvantaged communities each year. The cultural view that criminal justice is inequitable seems almost inevitable in communities where residents see large numbers of people cycling in and out of prison, especially since these (former) offenders are likely immersed in the community's social networks. In turn, constantly disrupted social networks and accompanying legal cynicism would seemingly pose a never-ending challenge to the development of collective efficacy, leading to its perpetual absence.

On the other hand, it also seems possible to conceive of legal cynicism *positively* affecting collective efficacy. In this regard, the recent social movement #BlackLivesMatter seems salient. #BlackLivesMatter emerged as a result of legal cynicism (e.g., the growing disenchantment with police tactics in Black neighborhoods or in encounters with Black individuals). However, the cynicism created this positive movement for social change—a movement that might well be viewed as a form of collective efficacy. Research on #BlackLivesMatter is still in its infancy. Thus, we lack strong empirical evidence to assess whether legal cynicism can in fact contribute to greater collective efficacy as suggested here. Nonetheless, we see this as an important new direction for collective efficacy theory, and one that seems more consistent with the spirit of community resilience that marks the era in which collective efficacy theory was born.

Conclusion

The turn of the twenty-first century was marked by a new image of community, setting the stage for new theoretical developments in criminology. The modern image of community is that it is resilient, its crime is reducible, and its residents can exert human agency in a concerted effort to solve neighborhood problems. Collective efficacy theory emerged out of this image. This chapter traced the development of collective efficacy theory, which presented a "fix" to the problem of the systemic model—namely, that dense private ties were not consistently linked to strong informal social control in empirical studies. Collective efficacy theory de-emphasized private ties as the key source of informal social control. Instead, primacy was placed on social cohesion (rooted in working trust rather than thick ties) in combination with shared values and expectations for action under certain conditions.

To date, collective efficacy theory has received substantial support in the research literature. At the same time, research has revealed a number of challenges to the theory including evidence suggesting the following: (1) the effects of collective efficacy may be attenuated in certain contexts, such as those in which law-abiding citizens and offenders coexist, or in relation to certain community problems; (2) collective efficacy may be as (or more) important for situationally controlling crime incidents as opposed to or controlling the development of criminality; (3) the time scale at which collective efficacy operates to reduce crime remains a question; and (4) it is unclear whether (and under what conditions) collective efficacy is fueled or stifled by legal cynicism.

Despite the unresolved technical issues that surround collective efficacy theory, it provides an optimistic view of cities and their communities. It thus offers an upbeat ending to our seven-part narrative regarding images of communities and crime. In Chapter 9, we review those seven images and discuss new images that appear on the horizon.

9

Communities and Crime

Looking Ahead

W e started our journey regarding historically situated images of
communities and crime in Chapter 2 with the image of *community as socially disorganized*. This pessimistic view of urban communities emerged in an era of turbulent change due to the fast-paced growth
of cities. Images discussed in many other chapters were popular during an
era marked by the decline of urban America. In the middle part of the twentieth century, prominent cities were shrinking instead of swelling, and what
remained was often in disarray. This era coincided with still more dire
images of communities and crime—such as *community as truly disadvantaged, community as a criminal culture*, or *community as a broken window*.

However, as discussed in Chapter 8, many once-declining cities are
making a comeback. They are reinventing themselves to compete in a complex
twenty-first-century global economy and to serve the needs of a new generation of residents wanting to reconnect with the urban cores all but forgotten
by their parents. The optimism regarding city life in this most recent era,
especially among younger generations, aligns well with the spirit of cooperation implicit in collective efficacy theory—that despite the complex, global
world in which we now live, community well-being can be achieved through
relationships built on working trust and a shared willingness to act for the
common good when problems arise.

How long will *community as collective efficacy* last as the prevailing
image of communities and crime? What compelling images of community
will succeed it? Of course, we do not yet know the answer to these questions.

But we speculate future images might be guided by the following four themes: (1) community as multicontextual; (2) community as overcriminalized; (3) community as a racial divide; and (4) community beyond the urban core. Several of these themes were touched on in earlier chapters—as emerging yet underdeveloped issues that either challenged or offered promise for extending certain images of community. Here, we discuss more explicitly how these four themes provide guidance for the images of community that we might see more fully developed in criminology moving forward.

Community as Multicontextual

What is "community" in the context of studying "communities and crime"? More fully, at what unit of social life are the "community" effects discussed throughout this book actually operating? Recall that we briefly addressed the ambiguity surrounding the definition of community in Chapter 1. Despite the long history of theory and research on community influence, the fundamental issue of clearly defining the unit of analysis from which processes such as social disorganization, street culture, criminal opportunity, and collective efficacy are expected to emerge is still unresolved (Hipp and Boessen, 2013). In fact, we argue here that the conceptualization of "community" for understanding crime has perhaps gotten more, as opposed to less, ambiguous. Recent work has questioned long-held assumptions about community influence and has introduced fresh approaches using a variety of units of analysis. As such, we see the field moving away from a community criminology that offers a single, appropriate unit of analysis. Rather, we see an inevitable movement toward a multicontextual community criminology— one that recognizes as key a variety of environmental units spanning the micro to macro continuum. In this section, we outline what we see as historical movement toward this image of the multicontextual community.

The Traditional Approach

Many neighborhood theorists discussed throughout this book implicitly embraced the idea that community processes related to crime operate at a meso-level scale. The term *meso level* is consistent with "a geographical section of a larger community or region (e.g., city) that usually contains residents or institutions and has socially distinctive characteristics" (Sampson, 2012, p. 56; see also Hipp and Boessen, 2013). Most of the scholars whose work was reviewed here operationalized this conceptualization of community through the use of administrative units such as census tracts, clusters of tracts, or areas similar to clusters of tracts (e.g., zip codes, political districts)—all created with "social distinctiveness" in mind. Although such administrative units probably do not represent an exact match to residents' perceptions of "community," they have historically been accepted as representing reasonable approximations. However, this nonspecific meso-level conceptualization and operationalization of community has its critics. First among the challengers are proponents of a "criminology of place."

The Crime-and-Place Challenge

As discussed in Chapter 7, research in the past three decades has increasingly pointed to patterns of crime concentration at small-scale units within communities (i.e., along certain streets or at specific locations). Crime-and-place scholars have used evidence of within-community hot spots as reason to challenge the traditional conceptualization of "community influence." In particular, they suggest that hot spots can be observed because environmental influences occur at small, sub-neighborhood units of analysis, such as street segments or specific addresses. The thinking is that this patterning of crime would not exist if there were not important theoretical processes operating at the level of such small-scale units. Criminology of place scholars further argue that small-scale units of analysis such as street blocks and places are preferable in comparison to traditional meso-level units because they are clearly defined, are easily recognized, and are particularly salient in that they represent the immediate settings of crime events (e.g., Groff, 2015; Sherman, Gartin, and Buerger, 1989; Weisburd, Bernasco, and Bruinsma, 2009; Weisburd, Groff, and Yang, 2012).

Place-based scholarship has relied heavily on the concept of criminal opportunity to account for differences in crime across micro-spatial units (again, see Chapter 7). However, others have broadened the explanation to include processes of informal social control or collective efficacy—concepts that they view as overlapping with criminal opportunity and also as useful in understanding high-crime places (Taylor, 1997, 1998; Weisburd, Groff, and Yang, 2012). For example, drawing upon environmental psychology (e.g., Wicker, 1987), Taylor (1997, p. 134) recognizes that within-neighborhood physical and social variation at the block level creates multiple, unique "behavior settings," with particular implications for behavior related to block-level informal social control. He states, "People are less likely to sit out on higher traffic volume streets . . . and thus know their neighbors less well on those blocks. On cul-de-sacs, the lowest traffic volume streets, residents appear to be more socially cohesive" (1997, p. 134).

Building on Taylor's influential work, Weisburd, Groff, and Yang (2012, pp. 23–24) embrace the street block as the most appropriate geographic unit of analysis for studying various processes underlying the spatial variation in crime, including criminal opportunity and collective efficacy. Their justification is built on the belief that people on a street block are familiar with one another, and that this "awareness of the standing patterns of behavior of neighbors provides a basis from which action can be taken." Additionally, they state that the street block is the most relevant unit for the development of shared norms regarding appropriate behavior, due to the ease of interaction and observation (see also Groff, 2015). Ultimately, their study does find significant relationships between street-level crime and street-level measures of criminal opportunity and collective efficacy.

In short, work in the crime-and-place tradition has challenged the traditional meso-level conceptualization and operationalization of "community influence" by illustrating that many so-called community processes actually operate at micro-level contextual units. Similarly, other research has challenged the traditional, meso-level conceptualization of community influence on crime by pointing not to sub-neighborhood, micro-spatial processes but to *broader-scale* influences instead—or, influences beyond the traditional community unit of analysis. We turn to this challenge next.

The Macro-Context Challenge

What we term the "macro-context challenge" asserts that community crime is not just a function of characteristics of any single, meso-level community unit (such as a census tract), but is also linked to the characteristics of adjacent areas and the broader urban locale. This view has been articulated in a number of the theoretical developments discussed in the book's previous chapters. For example, research on both collective efficacy theory and criminal opportunity theories recognizes that geographic units in spatial proximity to one another are interdependent due to "spatial diffusion"—with influence not necessarily being bound by "community" boundaries but dispersing instead into nearby areas (e.g., Morenoff, Sampson, and Raudenbush, 2001; Sampson, 2006). Thus, many scholars no longer see "community influence" as only coming from within a single spatial unit; it also can come from spatially adjacent or proximal areas.

Beyond considerations of spatial adjacency/proximity, a good deal of other work reviewed in this book recognizes that meso-level community units are embedded in larger sociocultural, political-economic structures (i.e., cities) that impact community life. For example, as reviewed in Chapter 3, scholarship in the tradition of the systemic model recognizes that "extra-community" linkages and investment and control from beyond the neighborhood are vital to understanding crime (e.g., Bursik and Grasmick, 1993; Carr, 2003; Ramey and Shrider, 2014; Vélez, 2001; Vélez, Lyons, and Boursaw, 2012). Similarly, Chapter 4 illustrates how larger macro-level patterns of economic restructuring had profound effects on local communities and crime during the 1970s and 1980s. As Wilson (1987) suggested, soaring crime rates and truly disadvantaged circumstances in the urban core resulted less from what was happening within neighborhood boundaries than the broader socioeconomic shifts occurring throughout the country.

This call to consider macro-level context is not new within communities and crime research. Dating back to the work of Blau and Blau (1982) and the macro-level scholarship that followed (Harer and Steffensmeier, 1992; Land et al., 1990; Messner and Golden, 1992; Sampson, 1987), criminologists have looked to city-level context to better understand the ways in which crime varies across space, place, and community. Likewise, scholars have long acknowledged that neighborhood-level processes might operate differently if the same neighborhood was located in a different macro-level setting (i.e., state or city). However, data limitations have often made it difficult to examine these types of *intersections* between macro- and meso-level environments and effects. Specifically, meso-level data on neighborhoods have typically been limited to a single city (e.g., Chicago, Los Angeles), and thus have not allowed researchers to examine how neighborhood processes vary across cities. In contrast, macro-level crime data covering the 100 or 125 largest cities have provided little information about crime and social circumstances across neighborhoods (e.g., census tracts or block groups) within city boundaries.

However, new data and research have begun to unpack the macro-meso intersection and explore the macro-context challenge. Perhaps the most ambitious effort has come from Peterson, Krivo, and colleagues' (2010) development of the NNCS data, which offers information on more than ninety-five hundred neighborhoods across ninety-one cities (see Chapter 5). Although research exploring these data are still in the early phases of development, several studies have shown that macro-level environment shapes how local communities and crime operate. For example, in their initial analysis of the NNCS data, Peterson and Krivo (2010) found that neighborhood conditions alone could not explain race differences in serious violence. It was only after they accounted for the structural conditions of the neighborhood, surrounding neighborhoods, *and* the larger city-level context that structural conditions could more fully account for neighborhood differences in Black and White violence. Similarly, Lyons, Vélez, and Santoro (2013) found that the neighborhood-level effects of immigration on crime are highly dependent on the larger city-level political climate toward immigration. Furthermore, emerging research using the NNCS data suggests that city-level patterns of racial segregation shape census tract-level relationships between race, racial composition, and crime (Krivo et al., 2015).

Although these studies offer key advances in our understanding of the macro-context challenge, many questions remain. As the NNCS data become more widely used and other data on both city-level and neighborhood-level contexts are developed, a door will open for further inquiries into the macro-meso intersection. Thus far, however, early evidence indicates that neighborhoods are not islands unto themselves and are, at least in part, a product of their surrounding environments.

Toward the Multicontextual Community

Altogether, the various lines of inquiry mentioned above—inquiry related to micro-spatial influence and scholarship focused on proximal or broader-area influences—have led to an emerging image of community as consisting of multiple, interdependent contexts. Sampson (2012, p. 55) captures that view with his description of communities as "large and small; overlapping or blurred in perceptual boundaries; relational; and ever changing in composition." In line with a complex, multilevel view of community, there is currently a small body of explicitly multilevel scholarship. For example, as reviewed in Chapter 7, scholarship on "multilevel criminal opportunity" considers criminal opportunity for crime and victimization events as merging from both place-level and neighborhood-level characteristics (e.g., Deryol et al., 2016; Taylor, 1997; Tillyer and Tillyer, 2014; Wilcox, Madensen, and Tillyer, 2007; Wilcox, Gialopsos, and Land, 2013). Further, as just mentioned above, there is a growing body of multilevel work that embeds neighborhoods into broader contexts to explore how meso-level effects on crime are shaped by larger macro-level patterns of racial segregation (Krivo et al., 2015; Peterson and Krivo, 2010), immigrant context (Ramey, 2013), and political climate (Lyons, Vélez, and Santoro, 2013).

Given such precedent, we anticipate that the study of "community" processes will continue to be less and less shackled by an outdated view that important contextual influences on crime emerge from within a single, independent unit of analysis. Regardless of whether one is studying America's largest cities, their smaller neighborhood environments, or the alleys, intersections, and buildings within these larger places, the concept of "community" can be used in each of these settings to inform our understanding of crime. Or, as Robert Sampson (2013, p. 7) noted in his 2012 presidential address to the American Society of Criminology: "Chicago is a place, but so is the Hyde Park community surrounding the University of Chicago, and within that 'Jimmy's,' a wonderful watering hole at East 55th and S. Woodlawn . . . The phenomenon of crime does not privilege any one type of place or ecological unit." Thus, rather than searching for community criminology's holy grail—the single definition of community that best aligns with potential community influence— the field appears to be increasingly embracing a multicontextual image of community (see also McNeeley and Wilcox, 2015).

Community as Overcriminalized

A major finding of the Chicago School was that crime is concentrated in certain neighborhoods. In particular, Shaw and McKay famously conveyed that there were, in fact, "delinquency areas" that differed from other areas in the city and beyond. As noted in Chapter 2, these delinquency areas were located in the inner city—in the so-called zone in transition that was populated by the socially disadvantaged. Over the years, this vision of the inner city as crime ridden has been reified in criminological writings. In each chapter of this book, we have discussed scholars' efforts to identify the key feature of the inner city—criminal codes or traditions, the quality of social networks and the capacity for informal social control, the concentration of disadvantage, "broken windows," and opportunity structures—that are theorized to make crime pervasive in these neighborhoods. Whatever their substantive differences, nearly all of these theories have, implicitly or explicitly, imagined inner-city communities to be predominantly criminalized.

This conception of the inner city as a crime area has more than a kernel of truth to it. Such neighborhoods produce the most serious criminals and forms of victimization by street crimes. They are places marked by grinding poverty, a host of social and physical ills, and lives filled with hardship. They are places marked as well by open-air drug markets and physical and social incivilities. And they are places where gun violence is a familiar occurrence, where residents see or hear about drive-by shootings or bodies of teens lying in the street. Still, these disquieting realities do not mean that inner-city communities are "delinquency areas." This image suggests two views of these communities that recent research and events suggest may be inaccurate and in need of reconsideration.

First, a delinquency area implies that crime is pervasive across the entire community. We call this the *assumption of homogeneity*. Second, a delinquency area implies that the community will always experience high crime rates—barring some unusual occurrence. We call this the *assumption of intractability*. Both of these assumptions are likely untrue: a high level of crime does not appear to the be present throughout or to be a permanent feature of inner-city areas. In this sense, scholars are embracing an *overcriminalized image* of these communities.

The Assumption of Homogeneity

In 1957, Walter Reckless, Simon Dinitz, and Ellen Murray examined the issue that had been largely ignored in their article titled, "The 'Good' Boy in a High Delinquency Area." Previous research, they observed, had ignored "those youths, who, though often handicapped by home background, area of residence, deviant companions and many other so-called causes of delinquency, manage to steer a course away from delinquent behavior" (p. 18). Similar to resiliency research today, they wanted to understand how these good boys somehow remained "'isolated' from the *pervasive delinquent patterns* of his area of residence" (p. 25, emphasis added). Reckless, Dinitz, and Murray (1956) would highlight how the "self concept" functions as an "insulator against delinquency."

Oddly, Reckless, Dinitz, and Murray (1957, p. 18) mentioned, but did not highlight, that only a "small quota of boys in a high delinquency area . . . experience contact with the police and juvenile court." Further, when they focused their attention on "areas of high white delinquency" in Columbus, Ohio, they discovered that the delinquency rate "ranged from 20 per 1,000 boys to well over 40 per 1,000" (1957, p. 18). It is at this point that the issue of overcriminalization becomes apparent. Again, these neighborhoods are described as "delinquency areas" marked by "pervasive delinquency patterns." Possessing this mindset, the theoretical task is to explain how "good boys" survive residence in this social context. An alternative empirical reality, however, is unmasked simply by flipping the delinquency rate of twenty to forty police or court contacts on its head: in the high delinquency areas, 960 to 980 out of 1,000 were, in fact, not delinquent. The vast majority of youths from these bad neighborhoods in Reckless, Dinitz, and Murray's investigation were thus good boys.

Although specific statistics may differ, it appears that a majority of those who grow up in inner-city neighborhoods avoid criminal involvement either fully or, in the least, do not become chronic or life-course-persistent offenders (Benson, 2013). In fact, the results produced by Shaw and McKay's (1969) mapping of crime across Chicago are instructive. They divided Chicago into "140 square-mile areas." In an analysis representative of other analyses for different years and outcome measures, they then computed the rates of "alleged delinquents taken to the Juvenile Court from each area during 1927–33, per hundred of the aged 10–16 male population in that area as of 1930" (p. 53). Across this seven-year period, they eliminated "duplicates"— that is, youths brought to court more than once.

These calculations revealed a citywide rate of 4.2 youths per hundred. But consistent with their social disorganization theory, they found much higher rates in some neighborhoods, such as those "close to the central business district" or "near the Stock Yards, the South Chicago steel mills, and other industrial sections" (1969, p. 55). Their computations showed that three areas had rates between 17.0 and 18.9, and twelve others more than 10.0. By contrast, fifty areas, mostly in residential neighborhoods, had rates less than 2.5. These data suggest two conclusions. First, community context matters, and some communities are far more criminogenic than others. Second, even in the most delinquent areas, the rate of court contact did not rise above one in five youths (for an alternative view, see Kobrin, 1951). Good boys, it might be said, were in the majority in these delinquency areas.

Admittedly, race, the war on drugs, zero-tolerance policing, and the dramatic expansion of mass imprisonment make the contemporary picture in urban areas more complicated (Clear, 2007; Frost and Clear, 2013). Research suggests that African American males have extensive contact with the justice system. One study estimated that the by age eighteen, nearly 30 percent of Black males have been arrested at least once, a figure that climbs to 49 percent by age twenty-three (Brame et al., 2014). Another study calculated that at then-current incarceration rates, as many as one in three African American men would spend some time in a state or federal prison during their lifetime (Bonczar, 2003). These figures could be bleaker in some urban neighborhoods. Still, by taking a step back, another reality is revealed. Most Black men are either not arrested or arrested multiple times, and two-thirds are not incarcerated. Black women, often ignored in discussions, are far less involved (e.g., a lifetime imprisonment rate of one in eighteen; see The Sentencing Project, 2017). Indeed, a danger lurks in criminologists' tendency to overcriminalize African Americans and their communities: they may reinforce, or at least leave unchallenged, stereotypes that closely align race with crime (see Tonry, 2011; Unnever and Gabbidon, 2011). This association is often so intertwined in public and policy discourse that Russell-Brown (2009) has referred to the prevailing stereotype as the "criminalblackman."

Beyond these considerations, a more fundamental challenge to the assumption of homogeneity comes from the "criminology of place," which was just discussed (see also Chapter 7). In a very real way, Shaw and McKay were predecessors to this contemporary paradigm because they mapped the distribution of crime by areas within the urban landscape, with their concern focused on "delinquency areas." Although praising their efforts, as noted, today's scholars critique Shaw and McKay for using a "unit of geography" that was too large (Weisburd et al., 2016, p. 8). By examining square-mile areas or zones, Shaw and McKay committed what amounted to "aggregation bias" in that they assumed that crime was evenly distributed across all places within their unit of analysis. Starting in particular with the work of Sherman, Gartin, and Buerger (1989) on "hot spots," it became apparent that crime within neighborhoods—including inner-city areas—was higher in some places and lower or absent in other places. Put another way, the communities were marked not by crime homogeneity but by crime heterogeneity.

The empirical research is so persuasive on this matter that scholars have formulated bold "laws" to describe this phenomenon. For example, Weisburd (2015, p. 133) has presented "the law of crime concentration," whereas

Wilcox and Eck (2011, p. 476) have proposed "the iron law of troublesome places." Wilcox and Eck have added three "articles" to their law, which are that "a few places have most of the trouble," "most places are no trouble," and "extreme skewness is the norm" in the distribution of crime (2011, pp. 476–477). The important insight is that these articles apply to all neighborhoods, including those in the inner city. It means that even in so-called delinquency areas, most streets and most places on streets are trouble-free. Once this insight is illuminated, the criminological enterprise must include a different type of analysis. The issue is transformed from asking what it is about an area that makes it pervasively criminal to asking what it is about specific street blocks or places (e.g., bars, houses) that make them criminogenic. This question does not mean that community-level factors are not important, but it does mean that one conduit for their effect is the nature of specific places that are facilitative of crime (Weisburd, Groff, and Yang, 2012). That is, as noted in Chapter 8 and in the preceding section of this chapter, a multi-level model is required.

The implications of this research for the overcriminalization of the inner-city is clear: even if crime is generally higher in inner-city communities, many of the places, and people who populate and frequent them, are conventional. To give one additional example, let us consider again Weisburd, Groff, and Yang's (2012) study of 24,023 "street segments" in Seattle, Washington, over a sixteen-year period (1989–2004). Street segments—or street "blocks"—are smaller ecological units that exist within a larger neighborhood. Weisburd, Groff, and Yang (2012, p. 23) define a *street segment* "as both sides of the street between two intersections." They see segments or blocks as "a social unit that has been recognized as important in the rhythms of everyday living in cities" (p. 23).

Their analysis yielded two important conclusions. First, consistent with Weisburd's (2015) law of concentration, they found that crime and place are "tightly coupled." In Seattle, they discovered that "about 50 percent of crime is found at just 5 to 6 percent of street segments" (2012, p. 168). Similarly, only 3 percent to 4 percent of the street blocks are home to 50 percent of high-risk delinquents (p. 175). Second, the data revealed that more than 80 percent of the street segments "had *very little or no crime* throughout the study period" (p. 172, emphasis added). Importantly, these safe blocks—or "spatial heterogeneity"—were present in neighborhoods seen as delinquency areas (p. 173). In fact, based on their data, Weisburd et al. explicitly rejected the simple distinction between "good" and "bad" neighborhoods, and the collateral idea that "chronic hot street segments means that crime-free segments are not to be found in the same area" (p. 174). In short, the criminology of place presents strong evidence that undermines the overcriminalized image of inner-city communities.

The Assumption of Intractability

The assumption of intractability is the view that crime rates in certain inner-city neighborhoods will always be high. The criminogenic forces in these communities are seen as deeply rooted and extreme. These might be the social disorganization experienced by immigrants coming to America in the first decades of the 1900s (Shaw and McKay, 1969) or perhaps the concentrated disadvantage experienced by the truly disadvantaged in the latter decades of the 1900s—and now beyond that time (Sampson and Wilson, 1995; Wilson, 1987). The intractability assumption suggests that the root causes of crime can only be reversed through systematic social reforms that revitalize the organization and socioeconomic welfare of these communities.

Shaw and McKay's social disorganization theory is the exemplar of this mode of thinking. As seen in Chapter 2, they argued that neighborhoods within the zone in transition were delinquency areas. In the process of immigration, ethnic succession, and eventually reorganization and assimilation, different groups would come to Chicago (and other cities) and settle in these criminogenic communities. As a consequence, they would face social disorganization—including a breakdown of informal controls and exposure to entrenched criminal traditions—and thus experience high criminal involvement. But because the source of crime was the community context and not a property of the individual settlers, groups that organized and moved to other, more crime-free zones would eventually escape the burden of crime. This thesis was meant to falsify the neo-Lombrosian view that any ethnic (or racial) group was innately inferior or wayward. As a result, it rejected the assumption of individual intractability in favor of the assumption of community intractability.

The assumption that crime in inner-city communities is intractable has been disputed in two ways—theoretically and then empirically. First, in their broken windows theory, Wilson and Kelling (1982) argue that the prime sources of crime were not so-called root causes (e.g., poverty) but rather incivilities that were malleable (see Wilson, 1975). As a result, neighborhoods could be transformed from unsafe into safe areas by the effective use of police tactics aimed at fixing these "broken windows" (see Chapter 6). Similarly, environmental or opportunity theories share this view that crime is not intractable. Because all crime events are situational and involve the intersection of motivated offenders, attractive targets, and an absence of guardians, crime can be decreased by prevention efforts that stop this intersection from taking place (see Chapter 7). And, although short on concrete crime-control prescriptions, collective efficacy theory suggests that residents' agency can find solutions to crime problems that might emerge (e.g., shut down a drug market that has been initiated) (see Chapter 8).

Second, in recent decades, crime rates in inner cities, including homicide rates, have been falling. This decrease is part of a general trend that, as noted in Chapter 6, Zimring (2007) calls "the Great American crime decline" (see also Blumstein and Waldman, 2000). Tonry (2014) notes that this is a general international phenomenon. "Almost no one except a handful of academic specialists," observes Tonry (2014, p. 1), "seems to have noticed that crime rates are falling throughout the Western world." In his *The Better Angels of Our Nature*, Steven Pinker (2011, p. 64) captures this flaw in the assumption of intractability even more broadly:

> Now let's consider the implications of the centuries-long decline in homicide in Europe. Do you think that city living, with its anonymity, crowding, immigrants, and jumble of cultures and classes, is a breeding ground for violence? What about the wrenching social changes brought on by capitalism and the Industrial Revolution? Is it your conviction that small-town life, centered on church, tradition, and fear of God, is our best bulwark against murder and mayhem? Well, think again. As Europe became more urban, cosmopolitan, commercial, industrialized, and secular, it got safer and safer.

Importantly, contemporary American inner-city areas have not been immune to these developments. Contrary to the assumption of intractability, crime has diminished there as well—though, admittedly, in some cities such as Chicago, it has recently risen (Brennan Center for Justice, 2016). This empirical reality thus cautions against overcriminalizing inner-city communities; high levels of crime are not inevitable.

This view has been expressed perhaps most poignantly by Franklin Zimring in *The City That Became Safe*. Writing in 2012, Zimring examined crime rates in New York City from 1985 and 1990 to 2009. He documents a remarkable drop in victimization, noting that "the important offenses in New York City's street crime portfolio were all subject to extensive downward variation in two decades" (p. 198). As Zimring reports, the homicide rate in the city declined 82 percent or, stated in the reverse, was only "18 percent of its 1990 total in 2009" (p. 4). Compared with peak rates after 1985, crime had decreased to 37 percent of that total for theft, 33 percent for assault, 23 percent for rape, 16 percent for robbery, 14 percent for burglary, and 6 percent for auto theft. These reductions occurred across the city. According to Zimring, "the first major benefit from a crime decline" occurred in "minority communities where crime is concentrated" (p. 207). These residents endured "less crime, less violence, and less fear of crime"—and less imprisonment (p. 207). For two high-risk male groups—Blacks and non-Black Hispanics fifteen to forty-four—the figures are stunning: they accounted for "63 percent of the lives saved between 1990 and 2009" or 1,005 of the total decline of 1,591 killings" (p. 206).

For Zimring, these findings undermine an overcriminalized view of inner-city crime as invariably high. In fact, he argues that New York's crime decline, shared by other cities though to a lesser extent, "requires a fundamental rethinking of the relationship between urban life and urban crime" (p. 196). He uses the phrase of "the inessentiality of urban crime" to capture the reality "that the *great majority* of street crimes are not a necessary part of modern big cities in the United States" (2012, p. 203, emphasis in the original). In the past, it had been assumed that crime was intractable—that the behavior of high-rate offenders was "fixed and predictable" (p. 196). According to Zimring, "one of the most important lessons of New York City's relentless march toward safety is that criminal offenders are more malleable and criminal events are easier to prevent than conventional wisdom had recognized" (p. 196). At the end of *The City That Became Safe*, he thus calls on criminological scholars "to accommodate the variable as well as the fixed" (p. 216), and he gives an important reason for doing so:

> Finding as we have that the operating forces that produce epidemic levels of serious crime in the city are relatively superficial, that they are not essential elements of urban life, provides a decisive response to one of the deepest fears generated in the last third of the 20th century. We now know that life-threatening crime is not an incurable urban disease in the United States. (p. 217)

In the time ahead, it thus might become increasingly likely to see cities as safer havens from crime and to embrace the image of the community as overcriminalized. Freed from the despairing sense that urban crime is too entrenched to ever be stopped, innovative ideas can emerge on how best to lower victimization even further (see, e.g., Eck and Madensen, in press).

This possibility, however, is not meant to imply that inner-city neighborhoods are crime free. These areas have more crime hot spots and still produce a high proportion of the nation's prison population (Clear, 2007). Homicides are concentrated within their boundaries and, due to social misfortune or diminished vigilance, can spike upward. And it is an unappreciated reality that it does not take too many predators to make a community dangerous— those willing to mug, do a drive-by shooting, traffic in drugs, or stand menacingly on a street corner. Still, the study of communities and crime will be enriched if the assumptions of homogeneity and intractability are no longer blindly accepted but carefully investigated.

Community as a Racial Divide

Although race has been woven into nearly all the perspectives on communities and crime discussed in the previous chapters, it has not been the focal point in any of these visions. As scholars described communities plagued by disorganization or disadvantage, race has been in the background rather than center stage. As a result, there has been growing demand for a "Black criminology" and for race-centered approaches to communities and crime, which recognize that White and non-White neighborhoods differ widely in their experiences, history, and worldviews toward crime and justice (Alexander, 2010; Russell, 1992; Unnever and Gabbidon, 2011).

Notably, scholars calling for race-centered theories are not suggesting that the race-neutral perspectives on communities and crime described in this book are wrong. They agree that these perspectives explain large portions of crime in minority neighborhoods (Russell, 1992). Furthermore, some of the theories described in the previous chapters were explicitly developed to help account for the sharp rises in crime seen in Black communities throughout the 1970s and 1980s (e.g., the community as truly disadvantaged) (Wilson, 1987). However, race-neutral theories may not tell the whole story of African American (or Latino) crime. They deal with race, but they are not *about* race. Instead, they describe general processes, such as social disorganization, weakening social controls, economic restructuring, and changes in disorder and opportunity that lead to increased crime and social dislocation *for everyone.* Yet relying on general theories with an "add Blacks and stir" approach may not fully capture the ways in which race and ethnicity shape communities and crime.

Toward a Black Criminology

Some of the most vocal calls for race-specific perspectives have come from scholars such as Katheryn Russell (1992) and from James Unnever and Shaun Gabbidon (2011; see also Noble, 2006; Onwudiwe and Lynch, 2000; Penn, 2003; Unnever, 2017; Unnever and Owusu-Bempah, in press), who have urged criminologists to embrace a Black criminology that explicitly examines the impact of race and racism on crime and justice. In their book, *A Theory of African American Offending*, Unnever and Gabbidon (2011, p. 10) explain that they "fundamentally disagree with the assumption . . . that African Americans, whites, and other minorities offend for identical reasons." Instead, they suggest that some of the sources of African American offending are distinct. They argue that the past and current experiences of African Americans in the United States are "peerless," with no parallel experience found among White or Latino communities. As a result, this has contributed to what Unnever and Gabbidon (2011, p. 1) describe as a "shared worldview" among African Americans that uniquely shapes Black offending and Black perceptions of the criminal justice system.

  As evidence, they and other scholars point to the unique history of African Americans in the United States. Although nearly all racial/ethnic minorities have experienced hardships, no group has faced the enduring disadvantages and barriers to integration seen among the Black community (Alexander, 2010; Healey, 2006; Unnever and Gabbidon, 2011). Unlike other race/ethnic groups, African Americans were subject to a brutal system of slavery that included beatings, rapes, mutilation, and lynchings. Following the abolition of slavery, Blacks were subject to Jim Crow laws that legally enforced segregation and maintained their disadvantaged and marginalized status. After the Jim Crow laws were struck down, African American communities have continued to face isolation and caste-like disadvantages that have been unparalleled among other minority groups. Although the most blatant forms of racism were curtailed by the civil rights movement, they have been replaced with more subtle forms of discrimination in the job market (Pager, 2003); the housing market (Charles, 2003; Massey and Denton, 1993); and, perhaps most notably, in the criminal justice system (Alexander, 2010; Tonry, 1995; Unnever and Gabbidon, 2011; Walker, Spohn, and Delone, 2012). At nearly every stage of the criminal justice system, African Americans receive worse treatment and outcomes than other groups, even when they have similar charges and offense histories. As a result of these cumulative disadvantages, Black communities now face a system of mass incarceration in which nearly one in three men can expect to face jail or prison time and will be saddled with criminal records for the rest of their lives (Alexander, 2010; Tonry, 1995).

  Although many minority groups in the United States have been subject to discrimination both within and beyond the criminal justice system, proponents of a Black criminology explain that the Black experience is different. It is not simply that the scope of Black disadvantage is greater. Black history and deprivation is different in "kind." For example, Irish immigrants that first arrived in the United States were treated as second-class citizens and often considered inferior to native-born Americans (Unnever and Gabbidon, 2011; Warner and Srole, 1945). Yet, within several decades, they had largely integrated and were considered model Americans. The same story could be told for Italians, Germans, Polish, Jewish, and other ethnic groups arriving in the United States at the turn of the twentieth century. However, the path toward integration was fundamentally different for African Americans, a point that Shaw and McKay (1942) and Merton (1938) realized even as Black populations first began to migrate to urban communities in the North and Midwest. They were never given the same guarantee of full citizenship that other racial/ethnic groups had received.

In light of these unique hardships both in the past and present, Unnever and Gabbidon (2011) argue that African Americans have developed a shared worldview that differs in many ways from the rest of American society. As evidence, Black and White communities have wide differences in their beliefs about whether there is equality in employment, educational opportunities, government actions, law enforcement activity, sentencing, incarceration, and application of the death penalty (Brunson and Weitzer, 2009; Unnever and Cullen, 2007, 2010; Unnever, Gabbidon, and Higgins, 2011). This divide in worldviews is perhaps most clearly illustrated by Black and White perceptions of the O. J. Simpson verdict, in which the vast majority of Whites were sure he was guilty and the vast majority of Blacks were sure he was not (Unnever and Gabbidon, 2011). In sum, the history of discrimination and racial subjugation of African Americans, especially within the criminal justice system, has contributed to a fraternal bond and collective view among Blacks in the United States that is unique and that impacts the thoughts, feelings, and everyday lived experiences of Black men and women.

Unnever and Gabbidon (2011, p. 10) argue that this shared worldview, which is "grounded in resistance to racial subordination," is a two-edged sword. On the one hand, it is a source of solidarity and strength that fosters a shared sense of community among Black men and women. On the other hand, it is a heavy burden and a constant source of strife that may contribute to African American offending in multiple ways. Specifically, both experiences and expectations of racial discrimination create strains, frustration, and a sense of alienation among African Americans, which may contribute to greater Black crime (McCord and Ensminger, 2003; Russell, 1992; Unnever and Gabbidon, 2011). Stereotypes could have a labeling effect on minority populations, whereby African Americans internalize the negative portrayals they encounter about Black criminality. Discriminatory practices may contribute to offending by weakening minority group members' social bonds with school, the labor force, and other protective institutions. In addition, discrimination within the criminal justice system could have particularly salient effects on Black (or Latino) offending by creating defiance, weakening beliefs in the legitimacy of law, and fostering widespread legal cynicism (Brunson and Weitzer, 2009; Sherman, 1993b; Unnever and Gabbidon, 2011). Or as Noble (2006, p. 91) suggests, miscarriages of justice can create a "reservoir of bad will" and a "sea of hostility" that may ultimately lead to less cooperation with criminal justice actors and greater crime and violence among minority communities.

Wither Racial Invariance?

There is clearly potential value in taking a more direct look at the way that race/ethnicity and racism have shaped communities and crime. A Black criminology could provide such opportunity by exposing sources of crime in minority neighborhoods that have been overlooked by race-neutral perspectives. However, there is also debate over the assumption that the causes of minority offending are unique, which is inherent to race-specific perspectives. Many criminologists have embraced the "racial invariance" perspective, which argues that the sources of crime are uniform across race and ethnic groups (see Steffensmeier et al., 2011). Rather than attributing Black (or Latino) crime to unique factors, the racial invariance perspective suggests that racial/ethnic differences in crime can be attributed almost entirely to the wide differences in structural conditions found in Black, White, and Latino communities. In fact, this idea was what prompted Sampson and Wilson's (1995, p. 41) defining statement on racial invariance, noting that "the sources of violent crime appear to be remarkably invariant across race and rooted instead in the structural differences among communities, cities, and states in economic and family organization."

On its surface, the racial invariance perspective appears to directly counter race-specific approaches that seek to highlight the unique conditions of urban Black neighborhoods (Unnever, 2017; Unnever and Owusu-Bempah, in press). However, these perspectives may complement one another in more ways than they first appear. Although the racial invariance perspective suggests that the causes of crime are similar across race/ethnicity, it also recognizes that the *circumstances* found in many Black and Latino communities are unparalleled in White neighborhoods. Yes, disadvantage may impact groups in similar ways, when all things are equal. However, proponents of the racial invariance position, such as Peterson and Krivo (2010) and Sampson and Wilson (1995), also clearly recognize that "all things" are almost never equal for Black and Latino communities. The degree of disadvantage found in the poorest White neighborhoods does not begin to approach the level of deprivation found in many minority communities, suggesting that Black and Latino neighborhoods exist in divergent social worlds from White America (Peterson and Krivo, 2010).

The Latino Paradox

In a similar vein to Black criminology positions, research on Latino communities has consistently observed a "Latino Paradox," indicating that structural disadvantages do not contribute to Latino crime in the same way that they impact White and Black offending. Despite the fact that Latino communities experience severe poverty, low wages, and low educational attainment, they maintain remarkably low levels of crime and appear to be insulated from the crime-generating effects of disadvantage seen among Whites and Blacks (Feldmeyer, Harris, and Scroggins, 2015; Feldmeyer and Steffensmeier, 2009; Sampson and Bean, 2006; Steffensmeier et al., 2011).

Like Black criminology positions, the Latino paradox would seem to undermine racial invariance arguments and suggests that Latino communities and crime operate under a different set of rules than Black and White communities. However, racial invariance proponents have embraced this finding and sought to integrate it with the invariance perspective.

Specifically, racial invariance proponents note that structural disadvantage remains a key source of crime for all race/ethnic groups, Latinos included. It is not that disadvantage has no effect on Latino crime, or that structural conditions are meaningless for Latino communities. Instead, it may simply be the case that Latino communities experience less severe concentrations of disadvantage or may rely on strong social support networks to counter the consequences of deprivation, which would align with racial invariance arguments (Peterson and Krivo, 2005; Vélez, 2006). However, given the fact that Latino communities are uniquely impacted by immigration, language differences, and distinct ethnic traditions and heritage, questions remain about whether the crime-generating processes in Latino and non-Latino communities can truly be considered invariant.

In summary, the debate over whether the sources of crime are "invariant" across race/ethnic groups will likely continue over the next few decades. It is not yet clear whether a Black (or Latino) criminology will gain traction and emerge as a new dominant vision of communities and crime alongside the perspectives described in the previous chapters. Likewise, it is too early to tell whether race-specific approaches will ultimately compete with the racial invariance perspective or whether they may be integrated with racial invariance as complementary positions. Regardless, it is clear from these perspectives that race/ethnicity and racism have shaped communities and crime in ways that have not been fully explored.

Community Beyond the Urban Core

A final emergent image of community in relation to crime is one that looks beyond the urban core, as traditionally conceived. As described in the previous chapters, the study of "communities and crime" has almost exclusively been a study of *urban American* communities and crime, though a precise definition of "community" has remained elusive (see above section on "The Multicontextual Community"). In particular, the focus has largely been on "inner ring" communities presumed to be the most problematic in U.S. cities. As a result, research on the topic has been closely tied to the urban model of concentric growth described in Chapter 2 and has largely focused on poor "slum areas" in the heart of large American cities.

However, the "American urban context" is ever changing. In particular, nonconcentric patterns of urban growth as well as gentrification and demographic inversion are evident, all with potential implications regarding shifts in the geographic concentration and causes of crime in inner-city versus suburban areas within large cities. Additionally, while many urban communities in large, heterogeneous cities are at the center of a prosperous, new twenty-first-century economy (described in Chapter 8), smaller cities, towns, and rural communities are still tied to the old industrial American economy and are suffering immensely. Finally, studies of communities and crime are increasingly looking at communities outside the United States that sometimes have entirely different histories, economies, and cultures. Collectively, these trends offer evidence of a broadening image of community (and community crime) beyond the traditional inner city, presumed to emerge from concentric urban growth in the United States. In this context, below we discuss four contemporary developments that are like to extend into the future: the dynamic urban core, new suburban forms of communities, forgotten "flyover" communities, and communities beyond the border.

The Dynamic Urban Core

The phrase *communities and crime* can hardly be uttered without bringing forth Park and Burgess's iconic picture of the city's concentric rings, expanding radially through the process of invasion and succession. As discussed in Chapter 2, Park and Burgess described the concentric zones model of growth as a natural and inevitable pattern of city structure and expansion. However, this model may not be as universal as its founders first thought (White, 1988). Although many cities across the east and Midwest resemble this picture of concentric zones, many others do not. For decades, urban sociologists have questioned elements of the Chicago School's model of the city, offering alternative visions of urban areas, such as the "LA model" (e.g., Dear, 2002, 2003; Soja, 2000). The LA model suggests that some urban areas (like Los Angeles) look less like the concentric rings of a tree than they do a game board, with communities interspersed throughout the city like tiles on a board game. Instead of growing radially outward from a single central nucleus, cities that developed after the industrial revolution often had multiple hubs. As cars became the dominant mode of transportation, streets (instead of spatial proximity) increasingly defined neighborhood boundaries and shaped local interaction (Grannis, 1998). Urban growth followed the arteries of the city, expanding along the highways and flourishing in satellite and suburban communities at the edges of the metropolis (Dear, 2002; Hughes, 1993; White, 1988). Cities such as Los Angeles became defined by sprawl, as opposed to the densely packed urban core described by the Chicago School. However, criminology has largely ignored these newer developments, and one would be hard pressed to find an introduction to criminology textbook that acknowledges alternatives to the classical Chicago School model of the city.

Likewise, neighborhoods within U.S. cities have experienced growing patterns of gentrification, which communities-and-crime research has yet to fully explore. As described in Chapter 8, a number of cities across the United States have seen an urban renewal, drawing many people back into the city center (Austen, 2014). Gentrification has brought new residents and businesses to urban neighborhoods that had been in sharp economic decline (Freeman, 2005; Zukin, 1987). The dominance of suburban sprawl has seen some reversal, as a mix of young populations, arts communities, and professionals have made their homes in the heart of the city. Abandoned factories and shuttered businesses have been repurposed as urban lofts, galleries, and restaurants. Urban neighborhoods that had been abandoned by all but the most disadvantaged residents have risen from the ashes and begun to see new life.

However, there is considerable ambiguity about how these patterns of urban renewal and gentrification will ultimately impact inner-city communities and crime. On the one hand, it could revitalize inner-city areas, bringing in new businesses, jobs, and residents who are invested in the success of their new urban homes (see Florida, 2002; Freeman, 2005; Zukin 1987). Gentrification may provide an injection of resources that can be used to combat the truly disadvantaged conditions and the broken windows (real and symbolic) that have plagued high-crime neighborhoods. On the other hand, there is also evidence that efforts at urban renewal either harm or do little to help the most disadvantaged residents in gentrified inner-city neighborhoods (see Atkinson, 2004; Papachristos et al., 2011; Smith, 1996; Zukin, 1987). Instead of bringing in new jobs and opportunities for upward mobility, current residents may be pushed out of their neighborhoods as a result of rising housing prices and pressure from outside interests to repurpose local spaces. Furthermore, even if gentrification provides some economic aid and crime reduction, it is unclear how widely this process will be felt across urban neighborhoods. For every one inner-city area that has experienced an "urban renewal," there remain dozens of disadvantaged neighborhoods that see no renewal in sight. Going forward, scholars will likely be faced with growing questions about how these patterns of change have reshaped communities and crime within central cities.

New Suburban Forms

Alternative patterns of urban growth (i.e., the LA model) and the gentrification of a number of older inner-city neighborhoods within concentric-growth cities have implications for community crime beyond the urban core—including crime in suburban communities. For example, gentrification in some cities has caused important demographic shifts, with well-to-do Whites buying up rehabbed inner-city housing. In turn, suburban communities are increasingly becoming communities of first settlement for poor immigrants. In his article, "Trading Places," Alan Ehrenhalt (2008, p. 20) describes this "inversion of the American city" as follows:

> We are moving toward a society in which millions of people with substantial earning power or ample savings can live wherever they want, and many will choose central cities over distant suburbs. As they do this, others will find themselves forced to live in less desirable places— now defined as those further from the center of the metropolis. And, as this happens, suburbs that never dreamed of being entry points for immigrants will have to cope with new realities.

At this point, we do not have evidence that the sort of inversion that Ehrenhalt describes in America's postindustrial big cities is anywhere near complete. He admits that many experts see the return to the urban center by wealthy Whites as "a minor demographic event" (p. 21). But the trend has begun. It does appear that important shifts are taking place that have potential implications for the images of twenty-first-century communities that will predominate in the future. If the inversion we are beginning to see is more than a blip, community criminology will undoubtedly need to expand its focus beyond "inner-ring" communities—as defined by an increasingly outdated, concentric-based view of growth in American cities—and examine community structure and process in suburban locales as well.

Forgotten "Flyover" Communities

Further beyond the urban core of America's large cities and its suburbs are the small cities and towns and outlying rural areas. As with the suburbs, most of the perspectives discussed in this book have ignored such communities. Small cities, towns, and rural communities have traditionally been considered relatively tranquil, easy-to-live places, with not enough crime to bother studying. In comparison, inner-city communities have often been viewed as dirty, gritty, crime-prone places, and that image of the inner-city prevailed for most of the twentieth century.

However, as described previously, that image is changing. Many large cities once built on strong manufacturing bases have been able to reinvent themselves with an alternative, often tech-based economy, and some of their inner-city communities have thrived as a result. In contrast, small cities and towns that were industry-reliant have become, instead, downwardly mobile communities (MacGillis and ProPublica, 2016). This feeling of "two

Americas"—"elite" urban versus "forgotten" rural—was glaringly high-lighted in the 2016 U.S. presidential race, where enthusiasm and voting for the two candidates fell starkly along rural-urban lines, reinforcing a rela-tionship between population density and partisanship that has been growing in America for the last half century (Badger, Bui, and Pierce, 2016). One candidate (and eventual winner), Donald Trump, used a bleak tone to effec-tively harness small-town and rural voters' anger over being left out of the new postindustrial U.S. economy. For example, his inaugural address, which hit on the themes of his entire campaign, infamously referenced the "American carnage" seen in "rusted-out factories scattered like tombstones across the landscape of our nation" (Trump, 2017).

In brief, the past several decades have brought economic devastation upon factory towns and rural communities while many urban areas have thrived under a twenty-first-century tech-driven job market. Recent accounts of "Small Town, USA" describe how residents of these once-tranquil com-munities have seen their hometowns experiencing the types of despair (e.g., chronic unemployment, substance abuse, and suicide) that was once thought to be reserved for the inner city (MacGillis and ProPublica, 2016). Can community criminology be relevant in understanding some of the problems facing small-town communities? Perhaps so, though up to this point, little community-focused crime research has studied rural areas (for notable exceptions, see Lee, 2008; Lee, Maume, and Ousey, 2003; Lee and Ousey, 2001; Osgood and Chambers, 2000; Petee and Kowalski, 1993; Weisheit, Fal-cone, and Wells, 2005). As such, there is a need for expanded scholarly effort in this regard—a need for exploring a wider swath of American locales and for invoking images of community that bridge the rural-urban divide.

Communities Beyond the Border

Still further beyond the urban core of America's large cities, suburbs, small towns, and rural areas are communities that lie outside the United States. This book has largely focused on images of American cities, as it is the Amer-ican context that has driven much of the thinking about crime. However, the field of criminology has become a much more global enterprise over the past several decades. For example, as reported in Chapters 7 and 8, a sub-stantial amount of research describing community patterns of criminal opportunity and collective efficacy has been generated outside the United States, including scholarship from Australia, China, England, Sweden, and the Netherlands, to name just a few examples (e.g., Bernasco and Luykx, 2003; Bruinsma et al., 2013; Jiang, Land, and Wang, 2013; Mazerolle, Wickes, and McBroom, 2010; Reynald et al., 2008; Sampson and Groves, 1989; Sampson and Wikström, 2008; Wickes et al., 2017).

To date, many of these international studies have drawn on community theory developed in the United States in an attempt to explore whether theoretical ideas about American communities generalize to communities beyond U.S. borders. There is mixed evidence in this regard. For example, collective efficacy theory has been supported in research on communities in Stockholm, Sweden (Sampson and Wikström, 2008), but the theory received little support in research on communities in the Dutch city The Hague (Bruinsma et al., 2013). It is yet unclear whether international work will continue to be framed as tests of the generalizability of theories that largely originated within the American communities-and-crime tradition. It is likely that many of the general themes and theories on communities and crime described in this book are at least somewhat applicable in communities outside of the United States. After all, social disorganization, structural disadvantage, crime opportunity, and weakened collective efficacy are not exclusively "American" experiences. However, these elements of community life and their effects on crime (if they do apply) are also likely to be experienced in unique ways in other nations. Furthermore, the distinct histories, cultures, economies, and sociopolitical environments across international contexts also make it likely that other counties will have their own unique visions of communities and crime, which have received remarkably little attention in criminology. Thus, future work might look to develop new, culturally specific community theories, or more fully adapt existing "American" theories to better fit other contexts (e.g., Chouhy, 2016). Regardless, this work will continue to add a new and vibrant dimension to the study of communities and crime.

Conclusion

Starting with the Chicago School, as represented most powerfully by Clifford Shaw and Henry McKay, the study of communities and crime has occupied a central place in the criminological enterprise. It is perhaps easy to forget that this line of inquiry is now a century old—and as vibrant as ever. The reality is that individuals, including those who choose to break the law, are not isolated figures who travel through life unaffected by their surroundings. Rather, humans live in communities, an array of smaller and larger social contexts. These multilevel contexts shape both the propensities to offend and the specific acts of crime that are committed—whether alone or in concert with others, whether in one place or another.

As we have seen, communities are dynamic, not static, always evolving in one way or another. The forces that shape community life may flow from broad sociohistorical changes or perhaps from people who choose to live in a particular area. Standing on the shoulders of the two original scholarly giants in this field—Shaw and McKay—subsequent scholars attempted to identify the core social processes that influenced the crime that they witnessed. They both captured and were captured by the times in which they wrote—expertly describing criminogenic factors heretofore invisible to prior investigators but also having their criminological vision narrowed by the context in which they were enmeshed. The result of their efforts was to construct theories that offered a particular image of the community that resonated with their academic, if not public, audiences and that explained in a convincing way why crime, at least in some places, was flourishing. Often, they proposed that this image not only contained a theory of crime but also a prescription for advancing community safety.

Our purpose in this volume has been to convey this intellectual history of communities and crime. Yet, unlike some histories, the story of communities and crime has not only a past but also a future. It is far too early to tell whether the emerging themes discussed in this concluding chapter will ultimately lose salience or whether they (or other depictions of communities) will gain enough traction to become the next defining vision of community. Although we cannot be certain what image of the community will dominate next, we are confident that thinking about communities and crime will continue to be an enduring American challenge.

References

Addams, J. (1960). *Twenty years at Hull-House*. New York: Signet. (Originally published 1910.)

Akers, R. L. (1996). Is differential association/social learning cultural deviance theory? *Criminology, 34*, 229–247.

Alarid, L. F., Burton, V. S., Jr., and Cullen, F. T. (2000). Gender and crime among felony offenders: Assessing the generality of social control and differential association theories. *Journal of Research in Crime and Delinquency, 37*, 171–199.

Alexander, M. (2010). *The new Jim Crow: Mass incarceration in the age of colorblindness*. New York: New Press.

Anderson, E. (1990). *Streetwise: Race, class, and change in an urban community*. Chicago: University of Chicago Press.

———. (1999). *Code of the street: Decency, violence, and the moral life of the inner city*. New York: W. W. Norton.

———. (2003). *A place on the corner* (2nd ed.). Chicago: University of Chicago Press.

Anderson, N. (1961). *The hobo: The sociology of the homeless man*. Chicago: University of Chicago Press. (Originally published 1923.)

Andresen, M. A., Linning, S. J., and Malleson, N. (2017). 2017. Crime at places and spatial concentrations: Exploring the spatial stability of property crime in Vancouver BC, 2003–2013. *Journal of Quantitative Criminology, 33*, 255–275.

Arnold, T. (2011). Why are Shaw and McKay (1942; 1969) given the credit for social disorganization theory? Unpublished manuscript, School of Criminal Justice, University of Cincinnati.

Atkinson, R. (2004). The evidence on the impact of gentrification: New lessons for the urban renaissance? *European Journal of Housing Policy, 4*, 107–131.

Austen, B. (2014). Detroit, through rose-colored glasses. *New York Times Magazine*, July 3, pp. 22–29, 37–38.

Badger, E., Bui, Q., and Pearce, A. (2016). The election highlighted a growing rural-urban split. *New York Times*, November 11. https://www.nytimes.com/2016/11/12/upshot/this-election-highlighted-a-growing-rural-urban-split.html?_r=0. Accessed March 29, 2017.

Bailey, W. C. (1984). Poverty, inequality, and city homicide rates. *Criminology, 22,* 531–550.

Ball-Rokeach, S. (1973). Values and violence: A test of the subculture of violence thesis. *American Sociological Review, 38,* 736–749.

Bartusch, D. J. (2010). Sampson, Robert J., and William Julius Wilson: Contextualized subculture. In F. T. Cullen and P. Wilcox (Eds.), *Encyclopedia of criminological theory* (pp. 812–815). Thousand Oaks, CA: Sage.

Becker, H. S. (1966). Introduction. In C. R. Shaw, *The jack-roller: A delinquent boy's own story* (pp. v–xviii). Chicago: University of Chicago Press.

Beckett, K., and Sasson, T. (2000). *The politics of injustice: Crime and punishment in America.* Thousand Oaks, CA: Sage.

Bellair, P. E. (1997). Social interaction and community crime: Examining the importance of neighbor networks. *Criminology, 35,* 677–703.

Bellair, P. E., and Browning, C. B. (2010). Contemporary disorganization research: An assessment and further test of the systemic model of neighborhood crime. *Journal of Research in Crime and Delinquency, 47,* 496–521.

Belluck, P. (1998). End of a ghetto: A special report; razing the slums to rescue the residents. *New York Times*, September 6. http://www.nytimes.com/1998/09/06/us/end-of-a-ghetto-a-special-report-razing-the-slums-to-rescue-the-residents.html. Accessed December 29, 2016.

Bennett, W. J., DiIulio, J. J., Jr., and Walters, J. P. (1996). *Body count: Moral poverty and how to win America's war against crime and drugs.* New York: Simon and Schuster.

Benson, M. L. (2013). *Crime and the life course: An introduction* (2nd ed.). New York: Routledge.

Berg, M. T., and Stewart, E. A. (2013). Street culture and crime. In F. T. Cullen and P. Wilcox (Eds.), *The Oxford handbook of criminological theory* (pp. 370–388). New York: Oxford University Press.

Bernasco, W. (2010). A sentimental journey to crime: Effects of residential history on crime location choice. *Criminology, 48,* 389–416.

Bernasco, W., and Block, R. (2009). Where offenders choose to attack: A discrete choice model of robberies in Chicago. *Criminology, 47,* 93–130.

———. (2011). Robberies in Chicago: A block-level analysis of the influence of crime generators, crime attractors, and offender anchor points. *Journal of Research in Crime and Delinquency, 48,* 33–57.

Bernasco, W., and Luykx, F. (2003). Effects of attractiveness, opportunity and accessibility to burglars on residential burglary rates of urban neighborhoods. *Criminology, 41,* 981–1002.

Bernasco, W., and Nieuwbeerta, P. (2005). How do residential burglars select target areas? A new approach to the analysis of criminal location choice. *British Journal of Criminology, 45,* 296–315.

Berry, B. J. L., and Kasarda, J. D. (1977). *Contemporary urban ecology.* New York: Macmillan.

Billingsley, A. (1989). Sociology of knowledge of William J. Wilson: Placing *The Truly Disadvantaged* in its sociohistorical context. *Journal of Sociology and Social Welfare, 16,* 7–40.

Bishop, B. (2008). *The big sort: Why the clustering of like-minded America is tearing us apart.* Boston, MA: Houghton Mifflin.

Blau, J. R., and Blau, P. M. (1982). The cost of inequality: Metropolitan structure and violent crime. *American Sociological Review, 47,* 114–129.

Blau, P. M. (1977). *Inequality and heterogeneity: A primitive theory of social structure.* New York: Free Press.

Blau, P. M., and Golden, R. M. (1986). Metropolitan structure and criminal violence. *Sociological Quarterly, 27,* 15–26.

Blumstein, A., and Wallman, J. (Eds.). (2000). *The crime drop in America.* New York: Cambridge University Press.

Boessen, A., and Hipp, J. R. (2015). Close-ups and the scale of ecology: Land uses and the geography of social context and crime. *Criminology, 53,* 399–462.

Bonczar, T. P. (2003). *Prevalence of imprisonment in the U.S. population, 1974–2001.* Washington, DC: Bureau of Justice Statistics, U.S. Department of Justice.

Bonta, J., and Andrews, D. A. (2017). *The psychology of criminal conduct* (6th ed.). New York: Routledge.

Bovenkerk, F. (2010). Robert Ezra Park (1864–1944). In K. Hayward, S. Maruna, and J. Mooney (Eds.), *Fifty key thinkers in criminology* (pp. 48–53). New York: Routledge.

Braga, A. A. (2012). High crime places, times, and offenders. In B. C. Welsh and D. P. Farrington (Eds.), *The Oxford handbook of crime prevention* (pp. 316–336). New York: Oxford University Press.

Braga, A. A., and Clarke, R. V. (2014). Explaining high-risk concentrations of crime in the city: Social disorganization, crime opportunities, and important next steps. *Journal of Research in Crime and Delinquency, 51,* 480–498.

Braga, A. A., Hureau, D. M., and Papachristos, A. V. (2011). The relevance of micro places to citywide robbery trends: A longitudinal analysis of robbery incidents at street corners and block faces in Boston. *Journal of Research in Crime and Delinquency, 48,* 7–32.

Braga, A. A., Papachristos, A. V., and Hureau, D. M. (2014). The effects of hot spots policing on crime: An updated systematic review and meta-analysis. *Justice Quarterly, 31,* 633–663.

Braga, A. A., and Weisburd, D. (2012). The effects of focused deterrence strategies on crime: A systematic review and meta-analysis of the empirical evidence. *Journal of Research in Crime and Delinquency, 49,* 323–358.

Braga, A. A., Welsh, B. C., and Schnell, C. (2015). Can policing disorder reduce crime? A systematic review and meta-analysis. *Journal of Research in Crime and Delinquency, 52,* 567–588.

Brame, R., Bushway, S. D., Paternoster, R., and Turner, M. G. (2014). Demographic patterns of cumulative arrest prevalence by ages 19 and 23. *Crime and Delinquency, 60,* 471–486.

Brantingham, P. J., and Brantingham, P. L. (Eds.). (1981). *Environmental criminology.* Beverly Hills, CA: Sage.

———. (2013). A theory of target search. In F. T. Cullen and P. Wilcox (Eds.), *The Oxford handbook of criminological theory* (pp. 535–553). New York: Oxford University Press.

Brantingham, P., L., and Brantingham, P. J. (1993). Nodes, paths and edges: Considerations on the complexity of crime and the physical environment. *Journal of Environmental Psychology, 13,* 3–28.

———. (1995). Criminality of place: Crime generators and crime attractors. *European Journal on Criminal Policy and Research, 3*, 1–26.

Breckinridge, S. P., and Abbott, E. (1912). *The delinquent child and the home.* Philadelphia, PA: Press of Wm F. Feld/Russell Sage Foundation.

Brennan Center for Justice. (2016). *Crime in 2016: Updated analysis.* https://www.brennancenter.org/sites/default/files/analysis/Crime_in_2016_Up.

Brezina, T., Agnew, R., Cullen, F. T., and Wright, J. P. (2004). Code of the street: A quantitative assessment of Elijah Anderson's subculture of violence thesis and its contribution to youth violence research. *Youth Violence and Juvenile Justice, 2*, 303–328.

Browning, C. R. (2002). The span of collective efficacy: Extending social disorganization theory to partner violence. *Journal of Marriage and Family, 64*, 833–850.

———. (2009). Illuminating the downside to social capital: Negotiated coexistence, property crime, and disorder in urban neighborhoods. *American Behavioral Scientist, 52*, 1556–1578.

Browning, C. R., Dietz, R., and Feinberg, S. (2004). The paradox of social organization: Networks, collective efficacy, and violent crime in urban neighborhoods. *Social Forces, 83*, 503–534.

Bruinsma, G. J. N., Pauwels, L. J. R., Weerman, F. M., and Bernasco, W. (2013). Social disorganization, social capital, collective efficacy and the spatial distribution of crime and offenders: An empirical test of six neighbourhood models for a Dutch city. *British Journal of Criminology, 53*, 942–963.

Brunson, R. K., and Weitzer, R. (2009). Police relations with Black and White youths in different urban neighborhoods. *Urban Affairs Review, 44*, 858–885.

Bulmer, M. (1984). *The Chicago School of sociology: Institutionalization, diversity, and the rise of sociological research.* Chicago: University of Chicago Press.

Burgess, E. W. (1942). Introduction. In C. R. Shaw and H. D. McKay, *Juvenile delinquency and urban areas* (pp. ix–xiii). Chicago: University of Chicago Press.

———. (1967). The growth of the city: An introduction to a research project. In R. E. Park, E. W. Burgess, and R. D. McKenzie (Eds.), *The city* (pp. 47–62). Chicago: University of Chicago Press. (Originally published 1925.)

Bursik, R. J. (1984). Urban dynamics and ecological studies of delinquency. *Social Forces, 63*, 393–413.

———. (1986). Ecological stability and the dynamics of delinquency. In A. J. Reiss, Jr. and M. Tonry (Eds.), *Communities and crime* (Crime and Justice: A Review of Research, vol. 8, pp. 35–66). Chicago: University of Chicago Press.

———. (1988). Social disorganization and theories of crime and delinquency: Problems and prospects. *Criminology, 26*, 519–552.

———. (2015). *Social Sources of Delinquency* and the second coming of Shaw and McKay. In F. T. Cullen, P, Wilcox, R. J. Sampson, and B. D. Dooley (Eds.), *Challenging criminological theory: The legacy of Ruth Rosner Kornhauser* (Advances in Criminological Theory, vol. 19, pp. 105–116). New Brunswick, NJ: Transaction.

Bursik, R. J., Jr., and Grasmick, H. G. (1993). *Neighborhoods and crime: The dimensions of effective community control.* New York: Lexington.

Bursik, R. J., Jr., and Webb, J. (1982). Community change and patterns of delinquency. *American Journal of Sociology, 88*, 24–42.

Carr, P. J. (2003). The new parochialism: The implications of the Beltway case for arguments concerning informal social control. *American Journal of Sociology, 108*, 1249–1291.

———. (2012). Citizens, community and crime control: The problems and prospects for negotiated order. *Criminology and Criminal Justice, 12,* 297–412.

Charles, C. Z. (2003). The dynamics of racial residential segregation. *Annual Review of Sociology, 29,* 167–207.

Chouhy, C. (2016). *Collective efficacy and community crime rates: A cross-national test of rival models.* Unpublished Ph.D. dissertation, University of Cincinnati.

Chouhy, C., Cullen, F. T., and Unnever, J. D. (2016). Mean streets revisited: Assessing the generality of rival criminological theories. *Victims and Offenders, 11,* 225–250.

Clarke, R. V. (2010). Crime science. In E. McLaughlin and T. Newburn (Eds.), *The Sage handbook of criminological theory* (pp. 271–283). London: Sage.

Clarke, R. V., and Cornish, D. (1985). Modeling offender's decisions: A framework for research and policy. In M. Tonry and N. Morris (Eds.), *Crime and justice: An annual review of research* (vol. 6, pp. 147–185). Chicago: University of Chicago Press.

Clarke R. V., and Felson, M. (2011). The origins of the routine activity approach and situational crime prevention. In F. T. Cullen, C. L. Jonson, A. J. Myer, and F. Adler (Eds.), *The origins of American criminology* (Advances in Criminological Theory, vol. 16, pp. 245–260). New Brunswick, NJ: Transaction.

Clear, T. R. (2007). *Imprisoning communities: How mass incarceration makes disadvantaged neighborhoods worse.* New York: Oxford University Press.

Cloward, R. A. (1959). Illegitimate means, anomie, and deviant behavior. *American Sociological Review, 24,* 164–176.

Cloward, R. A., and Ohlin, L. E. (1960). *Delinquency and opportunity: A theory of delinquent gangs.* New York: Free Press.

Cohen, A. K. (1955). *Delinquent boys: The culture of the gang.* New York: Free Press.

Cohen, A. K., and Short, J. F., Jr. (1958). Research in delinquent subcultures. *Journal of Social Issues, 14,* 20–37.

Cohen, L. E., and Felson, M. (1979). Social change and crime rate trends: A routine activity approach. *American Sociological Review, 44,* 588–608.

Cohen, L. E., Felson, M., and Land, K. C. (1980). Property crime rates in the United States: A macro-dynamic analysis, 1947–1977; with ex ante forecasts for the mid-1980s. *American Journal of Sociology, 86,* 90–118.

Cohen, L. E., Kluegel, J. R., and Land, K. C. (1981). Social inequality and predatory criminal victimization: An exposition and test of a formal theory. *American Sociological Review, 46,* 505–524.

Cohen, P. (2010). "Culture of poverty" makes a comeback. *New York Times,* October 17. http://www.nytimes.com/2010/10/18/us/18poverty.html. Accessed September 26, 2011.

Coleman, J. (1992). Columbia in the 1950s. In B. M. Berger (Ed.), *Authors of their own lives: Intellectual autobiographies by twenty American sociologists* (pp. 75–103). Berkeley: University of California Press.

Commager, H. S. (1960). Foreword. In J. Addams, *Twenty years at Hull-House* (pp. vii–xvi). New York: Signet.

Conzen, M. P. (2005). Global Chicago. In *The electronic encyclopedia of Chicago.* Chicago: Chicago Historical Society. http://www.encyclopedia.chicagohistory.org/pages/277.html. Accessed July 21, 2011.

Cooper, A., and Smith, E. L. (2011). *Homicide trends in the United States, 1980–2008.* Washington, DC: Bureau of Justice Statistics, U.S. Department of Justice.

Cornish, D. B., and Clarke, R. V. (Eds.). (1986). *The reasoning criminal: Rational choice perspectives on offending*. New York: Springer.

Corzine, J., and Huff-Corzine, L. (1992). Racial inequality and Black homicide: An analysis of felony, nonfelony and total rates. *Journal of Contemporary Criminal Justice, 8*, 150–165.

Coupe, T., and Blake, L. (2006). Daylight and darkness targeting strategies and the risks of being seen at residential burglaries. *Criminology, 44*, 431–464.

Covington, J. (1995). Racial classification in criminology: The reproduction of racialized crime. *Sociological Forum, 10*, 547–568.

Crowe, T. D. (2000). *Crime prevention through environmental design* (2nd ed.). Boston, MA: Butterworth-Heinemann.

Cullen, F. T. (1984). *Rethinking crime and deviance theory: The emergence of a structuring tradition*. Totowa, NJ: Rowman and Allanheld.

———. (1988). Were Cloward and Ohlin strain theorists? Delinquency and opportunity revisited. *Journal of Research in Crime and Delinquency, 25*, 214–241.

———. (2010). Cloward, Richard A., and Lloyd E. Ohlin: Delinquency and opportunity. In F. T. Cullen, and P. Wilcox (Eds.), *Encyclopedia of criminological theory* (vol. 1, pp. 170–174). Thousand Oaks, CA: Sage.

Cullen, F. T., Agnew, R., and Wilcox, P. (2014). *Criminological theory: Past to present* (5th ed.). New York: Oxford University Press.

Cullen, F. T., and Gendreau, P. (2001). From nothing works to what works: Changing professional ideology in the 21st century. *Prison Journal, 81*, 313–338.

Cullen, F. T., and Messner, S. M. (2007). The making of criminology revisited: An oral history of Merton's anomie paradigm. *Theoretical Criminology, 11*, 5–37.

Cullen, F. T., and Pratt, T. C. (2016). Toward a theory of police effects. *Criminology and Public Policy, 15*, 799–811.

Cullen, F. T., Wilcox, P., Sampson, R. J., and Dooley, B. D. (Eds.). (2015). *Challenging criminological theory: The legacy of Ruth Rosner Kornhauser* (Advances in Criminological Theory, vol. 19). New Brunswick, NJ: Transaction.

Curtis, L. A. (1975). *Violence, race, and culture*. Lexington, MA: Lexington Books.

Deakin, J., Smithson, H., Spencer, J., and Medina-Ariza, J. (2007). Taxing on the streets: Understanding the methods and process of street robbery. *Crime Prevention and Community Safety, 9*, 52–67.

Dear, M. (2002). Los Angeles and the Chicago School: Invitation to a debate. *City and Community, 1*, 5–32.

———. (2003). The Los Angeles school of urbanism: An intellectual History. *Urban Geography, 24*, 493–509.

Deryol, R., Wilcox, P., Logan, M., and Wooldredge, J. (2016). Crime places in context: An illustration of the multilevel nature of hotspot development. *Journal of Quantitative Criminology, 32*, 305–325.

Diary of a vandalized car. (1969). *Time*, February 28, pp. 62, 65.

DiIulio, J. J., Jr. (1995). The coming of super-predators. *Weekly Standard*, November 27, pp. 23–28.

Dill, B. T. (1989). Comments on William Wilson's the truly disadvantaged: A limited proposal for social reform. *Journal of Sociology and Social Welfare, 16*, 69–76.

DisasterCenter.com. (2016). *United States crime rates 1960-2014*. http://www.disastercenter.com/crime/uscrime.htm. Accessed May 6, 2016.

Donnelly, P. G., and Kimble, C. E. (1997). Community organizing, environmental change, and neighborhood crime. *Crime and Delinquency, 43*, 493–511.

Duneier, M. (2016). *Ghetto: The invention of a place, the history of an idea.* New York: Farrar, Straus, and Giroux.

Duru, H. (2010). *Crime on Turkish street blocks: An examination of the effects of high schools, on-premise alcohol outlets, and coffeehouses.* Unpublished Ph.D. dissertation, University of Cincinnati.

Eck, J. E., and Guerette, R. T. (2012). Place-based crime prevention: Theory, evidence, and policy. In B. C. Welsh and D. P. Farrington (Eds.), *The Oxford handbook of crime prevention* (pp. 354–383). New York: Oxford University Press.

Eck, J. E., and Madensen, T. D. (In press). Place management, guardianship and the establishment of order. In D. S. Nagin, F. T. Cullen, and C. L. Jonson (Eds.), *Deterrence, choice, and crime: Contemporary perspectives* (Advances in Criminological Theory). New York: Routledge.

Eck, J. E., and Maguire, E. R. (2000). Have changes in policing reduced crime? An assessment of the evidence. In A. Blumstein and J. Walman (Eds.), *The crime drop in America* (pp. 207–265). New York: Cambridge University Press.

Ehrenhalt, A. (2008). Trading places: The demographic inversion of the American city. *New Republic,* August 13, pp. 19–22.

Empey, L. T. (1982). *American delinquency: Its meaning and construction* (Rev. ed.). Homewood, IL: Dorsey.

Federal Bureau of Investigation. (2016). *Uniform crime reports.* Washington, DC: U.S. Government Printing Office.

Feldmeyer, B. (2009). Immigration and violence: The offsetting effects of immigration on Latino violence. *Social Science Research, 38,* 717–731.

———. (2010). The effects of racial/ethnic segregation on Latino and Black homicide. *Sociological Quarterly, 51,* 600–623.

Feldmeyer, B., Harris, C. T., and Scroggins, J. (2015). Enclaves of opportunity of ghettos of last resort? Assessing the effects of immigrant segregation on violent crime rates. *Social Science Research, 52,* 1–17.

Feldmeyer, B., Madero-Hernandez, A., Rojas-Gaona, C., and Sabon, L. C. (2017). Immigration, collective efficacy, social ties, and violence: Unpacking the mediating mechanisms in immigration effects on neighborhood-level violence. *Race and Justice.* Advance online publication. DOI: 10.1177/2153368717690563.

Feldmeyer, B., and Steffensmeier, D. (2009). Immigration effects on homicide offending for total and race/ethnicity-disaggregated populations (White, Black, and Latino). *Homicide Studies, 13,* 211–226.

Feldmeyer, B., Steffensmeier, D., and Ulmer, J. T. (2013). Racial/ethnic composition and violence: Size-of-place variations in percent Black and percent Latino effects on violence rates. *Sociological Forum, 28,* 811–841.

Felson, M. (1987). Routine activities and crime prevention in the developing metropolis. *Criminology, 25,* 911–931.

———. (1994). *Crime and everyday life: Insight and implications for society.* Thousand Oaks, CA: Pine Forge.

———. (1995). Those who discourage crime. In J. E. Eck and D. Weisburd (Eds.), *Crime places in crime theory, crime prevention studies* (vol. 4, pp. 53–66). Monsey, NY: Criminal Justice Press.

———. (2006). *Crime and nature.* Thousand Oaks, CA: Sage.

Felson, M., and Cohen, L. E. (1980). Human ecology and crime: A routine activity approach. *Human Ecology, 8,* 389–406.

Felson, M., and Eckert, M. A. (2016). *Crime and everyday life* (5th ed.). Thousand Oaks, CA: Sage.

Finestone, H. (1976). The delinquent and society: The Shaw and McKay tradition. In J. F. Short, Jr. (Ed.), *Delinquency, crime, and society* (pp. 23–49). Chicago: University of Chicago Press.

Fisher, B. S., Daigle, L. E., and Cullen, F. T. (2010). *Unsafe in the ivory tower: The sexual victimization of college women*. Thousand Oaks, CA: Sage.

Fisher, B. S., Reyns, B. W., and Sloan, J. J., III. (2016). *Introduction to victimology: Contemporary theory, research, and practice*. New York: Oxford University Press.

Fisher, B. S., Sloan, J. J., Cullen, F. T., and Lu, C. (1998). Crime in the ivory tower: The level and sources of student victimization. *Criminology, 36*, 671–710.

Florida, R. L. (2002). *The rise of the creative class: And how it's transforming work, leisure, community and everyday life*. New York: Basic Books.

Freeman, L. (2005). Displacement or succession? Residential mobility in gentrifying neighborhoods. *Urban Affairs Review, 40*, 463–491.

Frost, N. A., and Clear, T. R. (2013). Coercive mobility. In F. T. Cullen and P. Wilcox (Eds.), *The Oxford handbook of criminological theory* (pp. 691–708). New York: Oxford University Press.

Gans, H. J. (1990). Deconstructing the underclass the term's dangers as a planning concept. *Journal of the American Planning Association, 56*, 271–277.

Garland, D. (2001). *The culture of control: Crime and social order in contemporary society*. Chicago: University of Chicago Press.

Gastil, R. D. (1971). Homicide and a regional culture of violence. *American Sociological Review, 36*, 412–427.

Gau, J. M., and Pratt, T. C. (2008). Broken windows or window dressing? Citizens' (in)ability to tell the difference between disorder and crime. *Criminology and Public Policy, 7*, 163–184.

Gelsthorpe, L. (2010). Clifford Shaw (1895–1957). In K. Hayward, S. Maruna, and J. Mooney (Eds.), *Fifty key thinkers in criminology* (pp. 71–76). New York: Routledge.

Gilder, G. (1981). *Wealth and poverty*. New York: Basic Books.

Gill, C., Weisburd, D., Telep, C. W., Vitter, Z., and Bennett, T. (2014). Community-oriented policing to reduce crime, disorder and fear and increase satisfaction and legitimacy among citizens: A systematic review. *Journal of Experimental Criminology, 10*, 399–428.

Gottfredson, M. R., and Hindelang, M. J. (1981). Sociological aspects of criminal victimization. *Annual Review of Sociology, 7*, 107–128.

Gottfredson, M. R., and Hirschi, T. (1990). *A general theory of crime*. Stanford, CA: Stanford University Press.

Grannis, R. (1998). The importance of trivial streets: Residential streets and residential segregation. *American Journal of Sociology, 103*, 1530–1564.

Greenberg, S., Rohe, W., and Williams, J. (1982). Safety in urban neighborhoods: A comparison of physical characteristics and informal territorial control in high and low crime neighborhoods. *Population and Environment, 5*, 141–165.

Griggs, R. A. (2014). Coverage of the Stanford prison experiment in introductory psychology textbooks. *Teaching of Psychology, 41*, 195–203.

Groff, E. R. (2015). Informal social control and crime events. *Journal of Contemporary Criminal Justice, 31*, 90–106.

Groff, E. R., Weisburd, D., and Yang, S. (2010). Is it important to examine crime trends at a local "micro" level? A longitudinal analysis of street to street variability in crime trajectories. *Journal of Quantitative Criminology, 26*, 7–32.

Hackney, S. (1969). Southern violence. *American Historical Review, 74*, 906–925.

Hagan, J., and Palloni, A. (1999). Sociological criminology and the mythology of Hispanic immigration and crime. *Social Problems, 46*, 617–632.

Hall, M., Crowder, K., and Spring, A. (2015). Neighborhood foreclosures, racial/ethnic transitions, and residential segregation. *American Sociological Review, 80*, 526–549.

Hannerz, U. (1969). *Soulside: Inquiries into ghetto culture and community*. New York: Columbia University Press.

Harcourt, B. E. (2001). *Illusions of order: The false promise of broken windows policing*. Cambridge, MA: Harvard University Press.

Harer, M. D., and Steffensmeier, D. (1992). The differing effects of economic inequality on Black and White rates of violence. *Social Forces, 70*, 1035–1054.

Hart, T. C., and Miethe, T. D. (2014). Street robbery and public bus stops: A case study of activity nodes and situational risk. *Security Journal, 27*, 180–193.

Healey, J. F. (2006). *Race, ethnicity, gender, and class: The sociology of group conflict and change*. Thousand Oaks, CA: Sage.

Heitgerd, J. L., and Bursik, R. J., Jr. (1987). Extracommunity dynamics and the ecology of delinquency. *American Journal of Sociology, 92*, 775–787.

Hindelang, M. J., Gottfredson, M. R., and Garofalo, J. (1978). *Victims of personal crime: An empirical foundation for a theory of personal victimization*. Cambridge, MA: Ballinger.

Hipp, J. R. (2016). Collective efficacy: How is it conceptualized, how is it measured, and does it really matter for understanding perceived neighborhood crime and disorder? *Journal of Criminal Justice, 46*, 32–44.

Hipp, J. R., and Boessen, A. (2013). *Egohoods* as waves washing across the city: A new measure of "neighborhoods." *Criminology, 51*, 287–327.

Hipp, J. R., and Wickes, R. (In press). Violence in urban neighborhoods: A longitudinal study of collective efficacy and violent crime. *Journal of Quantitative Criminology*. DOI: 10.1007/s10940-016-9311-z.

Hirschi, T. (1969). *Causes of delinquency*. Berkeley: University of California Press.

———. (1986). On the compatibility of rational choice and social control theories of crime. In D. B. Cornish and R. V. Clarke (Eds.), *The reasoning criminal: Rational choice perspectives on offending* (pp. 105–118). New York: Springer.

———. (1996). Theory without ideas: Reply to Akers. *Criminology, 34*, 249–256.

Hughes, H. L. (1993). Metropolitan structure and the suburban hierarchy. *American Sociological Review, 58*, 417–433.

Hunter, A. (1985). Private, parochial and public social orders: The problem of crime and incivility in urban communities. In G. Suttles and M. Zald (Eds.), *The challenge of social control: Citizenship and institution building in modern society* (pp. 230–242). Norwood, NJ: Ablex.

Jacobs, J. (1961). *The death and life of great American cities*. New York: Random House.

Jeffery, C. R. (1971). *Crime prevention through environmental design*. Beverly Hills, CA: Sage.

Jiang, S., Land, K. C., and Wang, J. (2013). Social ties, collective efficacy and perceived neighborhood property crime in Guangzhou, China. *Asian Criminology, 8*, 207–223.

Jonassen, C. T. (1949). A re-evaluation and critique of the logic and some methods of Shaw and McKay. *American Sociological Review, 14*, 608–617.

Jonson, C. L., McArthur, R., Cullen, F. T., and Wilcox, P. (2012). Unraveling the sources of adolescent substance use: A test of rival theories. *International Journal of School Disaffection, 9*, 53–90.

Kanigel, R. (2016). *Eyes on the street: The life of Jane Jacobs*. New York: Alfred A. Knopf.

Kasarda, J. D., and Janowitz, M. (1974). Community attachment in mass society. *American Sociological Review, 39*, 328–339.

Kelling, G. L., and Coles, C. M. (1997). *Fixing broken windows: Restoring order and reducing crime in our communities*. New York: Touchstone.

Kelling, G. L., and Sousa, W. H., Jr. (2001). *Do police matter? An analysis of the impact of New York City's police reforms*. New York: Manhattan Institute.

Kennedy, L. W., and Forde, D. R. (1990). Routine activities and crime: An analysis of victimization in Canada. *Criminology, 28*, 137–152.

Kirk, D. S. (2008). The neighborhood context of racial and ethnic disparities in arrest. *Demography, 45*, 55–77.

———. (2009). Unraveling the contextual effects on student suspension and juvenile arrest: The independent and interdependent influences of school, neighborhood, and family social context. *Criminology, 47*, 479–520.

Kirk, D. S., and Papachristos, A. V. (2011). Cultural mechanisms and the persistence of neighborhood violence. *American Journal of Sociology, 116*, 1190–1233.

———. (2015). Concentrated disadvantage and the persistence of legal cynicism. In F. T. Cullen, P., Wilcox, R. J. Sampson, and B. D. Dooley (Eds.), *Challenging criminological theory: The legacy of Ruth Rosner Kornhauser* (Advances in Criminological Theory, vol. 19, pp. 259–274). New Brunswick, NJ: Transaction.

Kobrin, S. (1951). The conflict of values in delinquency areas. *American Sociological Review, 16*, 653–661.

———. (1959). The Chicago Area Project: A 25-year assessment. *Annals of the American Academy of Political and Social Sciences, 332*, 19–29.

Kornhauser, R. R. (1963). Theoretical issues in the sociological study of juvenile delinquency. Mimeographed Paper. Center for the Study of Law and Society, University of California, Berkeley. http://www.asc41.com/hisotry/Oral_History/Kornahsuer_63.pdf.

———. (1978). *Social sources of delinquency: An appraisal of analytical models*. Chicago: University of Chicago Press.

———. (1984). *Social sources of delinquency: An appraisal of analytic models* (Paperback ed.). Chicago: University of Chicago Press.

Kozol, J. (1991). *Savage inequalities: Children in America's schools*. New York: Crown.

Krivo, L. J., Byron, R. A., Calder, C. A., Peterson, R. D., Browning, C. R., Kwan, M., and Lee, J. Y. (2015). Patterns of local segregation: Do they matter for neighborhood crime? *Social Science Research, 54*, 303–318.

Krivo, L. J., and Peterson, R. D. (1996). Extremely disadvantaged neighborhoods and urban crime. *Social Forces, 75*, 619–650.

———. (2000). The structural context of homicide: Accounting for racial differences in process. *American Sociological Review, 65*, 547–559.

Kubrin, C. E. (2008). Making order of disorder: A call for conceptual clarity. *Criminology and Public Policy, 7*, 203–214.

———. (2013). Immigration and crime. In F. T. Cullen and P. Wilcox (Eds.), *The Oxford handbook of criminological theory* (pp. 440–455). New York: Oxford University Press.

Kubrin, C. E., Squires, G. D., Graves, S. M., and Ousey, G. C. (2011). Does fringe banking exacerbate neighborhood crime rates? *Criminology and Public Policy, 10*, 437–466.

Kulig, T. C., Pratt, T. C., and Cullen, F. T. (2017). Revisiting the Stanford Prison Experiment: A case study in organized skepticism. *Journal of Criminal Justice Education, 28*, 74–111.

Kurtz, E. M., Koons, B. A., and Taylor, R. B. (1998). Land use, physical deterioration, resident-based control and calls for service on urban streetblocks. *Justice Quarterly, 15,* 121–149.

Kurtz, L. R. (1984). *Evaluating Chicago sociology: A guide to the literature, with an annotated bibliography.* Chicago: University of Chicago Press.

LaFree, G., Drass, K. A., and O'Day, P. (1992). Race and crime in postwar America: Determinants of African-American and White rates, 1957–1988. *Criminology, 30,* 157–185.

LaGrange, T. C. (1999). The impact of neighborhoods, schools, and malls on the spatial distribution of property damage. *Journal of Research in Crime and Delinquency, 36,* 393–422.

Lamont, M., and Small, M. L. (2008). How culture matters: Enriching our understanding of poverty. In A. C. Lin and D. R. Harris (Eds.), *The colors of poverty: Why racial and ethnic disparities persist* (pp. 76–102). New York: Russell Sage Foundation.

Land, K. C., and Felson, M. (1976). A general framework for building dynamic macro social indicator models: Including an analysis of changes in crime rates and police expenditures. *American Journal of Sociology, 82,* 565–604.

Land, K. C., McCall, P. L., and Cohen, L. E. (1990). Structural covariates of homicide rates: Are there any invariances across time and space? *American Journal of Sociology, 95,* 922–963.

Lee, M. R. (2008). Civic community in the hinterland: Toward a theory of rural social structure and violence. *Criminology, 46,* 447–478.

Lee, M. R., Maume, M. O., and Ousey, G. C. (2003). Social isolation and lethal violence across the metro/nonmetro divide: The effects of socioeconomic disadvantage and poverty concentration on homicide. *Rural Sociology, 68,* 107–131.

Lee, M. R., and Ousey, G. C. (2001). Size matters: Examining the link between small manufacturing, socioeconomic deprivation, and crime rates in nonmetropolitan communities. *Sociological Quarterly, 42,* 581–602.

Lee, M. T., Martinez, R., Jr., and Rosenfeld, R. (2001). Does immigration increase homicide? Negative evidence from three border cities. *Sociological Quarterly, 42,* 559–580.

Lee, Y., Eck, J. E., and Corsaro, N. (2016). Conclusions from the history of research into the effects of police force size on crime—1968 through 2013: A historical systematic review. *Journal of Experimental Criminology, 12,* 431–451.

Link, N. W., Kelly, J. M., Pitts, J. R., Waltman-Spreha, K., and Taylor, R. B. (2017). Reversing broken windows: Evidence of lagged, multilevel impacts of risk perceptions on perceptions of incivility. *Crime and Delinquency, 63,* 659–682.

Lockwood, D. (2007). Mapping crime in Savannah: Social disadvantage, land use, and violent crimes reported to the police. *Social Science Computer Review, 25,* 194–209.

Loftin, C., and Parker, R. N. (1985). An errors-in-variable model of the effect of poverty on urban homicide rates. *Criminology, 23,* 269–288.

Logan, J. R., Stults, B. J., and Farley, R. (2004). Segregation of minorities in the metropolis: Two decades of change. *Demography, 41,* 1–22.

Lowenkamp, C. T., Cullen, F. T., and Pratt, T. C. (2003). Replicating Sampson and Groves's test of social disorganization theory: Revisiting a criminological classic. *Journal of Research in Crime and Delinquency, 40,* 351–373.

Lyons, C. J., Vélez, M. B., and Santoro, W. A. (2013). Neighborhood immigration, violence, and city-level immigrant political opportunities. *American Sociological Review, 78,* 604–632.

Maccoby, E. E., Johnson, J. P., and Church, R. M. (1958). Community integration and the social control of juvenile delinquency. *Journal of Social Issues, 14*, 38–51.

MacGillis, A., and ProPublica. (2016). The original underclass. *The Atlantic*, September. https://www.theatlantic.com/magazine/archive/2016/09/the-original-underclass /492731/. Accessed March 3, 2017.

MacKenzie, R. D. (1967). The ecological approach to the study of the community. In R. E. Park, E. W. Burgess, and R. D. McKenzie (Eds.), *The city* (pp. 63–79). Chicago: University of Chicago Press. (Originally published 1925.)

Madensen, T. D., and Eck, J. E. (2013). Crime places and place management. In F. T. Cullen and P. Wilcox (Eds.), *The Oxford handbook of criminological theory* (pp. 554–578). New York: Oxford University Press.

Maimon, D., and Browning, C. R. (2010). Unstructured socializing, collective efficacy, and violent behavior among urban youth. *Criminology, 48*, 443–474.

Manza, J., and Uggen, C. (2006). *Locked out: Felon disenfranchisement and American democracy.* New York: Oxford University Press.

Markowitz, F. E., Bellair, P. E., Liska, A. E., and Liu, J. (2001). Extending social disorganization theory: Modeling the relationships between cohesion, disorder, and fear. *Criminology, 39*, 293–319.

Martin, D. (2006). Jane Jacobs, urban activist, is dead at 89. *New York Times*, April 25. http://www.nytimes.com/2006/04/25/books/25cnd-jacobs.html. Accessed October 10, 2010.

Martinez, R., Jr. (2002). *Latino homicide: Immigration, violence, and community.* New York: Routledge.

Martinez, R., Jr., and Lee, M. (2000). Comparing the context of immigrant homicides in Miami: Haitians, Jamaicans, and Mariels. *International Migration Review, 34*, 794–812.

Massey, D. S., and Denton, N. A. (1993). *American apartheid: Segregation and the making of the underclass.* Cambridge, MA: Harvard University Press.

Matsueda, R. L. (2015). Social structure, culture, and crime: Assessing Kornhauser's challenge to criminology. In F. T. Cullen, P, Wilcox, R. J. Sampson, and B. D. Dooley (Eds.), *Challenging criminological theory: The legacy of Ruth Rosner Kornhauser* (Advances in Criminological Theory, vol. 19, pp. 117–143). New Brunswick, NJ: Transaction.

Matza, D. (1969). *Becoming deviant.* Englewood Cliffs, NJ: Prentice Hall.

Mazerolle, L., Wickes, R., and McBroom, J. (2010). Community variations in violence: The role of social ties and collective efficacy in comparative context. *Journal of Research in Crime and Delinquency, 47*, 3–30.

McCord, J., and Ensminger, M. E. (2003). Racial discrimination and violence: A longitudinal perspective. In D. F. Hawkins (Ed.), *Violent crime: Assessing race and ethnic differences* (pp. 319–330). Cambridge: Cambridge University Press.

McKay, H. D. (1949). The neighborhood and child conduct. *Annals of the American Academy of Political and Social Science, 261*, 32–41.

McNeeley, S., and Wilcox. P. (2015). Neighborhoods and delinquent behavior. In M. D. Krohn and J. Lane (Eds.), *Handbook of juvenile delinquency and juvenile justice* (pp. 217–235). West Sussex: Wiley-Blackwell.

Merry, S. E. (1981). Defensible space undefended: Social factors in crime control through environmental design. *Urban Affairs Quarterly, 16*, 397–422.

Merton, R. K. (1938). Social structure and anomie. *American Sociological Review, 3*, 672–682.

———. (1995). Opportunity structure: The emergence, diffusion, and differentiation of a sociological concept, 1930s-1950s. In F. Adler and W. S. Laufer (Eds.), *The legacy of anomie theory* (Advances in Criminological Theory, vol. 6, pp. 3–78). New Brunswick, NJ: Transaction.

Messner, S. F., and Golden, R. M. (1992). Racial inequality and racially disaggregated homicide rates: An assessment of alternative theoretical explanations. *Criminology, 30*, 421–448.

Messner, S. F., and Sampson, R. J. (1991). The sex ratio, family disruption, and rates of violent crime: The paradox of demographic structure. *Social Forces, 69*, 693–714.

Miethe, T. D., and McDowall, D. (1993). Contextual effects in models of criminal victimization. *Social Forces, 71*, 741–759.

Miethe, T. D., and Meier, R. F. (1990). Opportunity, choice, and criminal victimization: A test of a theoretical model. *Journal of Research in Crime and Delinquency, 27*, 243–266.

———. (1994). *Crime and its social context: Toward an integrated theory of offenders, victims, and situations*. Albany: State University of New York Press.

Miethe, T. D., Stafford, M. C., and Long, J. S. (1987). Social differentiation in criminal victimization: A test of routine activities/lifestyle theories. *American Sociological Review, 52*, 184–194.

Miller, J. (2008). *Getting played: African American girls' urban inequality and gendered violence*. New York: New York University Press.

Miller, W. B. (1958). Lower class culture as a generating milieu of gang delinquency. *Journal of Social Issues, 14*, 5–19.

Morenoff, J. D., Sampson, R. J., and Raudenbush, S. W. (2001). Neighborhood inequality, collective efficacy, and the spatial dynamics of urban violence. *Criminology, 39*, 517–560.

Moynihan, D. P. (1965). *The Negro family: The case for national action. Office of Policy Planning Research*. Washington, DC: U.S. Department of Labor.

Muller, T. (1993). *Immigrants and the American city*. New York: New York University Press.

Murray, C. A. (1984). *Losing ground: American social policy, 1950–1980*. New York: Basic Books.

Mustaine, E. E., and Tewksbury, R. (1998). Predicting risks of larceny theft victimization: Routine activity analysis using refined lifestyle measures. *Criminology, 36*, 829–857.

Newby, R. G. (1989). Problems of pragmatism in public policy: Critique of William Wilson's *The Truly Disadvantaged. Journal of Sociology and Social Welfare, 16*, 123–132.

Newman, O. (1972). *Defensible space: Crime prevention through urban design*. New York: Macmillan.

———. (1996). *Creating defensible space*. Washington, DC: U.S. Department of Housing and Urban Development.

Noble, R. (2006). *Black rage in the American prison system*. New York: LFB Scholarly Pub.

Olasky, M. (1992). *The tragedy of American compassion*. Washington, DC: Regnery.

O'Neil, T. (2010). A look back: Pruitt and Igoe started strong, but in the end failed. *St. Louis Post-Dispatch*, July 25. http://www.stltoday.com/news/local/metro/a-look-back-pruitt-and-igoe-started-strong-but-in/article_e2a30e7c-f180–5770–8962-bf6e8902efc1.html. Accessed December 28, 2010.

Onwudiwe, I. D., and Lynch, M. J. (2000). Reopening the debate: A reexamination of the need for a Black criminology. *Social Pathology, 6*, 182–198.

Osgood, D. W., and Chambers, J. M. (2000). Social disorganization outside the metropolis: An analysis of rural youth violence. *Criminology, 38*, 81–115.

Ousey, G. C. (1999). Homicide, structural factors, and the racial invariance assumption. *Criminology, 37*, 405–426.

———. (2000). Explaining regional and urban variation in crime: A review of research. In G. LaFree (Ed.), *The nature of crime: Continuity and change* (vol. 1, pp. 261–308). Washington, DC: Office of Justice Programs, U.S. Department of Justice.

Ousey, G. C., and Kubrin, C. E. (2009). Exploring the connection between immigration and violent crime rates in US cities, 1980–2000. *Social Problems, 56*, 447–473.

———. (In press). Immigration and crime: Assessing a contentious issue. *Annual Review of Criminology.*

Pager, D. (2003). The mark of a criminal record. *American Journal of Sociology, 108*, 937–975.

———. (2007). *Marked: Race, crime, and finding work in an era of mass incarceration.* Chicago: University of Chicago Press.

Papachristos, A. V., Smith, C. M., Scherer, M. L., and Fugiero, M. A. (2011). More coffee, less crime? The relationship between gentrification and neighborhood crime rates in Chicago, 1991 to 2005. *City and Community, 10*, 215–240.

Park, R. E. (1961). Editor's preface. In N. Anderson, *The hobo: The sociology of the homeless man* (pp. xx111–xxvi). Chicago: University of Chicago Press. (Originally published 1923.)

———. (1967a). The city: Suggestions for the investigation of human behavior in the urban environment. In R. E. Park, E. W. Burgess, and R. D. McKenzie (Eds.), *The city* (pp. 1–46). Chicago: University of Chicago Press. (Originally published 1925.)

———. (1967b). Community organization and juvenile delinquency. In R. E. Park, E. W. Burgess, and R. D. McKenzie (Eds.), *The city* (pp. 99–112). Chicago: University of Chicago Press. (Originally published 1925.)

Park, R. E., and Burgess, E. W. (1969). *Introduction to the science of sociology* (3rd and Rev. ed.). Chicago: University of Chicago Press. (Originally published 1921.)

Parker, K. F. (2008). *Unequal crime decline: Theorizing race, urban inequality and criminal violence.* New York: New York University Press.

Pattillo, M. E. (1998). Sweet mother and gangbangers: Managing crime in a middle-class neighborhood. *Social Forces, 76*, 747–774.

Pattillo-McCoy, M. (1999). *Black picket fences: Privilege and peril among the Black middle class.* Chicago: University of Chicago Press.

Paulsen, D. J., and Robinson, M. B. (2004). *Spatial aspects of crime: Theory and practice.* Boston, MA: Allyn and Bacon.

Penn, E. (2003). On Black criminology: Past, present, and future. *Criminal Justice Studies, 16*, 317–327.

Perkins, K. L., and Sampson, R. J. (2015). Compounded deprivation in the transition to adulthood: The intersection of racial and economic inequality among Chicagoans, 1995–2013. *RSF: The Russell Sage Foundation Journal of the Social Sciences, 1* (1), 35–54.

Petee, T. A., and Kowalski, G. S. (1993). Modeling rural violent crime rates: A test of social disorganization theory. *Sociological Focus, 26*, 87–89.

Peterson, R. D., and Krivo, L. J. (1993). Racial segregation and Black urban homicide. *Social Forces, 71*, 1001–1026.

———. (1999). Racial segregation, the concentration of disadvantage, and Black and White homicide victimization. *Sociological Forum, 14*, 465–493.

———. (2005). Macrostructural analyses of race, ethnicity, and violent crime: Recent lessons and new directions for research. *Annual Review of Sociology, 31*, 331–356.

———. (2010). *Divergent social worlds: Neighborhood crime and the racial-spatial divide.* New York: Russell Sage Foundation.

Pfohl, S. J. (1985). *Images of deviance and social control. A sociological history.* New York: McGraw-Hill.

Phillips, J. A. (2002). White, Black, and Latino homicide rates: Why the difference? *Social Problems, 49*, 349–373.

Pinker, S. (2011). *The better angels of our nature: Why violence has declined.* New York: Penguin.

Platt, A. R. (1969). *The child savers: The invention of the juvenile court.* Chicago: University of Chicago Press.

Portes, A., and Rumbaut, R. G. (2006). *Immigrant America: A portrait.* Berkeley: University of California Press.

Pratt, T. C., and Cullen, F. T. (2005). Assessing macro-level predictors and theories of crime: A meta-analysis. In M. Tonry (Ed.), *Crime and justice: A review of research* (vol. 32, pp. 373–450). Chicago: University of Chicago Press.

Putnam, R. (2000). *Bowling alone: The collapse and renewal of American community.* New York: Simon and Schuster.

Quillian, L. (1999). Migration patterns and the growth of high-poverty neighborhoods, 1970–1990. *American Journal of Sociology, 105*, 1–37.

Rainwater, L. (1967). Lessons of Pruitt-Igoe. *Public Interest, 8*, 116–126.

Ramey, D. M. (2013). Immigrant revitalization and neighborhood violent crime in established and new destination cities. *Social Forces, 92*, 597–629.

Ramey, D. M., and Shrider, E. A. (2014). New parochialism, sources of community investment, and the control of street crime. *Criminology and Public Policy, 13*, 193–216.

Reckless, W. C., Dinitz, S., and Murray, E. (1956). Self concept as an insulator against delinquency. *American Sociological Review, 21*, 744–746.

———. (1957). The "good" boy in the high delinquency area. *Journal of Criminal Law, Criminology, and Police Science, 48*, 18–25.

Rengert, G. F. (1989). Spatial justice and criminal victimization. *Justice Quarterly, 6*, 543–564.

Rengert, G. F., and Wasilchick, J. (2000). *Suburban burglary: A tale of two suburbs* (2nd ed.). Springfield, IL: Charles C. Thomas.

Reynald, D. (2015). Environmental design and crime events. *Journal of Contemporary Criminology, 31*, 71–89.

Reynald, D., Averdijk, M., Elffers, H., and Bernasco, W. (2008). Do social barriers affect urban crime trips? The effects of ethnic and economic neighbourhood compositions on the flow of crime in The Hague, the Netherlands. *Built Environment, 34*, 21–31.

Rice, K. J., and Smith, W. R. (2002). Socioecological models of automotive theft: Integrating routine activity and social disorganization approaches. *Journal of Research in Crime and Delinquency, 39*, 304–336.

Roncek, D. W., and Bell, R. (1981). Bars, blocks, and crimes. *Journal of Environmental Systems, 11*, 35–47.

Roncek, D. W., and Faggiani, D. (1985). High schools and crime: A replication. *Sociological Quarterly, 26*, 491–505.

Roncek, D. W., and LoBosco, A. (1983). The effect of high schools in their neighborhoods. *Social Science Quarterly, 64*, 599–613.

Roncek, D. W., and Maier, P. A. (1991). Bars, blocks, and crimes revisited: Linking the theory of routine activities to the empiricism of "hot spots." *Criminology, 29*, 725–753.

Roncek, D. W., and Pravatiner, M. A. (1989). Additional evidence that taverns enhance nearby crime. *Sociology and Social Research, 73*, 185–188.

Rose, D. R., and Clear, T. R. (1998). Incarceration, social capital, and crime: Implications for social disorganization theory. *Criminology, 36*, 441–480.

Ross, C. E., and Jang, S. J. (2000). Neighborhood disorder, fear, and mistrust: The buffering role of social ties with neighbors. *American Journal of Community Psychology, 28*, 401–420.

Rothman, D. J. (1971). *The discovery of the asylum: Social order and disorder in the new republic.* Boston, MA: Little, Brown.

———. (1980). *Conscience and convenience: The asylum and its alternatives in Progressive America.* Boston, MA: Little, Brown.

Rumbaut, R. G., and Ewing, W. A. (2007). *The myth of immigrant criminality and the paradox of assimilation: Incarceration rates among native and foreign-born men.* Washington, DC: Immigration Policy Center, American Immigration Law Foundation.

Russell, K. K. (1992). Development of a Black criminology and the role of the Black criminologist. *Justice Quarterly, 9*, 667–683.

Russell-Brown, K. (2009). *The color of crime: Racial hoaxes, White fear, Black protectionism, police harassment, and other microaggressions* (2nd ed.). New York: New York University Press.

Sam, D. L., Vedder, P., Ward, C., and Horenczyk, G. (2006). Psychological and sociocultural adaptation of immigrant youth. In J. W. Berry, J. S. Phinney, D. L. Sam, and P. Vedder (Eds.), *Immigrant youth in cultural transition: Acculturation, identity, and adaptation across national contexts* (pp. 117–141). Mahwah, NJ: Lawrence Erlbaum.

Sampson, R. J. (1983). Structural density and criminal victimization. *Criminology, 21*, 276–293.

———. (1985). Neighborhood and crime: The structural determinants of personal victimization. *Journal of Research in Crime and Delinquency, 22*, 7–40.

———. (1986). Effects of inequality, heterogeneity, and urbanization on intergroup victimization. *Social Science Quarterly, 67*, 751–766.

———. (1987). Urban Black violence: The effect of male joblessness and family disruption. *American Journal of Sociology, 93*, 348–382.

———. (1988). Local friendship ties and community attachment in mass society: A multi-level systemic model. *American Sociological Review, 53*, 766–779.

———. (1997). Collective regulation of adolescent misbehavior: Validation results from eighty Chicago neighborhoods. *Journal of Adolescent Research, 12*, 227–244.

———. (2002). Transcending tradition: New direction in community research, Chicago style. *Criminology, 40*, 213–230.

———. (2006). Collective efficacy theory: Lessons learned and directions for future inquiry. In F. T. Cullen, J. P. Wright and K. R. Blevins (Eds.), *Taking stock: The status of criminological theory* (Advances in Criminological Theory, vol. 15, pp. 149–167). Somerset, NJ: Transaction.

———. (2008). Rethinking crime and immigration. *Contexts, 7* (1), 28–33.

———. (2009). Racial stratification and the durable tangle of neighborhood inequality. *Annals of the American Academy of Political and Social Science, 621*, 260–280.

———. (2011). Communities and crime revisited: Intellectual trajectory of a Chicago School education. In F. T. Cullen, C. L. Jonson, A. J. Myer, and F. Adler (Eds.), *The origins of American criminology* (Advances in Criminological Theory, vol. 16, pp. 63–88). New Brunswick, NJ: Transaction.

———. (2012). *Great American city: Chicago and the enduring neighborhood effect.* Chicago: University of Chicago Press.

———. (2013). The place of context: A theory and strategy for criminology's hard problems. *Criminology, 51*, 1–31.

Sampson, R. J., and Bartusch, D. J. (1998). Legal cynicism and (subcultural?) tolerance of deviance: The neighborhood context of racial differences. *Law and Society Review, 32*, 777–804.

Sampson, R. J., and Bean, L. (2006). Cultural mechanisms and killing fields: A revised theory of community-level racial inequality. In R. D. Peterson, L. J. Krivo, and J. Hagan (Eds.), *The many colors of crime: Inequalities of race, ethnicity, and crime in America* (pp. 8–36). New York: New York University Press.

Sampson, R. J., and Castellano, T. C. (1982). Economic inequality and personal victimization. *British Journal of Criminology, 22*, 363–385.

Sampson, R. J., and Groves, W. B. (1989). Community structure and crime: Testing social disorganization theory. *American Journal of Sociology, 94*, 774–802.

Sampson, R. J., Morenoff, J. D., and Raudenbush, S. (2005). Social anatomy of racial and ethnic disparities in violence. *American Journal of Public Health, 95*, 224–232.

Sampson, R. J., and Raudenbush, R. W. (1999). Systematic social observation of public spaces: A new look at disorder in urban neighborhoods. *American Journal of Sociology, 3*, 603–651.

———. (2001). *Disorder in urban neighborhoods: Does it lead to crime?* Washington, DC: National Institute of Justice, U.S. Department of Justice.

———. (2004). Social disorder: Neighborhood stigma and the social construction of "broken windows." *Social Psychology Quarterly, 67*, 319–342.

Sampson, R. J., Raudenbush, S. W., and Earls, F. (1997). Neighborhoods and violent crime: A multilevel study of collective efficacy. *Science, 277*, 918–924.

Sampson, R. J., and Wikström, P. O. (2008). The social order of violence in Chicago and Stockholm neighborhoods: a comparative inquiry. In S. N. Kalyvas, I. Shapiro, and T. Masoud (Eds.), *Order, conflict, and violence* (pp. 97–119). New York: Cambridge University Press.

Sampson, R. J., and Wilson, W. J. (1995). Toward a theory of race, crime and urban inequality. In J. Hagan and R. D. Peterson (Eds.), *Crime and inequality* (pp. 37–54). Stanford, CA: Stanford University Press.

Sampson, R. J., and Wooldredge, J. D. (1987). Linking the micro- and macro-level dimensions of lifestyle-routine activity and opportunity models of predatory victimization. *Journal of Quantitative Research, 3*, 371–393.

Schlossman, S., Zellman, G., and Shavelson, R., with Sedlak, M., and Cobb, J. (1984). *Delinquency prevention in South Chicago: A fifty-year assessment of the Chicago Area Project.* Santa Monica, CA: Rand.

Shaw, C. R. (1929a). Delinquency and the social situation. *Religious Education, 24*, 409–417.

———. (1929b). *Delinquency areas: A study of the geographic distribution of school truants, juvenile delinquency, and adult offenders in Chicago.* Chicago: University of Chicago Press.

———. (1966). *The jack-roller: A delinquent boy's own story.* Chicago: University of Chicago Press. (Originally published 1930.)

Shaw, C. R., and McKay, H. D. (1942). *Juvenile delinquency and urban areas.* Chicago: University of Chicago Press.

———. (1969). *Juvenile delinquency and urban areas* (Rev. ed.). Chicago: University of Chicago Press.

Shaw, C. R., with McKay, H. D., and McDonald, J. F. (1938). *Brothers in crime.* Chicago: University of Chicago Press.

Shaw, C. R., with Moore, M. E. (1976). *The natural history of a delinquent career.* Chicago: University of Chicago Press. (Originally published 1931.)

Sherman, L. W. (1993a). Why crime control is not reactionary. In D. Weisburd and C. Uchida (Eds.), *Police innovation and control of the police* (pp. 171–189). New York: Springer.

———. (1993b). Defiance, deterrence, and irrelevance: A theory of the criminal sanction. *Journal of Research in Crime and Delinquency, 30*, 445–473.

———. (1998). *Evidence-based policing.* Washington, DC: Police Foundation.

Sherman, L. W., Gartin, P., and Buerger, M. E. (1989). Hot spots of predatory crime: Routine activities and the criminology of place. *Criminology, 27*, 27–56.

Shihadeh, E. S., and Ousey, G. C. (1998). Industrial restructuring and violence: The link between entry-level jobs, economic deprivation, and Black and White homicide. *Social Forces, 77*, 185–206.

Shihadeh, E. S., and Shrum, W. (2004). Serious crime in urban neighborhoods: Is there a race effect? *Sociological Spectrum, 24*, 507–533.

Shihadeh, E. S., and Steffensmeier, D. J. (1994). Economic inequality, family disruption, and urban Black violence: Cities as units of stratification and social control. *Social Forces, 73*, 729–751.

Short, J. F., Jr., and Strodtbeck, F. L. (1965). *Group process and gang delinquency.* Chicago: University of Chicago Press.

Shover, N. (1996). *Great pretenders: Pursuits and careers of persistent thieves.* Boulder, CO: Westview.

Sidebottom, A., Tompson, L., Thornton, A., Bullock, K., Tilley, N., Bowers, K., and Johnson, S. D. (In press). Gating alleys to reduce crime: A meta-analysis and realist synthesis. *Justice Quarterly.* http://dx.doi.org/10.1080/07418825.2017.1293135.

Simcha-Fagan, O. M., and Schwartz, J. E. (1986). Neighborhood and delinquency: An assessment of contextual effects. *Criminology, 24*, 667–699.

Simon, J. (2007). *Governing through crime: How the war on crime transformed American democracy and created a culture of fear.* New York: Oxford University Press.

Sinclair, U. (1960). *The jungle.* New York: Signet. (Originally published 1906.)

Skogan, W. G. (1990). *Disorder and decline: Crime and the spiral of decade in American neighborhoods.* Berkeley: University of California Press.

Slocum, L.A., Rengifo, A. F., Choi, T., and Herrmann, C. R. (2013). The elusive relationship between community organizations and crime: An assessment across disadvantaged areas of the South Bronx. *Criminology, 51*, 167–216.

Small, M. L., Harding, D. J., and Lamont, M. (2010). Reconsidering culture and poverty. *Annals of the American Academy of Political and Social Science, 629*, 6–27.

Smith, D. A., and Jarjoura, G. R. (1989). Household characteristics, neighborhood composition, and burglary victimization. *Social Forces, 68*, 621–640.

Smith, M. D. (1992). Variations in correlates of race-specific urban homicide rates. *Journal of Contemporary Criminal Justice, 8*, 137–149.

Smith, M. J., and Clarke, R. V. (2012). Situational crime prevention: Classifying techniques using "good enough" theory. In B. C. Welsh and D. P. Farrington (Eds.), *The Oxford handbook of crime prevention* (pp. 291–315). New York: Oxford University Press.

Smith, N. (1996). *The new urban frontier: Gentrification and the revanchist city.* New York: Routledge.

Smith, W. R., Frazee, S. G., and Davison, E. L. (2000). Furthering the integration of routine activity and social disorganization theories: Small units of analysis and the study of street robbery as a diffusion process. *Criminology, 38*, 489–523.

Snodgrass, J. D. (1972). *The American criminological tradition: Portraits of the men and ideology in a discipline.* Unpublished Ph.D. dissertation, University of Pennsylvania.

———. (1976). Clifford R. Shaw and Henry D. McKay: Chicago criminologists. *British Journal of Criminology, 16*, 1–19.

Soja, E. W. (2000). *Postmetropolis: Critical studies of cities and regions.* Oxford: Blackwell.

Steffensmeier, D., Feldmeyer, B., Harris, C. T., and Ulmer, J. T. (2011). Reassessing trends in Black violent crime, 1980–2008: Sorting out the "Hispanic effect" in uniform crime reports arrests, national crime victimization survey offender estimates, and U.S. prisoner counts. *Criminology, 49*, 197–251.

Steffensmeier, D., Ulmer, J. T., Feldmeyer, B., and Harris, C. (2010). Scope and conceptual issues in testing the race-crime invariance thesis: Black, White, and Hispanic comparisons. *Criminology, 48*, 1133–1170.

Stewart, E. A., and Simons, R. L. (2006). Structure and culture in African-American adolescent violence: A partial test of code of the streets thesis. *Justice Quarterly, 23*, 1–33.

———. (2010). Race, code of the street, and violent delinquency: A multilevel investigation of neighborhood street culture and individual norms of violence. *Criminology, 42*, 569–605.

Stewart, E. A., Simons, R. L., and Conger, R. D. (2002). Assessing neighborhood and social psychological influences on childhood violence in an African American sample. *Criminology, 40*, 801–830.

Stucky, T. D., and Ottensmann, J. R. (2009). Land use and violent crime. *Criminology, 47*, 1223–1264.

Sugrue, T. J. (2010). *Not even past: Barack Obama and the burden of race.* Princeton, NJ: Princeton University Press.

Sutherland, E. H. (1937). *The professional thief: By a professional thief.* Chicago: University of Chicago Press.

———. (1947). *Principles of criminology* (3rd ed.). Philadelphia, PA: J. B. Lippincott.

Sutherland, E. H., and Cressey, D. R. (1955). *Principles of criminology* (5th ed.). Philadelphia, PA: J. B. Lippincott.

Suttles, G. D. (1968). *The social order of the slum: Ethnicity and territory in the inner city.* Chicago: University of Chicago Press.

Swidler, A. (1986). Culture in action: Symbols and strategies. *American Sociological Review, 51*, 273–286.

Taylor, R. B. (1997). Social order and disorder of street-blocks and neighborhoods: Ecology, micro-ecology and the systemic model of social disorganization theory. *Journal of Research in Crime and Delinquency, 34*, 113–155.

———. (1998). Crime and small-scale place: What we know, what we can prevent, and what else we need to know. In *Crime and place: Plenary Papers of the 1997 Conference on Criminal Justice Research and Evaluation* (pp. 1–22). Washington, DC: NIJ.

———. (2001). *Breaking away from broken windows: Baltimore neighborhoods and the nationwide fight against crime, grime, fear, and decline.* Boulder, CO: Westview.

Taylor, R. B., and Gottfredson, S. (1986). Environmental design, crime, and prevention—an examination of community dynamics. In A. J. Reiss, Jr. and M. Tonry (Eds.), *Communities and crime* (Crime and Justice: A Review of Research, vol. 8, pp. 387–416). Chicago: University of Chicago Press.

Taylor, R. B., and Harrell, A. V. (1996). *Physical environment and crime.* Washington, DC: Office of Justice Programs, National Institute of Justice, U.S. Department of Justice, NCJ 157311.

Telep, C., and Weisburd, D. (2012). What is known about the effectiveness of police practices in reducing crime and disorder? *Police Quarterly, 15*, 331–357.

The Sentencing Project. (2017). *Fact sheet: Trends in U.S. corrections.* Washington, DC: Author.

Thomas, W. I. (1969). The person and his wishes. In R. E. Park and E. W. Burgess (Eds.), *Introduction to the science of sociology* (3rd and Rev. ed.) (pp. 488–490). Chicago: University of Chicago Press. (Originally published 1921.)

Thomas, W. I., and Znaniecki, F. (1984). *The Polish peasant in Europe and America* (Edited and abridged by E. Zaretsky). Urbana: University of Illinois Press. (Original five volumes published between 1918 and 1920.)

Thrasher, F. M. (1927). *The gang: A study of 1,313 gangs in Chicago.* Chicago: University of Chicago Press.

———. (1963). *The gang: A study of 1,313 gangs in Chicago* (Abridged ed.). Chicago: University of Chicago Press. (Originally published 1927.)

Tillyer, M. S., and Tillyer, R. (2014). Violence in context: A multilevel analysis of victim injury in robbery incidents. *Justice Quarterly, 31*, 767–791.

Tonry, M. (1995). *Malign neglect: Race, crime, and punishment in America.* New York: Oxford University Press.

———. (2011). *Punishing race: A continuing American dilemma.* New York: Oxford University Press.

———. (2014). Why crime rates are falling throughout the Western world. In M. Tonry (Ed.), *Why crime rates fall and why they don't* (Crime and Justice: A Review of Research, vol. 43, pp. 1–63). Chicago: University of Chicago Press.

Trump, D. J. (2017). Inaugural address. January 20. http://www.cnn.com/2017/01/20/politics/trump-inaugural-address/. Accessed March 22, 2017.

Unnever, J. D. (2017). The racial invariance thesis in criminology: Toward a Black criminology. Manuscript submitted for publication.

Unnever, J. D., and Cullen, F. T. (2007). The racial divide in support for the death penalty: Does White racism matter? *Social Forces, 85*, 1281–1301.

———. (2010). Social sources of Americans' punitiveness: A test of three competing models. *Criminology, 48*, 99–129.

Unnever, J. D., and Gabbidon, S. L. (2011). *A theory of African American offending: Race, racism, and crime.* New York: Routledge.

Unnever, J. D., Gabbidon, S. L., and Higgins, G. E. (2011). The election of Barack Obama and perceptions of criminal injustice. *Justice Quarterly, 28*, 23–45.

Unnever, J. D., and Owusu-Bempah, A. (In press). A Black criminology matters. In J. D. Unnever, S. L. Gabbidon, and C. Chouhy (Eds.), *Building a Black criminology: Race, theory, and crime* (Advances in Criminological Theory). New York: Routledge.

U.S. Bureau of Labor Statistics. (2016). *Labor force statistics from the Current Population Survey* [Data File]. http://data.bls.gov/pdq/SurveyOutputServlet.

U.S. Census Bureau. (1983). *Current population reports*. Washington, DC: U.S. Government Printing Office.

———. (2010). *Current population reports*. Washington, DC: U.S. Government Printing Office.

———. (2015). *Current population reports*. Washington, DC: U.S. Government Printing Office.

Vaughn, M. G., Salas-Wright, C. P., DeLisi, M., and Maynard, B. R. (2014). The immigrant paradox: Immigrants are less antisocial than native-born Americans. *Social Psychiatry and Psychiatric Epidemiology, 49*, 1129–1137.

Vélez, M. B. (2001). The role of public social control in urban neighborhoods: A multilevel analysis of victimization risk. *Criminology, 39*, 837–864.

———. (2006). Toward an understanding of the lower rates of homicide in Latino versus Black neighborhoods: A look at Chicago. In R. D. Peterson, L. J. Krivo, and J. Hagan (Eds.), *Many colors of crime: Inequalities of race, ethnicity, and crime in America* (pp. 91–107). New York: New York University Press.

Vélez, M. B., Lyons, C. J., and Boursaw, B. (2012). Neighborhood housing investments and violent crime in Seattle, 1981–2007. *Criminology, 50*, 1025–1056.

Venkatesh, S. (1997). The social organization of street gang activity in an urban ghetto. *American Journal of Sociology, 103*, 82–111.

Veysey, B. M., and Messner, S. F. (1999). Further testing of social disorganization theory: An elaboration of Sampson and Groves's "community structure and crime." *Journal of Research in Crime and Delinquency, 36*, 156–174.

Walker, S., Spohn, C., and DeLone, M. (2012). *The color of justice: Race, ethnicity, and crime in America*. Belmont, CA: Wadsworth.

Warner, B. D. (2003). The role of attenuated culture in social disorganization theory. *Criminology, 41*, 73–97.

———. (2007). Directly intervene or call the authorities? A study of forms of neighborhood social control within a social disorganization framework. *Criminology, 45*, 99–129.

Warner, B. D., and Burchfield. K. (2011). Misperceived neighborhood values and informal social control. *Justice Quarterly, 28*, 606–630.

Warner, B. D., and Sampson, R. J. (2015). Social disorganization, collective efficacy, and macro-level theories of social control. In F. T. Cullen, P, Wilcox, R. J. Sampson, and B. D. Dooley (Eds.), *Challenging criminological theory: The legacy of Ruth Rosner Kornhauser* (Advances in Criminological Theory, vol. 19, pp. 215–234). New Brunswick, NJ: Transaction.

Warner, B. D., and Wilcox Rountree, P. (1997). Local social ties in a community and crime model: Questioning the systemic nature of informal social control. *Social Problems, 44*, 520–536.

———. (2000). Implications of ghetto-related behavior for a community and crime model: Defining the process of cultural attenuation. *Sociology of Crime, Law, and Deviance, 2*, 39–62.

Warner, W. L., and Srole, L. (1945). *The social systems of American ethnic groups*. New Haven, CT: Yale University Press.

Weisburd, D. (2015). The law of concentration and the criminology of place. *Criminology, 53,* 133–157.

Weisburd, D., and Braga, A. A. (Eds.). (2006). *Police innovation: Contrasting perspectives*. New York: Cambridge University Press.

Weisburd, D., Bernasco, W., and Bruinsma, G. J. N. (Eds.). (2009). *Putting crime in its place: Units of analysis in spatial crime research*. New York: Springer.

Weisburd, D., Bushway, S., Lum, C., and Yang, S. M. (2004). Trajectories of crime at places: A longitudinal study of street segments in the city of Seattle. *Criminology, 42,* 283–321.

Weisburd, D., Eck, J. E., Braga, A. A., Telep, C. W., Cave, B., Bowers, K., . . . , Yang, S-M. (2016). *Place matters: Criminology for the twenty-first century*. New York: Cambridge University Press.

Weisburd, D., Groff, E. R., and Yang, S-M. (2012). *The criminology of place: Street segments and our understanding of the crime problem*. New York: Oxford University Press.

Weisheit, R. A., Falcone, D. N. and Wells, L. E. (2005). *Crime and policing in rural and small-town America*. Long Grove, IL: Waveland Press.

Welsh, B. C., and Farrington, D. P. (2009). *Making public places safer: Surveillance and crime prevention*. New York: Oxford University Press.

Western, B. (2006). *Punishment and inequality in America*. New York: Russell Sage Foundation.

White, G. F. (1990). Neighborhood permeability and burglary rates. *Justice Quarterly, 7,* 57–67.

White, M. J. (1988). *American neighborhoods and residential differentiation*. New York: Russell Sage Foundation.

Wicker, A. W. (1987). Behavior settings reconsidered: Temporal stages, resources, internal dynamics, context. In D. Stokols and I. Altman (Eds.), *Handbook of environmental psychology* (pp. 613–653). New York: John Wiley.

Wickes, R., Hipp, J. R., Sargeant, E., and Hommel, R. (2013). Collective efficacy as a task specific process: Examining the relationship between social ties, neighborhood cohesion and the capacity to respond to violence, delinquency and civic problems. *American Journal of Community Psychology, 52,* 115–127.

Wickes, R., Hipp, J. R., Sargeant, E., and Mazerolle, L. (2017). Neighborhood social ties and shared expectations for informal social control: Do they influence informal social control actions? *Journal of Quantitative Criminology, 33,* 101–129.

Wilcox, P. (2010). Theories of victimization. In B. S. Fisher and S. Lab (Eds.), *Encyclopedia of victimology and crime prevention* (pp. 978–986). Thousand Oaks, CA: Sage.

———. (2015). Routine activities, criminal opportunities, crime and crime prevention. In J. D. Wright (Ed.), *International encyclopedia of the social and behavioral sciences* (vol. 20, 2nd ed., pp. 772–779). Oxford: Elsevier.

Wilcox, P., and Eck, J. E. (2011). Criminology of the unpopular: Implications for policy aimed at payday lending facilities. *Criminology and Public Policy, 10,* 473–482.

Wilcox, P., Gialopsos, B.M., and Land, K.C. (2013). Multilevel criminal opportunity. In F. T. Cullen and P. Wilcox (Eds.), *The Oxford handbook of criminological theory* (pp. 579–601). New York: Oxford University Press.

Wilcox, P., and Land, K. C. (2015). Social disorganization and criminal opportunity. In F. T. Cullen, P. Wilcox, R. J. Sampson, and B. Dooley (Eds.), *Challenging crimi-*

nological theory: The legacy of Ruth Rosner Kornhauser (Advances in Criminological Theory, vol. 19, pp. 237–257). New Brunswick, NJ: Transaction.

Wilcox, P., Land, K. C., and Hunt, S. A. (2003). *Criminal circumstances: A dynamic multi-contextual criminal opportunity theory.* New York: Aldine de Gruyter.

Wilcox, P., Madensen, T. D., and Tillyer, M. S. (2007). Guardianship in context: Implications for burglary victimization risk and prevention. *Criminology, 45,* 771–804.

Wilcox, P., Quisenberry, N., Cabrera, D. T., and Jones, S. (2004). Busy places and broken windows? Towards defining the role of physical structure and process in community crime models. *Sociological Quarterly, 45,* 185–207.

Wilcox, P., and Swartz K. (In press). Social spatial influences. In G. J. N. Bruinsma and S. D. Johnson (Eds.), *The Oxford handbook of environmental criminology.* Oxford: Oxford University Press.

Wilcox Rountree, P., and Land, K. C. (2000). The generalizability of multilevel models of burglary victimization: A cross-city comparison. *Social Science Research, 29,* 284–305.

Wilcox Rountree, P., Land, K. C., and Miethe, T. D. (1994). Macro-micro integration in the study of victimization: A hierarchical logistic model analysis across Seattle neighborhoods. *Criminology, 32,* 387–414.

Wilcox Rountree, P., and Warner, B. D. (1999). Social ties and crime: Is the relationship gendered? *Criminology, 37,* 789–814.

Wilkinson, D. L. (2007). Local social ties and willingness to intervene: Textured views among violent urban youth of neighborhood social control dynamics and situations. *Justice Quarterly, 24,* 185–220.

Wilson, J. Q. (1975). *Thinking about crime.* New York: Basic Books.

Wilson, J. Q., and Kelling, G. L. (1982). Broken windows: The police and neighborhood safety. *Atlantic Monthly,* March, pp. 29–38.

Wilson, W. J. (1980). *The declining significance of race: Blacks and changing American institutions.* Chicago: University of Chicago Press.

———. (1987). *The truly disadvantaged: The inner city, the underclass, and public policy.* Chicago: University of Chicago Press.

———. (1996). *When work disappears: The world of the new urban poor.* New York: Vintage.

———. (2009). *More than just race: Being Black and poor in the inner city (issues of our time).* New York: Norton.

———. (2011). Reflections on a sociological career that integrates social science with social policy. *Annual Review of Sociology, 37,* 1–18.

Wo, J. C., Hipp, J. R., and Boessen, A. (2016). Voluntary organizations and neighborhood crime: A dynamic perspective. *Criminology, 54,* 212–241.

Wolfgang, M. E., and Ferracuti, F. (Eds.). (1967). *The subculture of violence: Towards an integrated theory in criminology.* London: Social Science Paperbacks.

Wright, E. M., and Benson, M. L. (2011). Clarifying the effects of neighborhood context on violence "behind closed doors." *Justice Quarterly, 28,* 775–798.

Wright, R., Brookman, F., and Bennett, T. (2006). The foreground dynamics of street robbery in Britain. *British Journal of Criminology, 46,* 1–15.

Wright, R. T., and Decker, S. H. (1994). *Burglars on the job: Streetlife and residential break-ins.* Boston, MA: Northeastern University Press.

———. (1997). *Armed robbers in action: Stickups and street culture.* Boston, MA: Northeastern University Press.

Zacks, R. (2012). *Island of vice: Theodore Roosevelt's quest to clean up sin-loving New York.* New York: Anchor Books.

Zaretsky, E. (1984). Editor's introduction. In W. I. Thomas and F. Znaniecki, *The Polish peasant in Europe and America* (edited and abridged by E. Zaretsky). Urbana: University of Illinois Press. (Original five volumes published between 1918 and 1920.)

Zhang, L., Messner, S. F., and Liu, J. (2007). A multilevel analysis of the risk of household burglary in the city of Tianjin, China. *British Journal of Criminology, 47*, 918–937.

Zimbardo, P. G. (2007). *The Lucifer effect: Understanding how good people turn evil.* New York: Random House.

Zimbardo, P. G., Banks, W. C., Haney, C., and Jaffe, D. (1973). A Pirandellian prison: The mind is a formidable jailer. *New York Times Magazine, 8,* 38–60.

Zimring, F. E. (2007). *The great American crime decline.* New York: Oxford University Press.

———. (2012). *The city that became safe: New York's lessons for urban crime and its control.* New York: Oxford University Press.

———. (2013). American youth violence: A cautionary tale. In M. Tonry (Ed.), *Crime and justice in America, 1975–2025* (Crime and Justice: A Review of Research, vol. 42, pp. 263–298). Chicago: University of Chicago Press.

Zorbaugh, H. W. (1976). *The Gold Coast and the slum: A sociological study of Chicago's near north side.* Chicago: University of Chicago Press. (Originally published 1929.)

Zukin, S. (1987). Gentrification: Culture and capital in the urban core. *Annual Review of Sociology, 13,* 129–147.

Index

Pamela Wilcox is Professor of Criminal Justice and Fellow of the Graduate School at the University of Cincinnati. She is the co-author of *Criminal Circumstance: A Dynamic Multicontextual Criminal Opportunity Theory* and co-editor of *Challenging Criminological Theory: The Legacy of Ruth Rosner Kornhauser.*

Francis T. Cullen is Distinguished Research Professor Emeritus and Senior Research Associate in the School of Criminal Justice at the University of Cincinnati. He is co-author of *Criminological Theory: Context and Consequences* and co-editor of *The Oxford Handbook of Criminological Theory.*

Ben Feldmeyer is Associate Professor in the School of Criminal Justice at the University of Cincinnati.